EMERSON
and the
DEFENSE
OF EQUALITY

EMERSON *and the* DEFENSE OF EQUALITY

GREG GARVEY

University of Massachusetts Press
AMHERST AND BOSTON

Copyright © 2025 by University of Massachusetts Press
All rights reserved
Printed in the United States of America

ISBN 978-1-62534-893-7 (paper); 894-4 (hardcover)

Designed by Jen Jackowitz
Set in Minion Pro
Printed and bound by Books International, Inc.

Cover design by adam b. bohannon

Library of Congress Cataloging-in-Publication Data
A catalog record for this book is available from the Library of Congress.

British Library Cataloguing-in-Publication Data
A catalog record for this book is available from the British Library.

The authorized representative in the EU for product safety and
compliance is Mare-Nostrum Group.
Email: gpsr@mare-nostrum.co.uk
Physical address: Mare-Nostrum Group B.V., Mauritskade 21D,
1091 GC Amsterdam, The Netherlands

For
Abigail Jean Garvey

Contents

Frequently Cited Texts ix

Prologue
Alexander Stephens and the Assault on Equality xi

INTRODUCTION
Emerson and the Meanings of Equality 1

1
*Political Equality
and the "Furious Democracy"* 25

2
*Marriage, Friendship,
and the Domestication of Culture* 61

3
*Emerson's Cosmopolitan Anthropology
and the Polygenesis Debate* 104

4
Liberty, Property, and Socialism 157

CONCLUSION
Emerson's Culture War 204

Acknowledgments 215

Notes 217

Index 243

Frequently Cited Texts

AW

Emerson's Antislavery Writings. Ed. Len Gougeon and Joel Myerson. New Haven: Yale University Press, 1995.

CW

The Collected Works of Ralph Waldo Emerson. Ed. Alfred R. Ferguson et al. 10 vols. Cambridge: Belknap Press of Harvard University Press, 1971–2013.

EL

The Early Lectures of Ralph Waldo Emerson. Ed. Robert E. Spiller et al. 3 vols. Cambridge: Harvard University Press, 1959–1972.

JMN

The Journals and Miscellaneous Notebooks of Ralph Waldo Emerson. Ed. William H. Golman et al. 16 vols. Cambridge: Harvard University Press, 1962–1982.

L

The Letters of Ralph Waldo Emerson. Ed. Ralph L. Rusk and Eleanor M. Tilton. 10 vols. New York: Columbia University Press, 1939–1995.

LL

The Later Lectures of Ralph Waldo Emerson: 1843–1871. Ed. Ronald Bosco and Joel Myerson. 2 vols. Athens: University of Georgia Press, 2001.

W

The Works of Ralph Waldo Emerson. Ed. Edward W. Emerson. 14 vols. Cambridge, MA: Riverside, 1883.

Prologue

Alexander Stephens and the Assault on Equality

Elated that he had passed a bill allowing slavery to expand westward, Congressman Alexander H. Stephens of Georgia exulted, "Nebraska is through the House," adding: "I took the reins in my hand, applied the whip and spur, and brought the 'wagon' out at eleven o'clock P.M. Glory enough for one day."[1] It was May of 1854. Cadaverously gaunt but personable and well liked, Stephens would soon become vice president of the Confederate States of America.

Alexander Stephens was a southern unionist with a record of resisting the secessionist spirit that was taking hold in the slave states during the 1850s. By the standards of the time, he was also a moderate, who, like Abraham Lincoln, had long been a member of the Whig Party. The Georgia congressman and the former representative from Illinois both admired the Whigs' desire to promote national unity through government-funded infrastructure projects like building canals and subsidizing railroads. The passage of the Kansas-Nebraska Act might have been a cause for Stephens to celebrate, but it also heralded the collapse of his political party and fueled the rise of the Republicans. By the time Lincoln became their candidate for president almost exactly six years later, Republicans opposed any expansion of slavery.

During the campaign of 1860, Stephens traveled to Illinois, where he tried to broker a deal to unite rival factions of Democrats and undercut the Republicans. By his thinking, a strong showing by the Democrats might stop the rise of Lincoln and the new Republican Party.[2] His mission failed, and Lincoln won the election with a plurality of slightly less than forty percent of the national vote. Unlike his equally personable colleague from Illinois, Stephens sided with the proslavery Democrats, who ultimately came out on the losing side. The nation now faced the long-feared and repeatedly deferred secession crisis.

In the months between Lincoln's election and his inauguration, seven slaveholding states seceded from the Union and created a political compact based on inequality between races. Yet even during these critical months of negotiation and coercion, Stephens tried to slow down the momentum of secession and hold the Union together. As the election results were sinking in and outrage at Lincoln's victory was growing throughout the South, Stephens gave a speech to the Georgia legislature that created a brief window for negotiation. "Before looking to extreme measures," he advised, "let us first see, as Georgians, that everything that can be done to preserve our rights, our interests, and our honor, as well as the peace of the country in the Union, be first done." He emphasized that Lincoln's election was valid according to the Constitution. How could Georgia leave the Union if the Constitution was intact? "If all our hopes are to be blasted," Stephens argued, "if the republic is to go down, let us be found to the last moment standing on the deck with the Constitution of the United States waving over our heads. Let the fanatics of the North break down the Constitution." If, in the future, President Lincoln did violate the Constitution, Stephens assured his colleagues that he "would aid in hanging him higher than the Virginians hung John Brown." Ironically, though, as Georgia followed its neighbors in choosing secession, it was Stephens's reputation as a genial moderate that propelled him to high office in the newly formed Confederacy.[3]

Shortly after his appointment as vice president, Stephens gave another, now infamous speech that reveals much about the corrosive toll that a thirty-year-long campaign to undermine belief in equality had taken on the values of the nation. Stephens's "Cornerstone Speech" dramatizes just how vulnerable the idea that all human beings are created equal had become in 1860 America. In this speech, Stephens references research in history, religion, science, and anthropology that rejected universal human equality as a naïve fantasy of Enlightenment idealists. Taking the long view of history, Stephens argues, shows that the Founders had made a mistake by holding that universal equality was a necessary principle for a just society. Equality itself, he insists, is a false value. Influential people like Stephens had been making the case against equality for decades.

Nevertheless, as the election of a president who opposed the expansion of slavery seemed to prove, the assault on equality had failed to persuade a majority of Americans to repudiate equality. Hence, Stephens and his secessionist peers had been compelled to nullify the old compact and try to constitute a smaller nation under an updated Constitution that defined the inherent *inequality* of its members as its primary guiding belief. Stephens is unambiguous in defining acceptance or rejection of equality as the crucial issue—not slavery or ambiguities in the right to liberty, but a difference of opinion on the belief that equality was an essential civic and spiritual value. The belief in equality, he held, had set the nation on a path to inevitable self-destruction. As he saw it, regrettably, "the errors of the past still clung to many" persons even as evidence against equality accumulated. But, Stephens announces, ultimate victory in the assault on equality was assured because "it was as impossible to war successfully against a principle in politics as it was in physics and mechanics." With the belief in equality already eradicated "throughout the length and breadth of the Confederate States," Stephens assures his hearers that the "social fabric" of the Confederacy "is firmly planted" internally. With the opportunities that will result from replacing equality with *inequality* as a foundational value, he is sure that the Confederacy will become a new city on a hill, broadcasting "the ultimate success of a full recognition of this principle throughout the civilized world."[4]

Ralph Waldo Emerson singles out the Cornerstone Speech in his December 1863 lecture "The Fortune of the Republic" as a great asset in the defense of equality. Speaking as the war dragged on after Gettysburg that summer, Emerson had begun to feel that the Union might go weak in the knees. He calls Stephens an "eminent benefactor of the Union in this war" because he admitted in the Cornerstone Speech the core value that was under threat. Stephens had declared to his fellow Georgians that slavery was not only consistent with "the theory and policy of his government" but also the "cornerstone of their State." Other than the Emancipation Proclamation, Emerson concludes, "no other public act has served us so much at home and abroad" (*AW* 148). Stephens's words were perfect reminders of what was at stake in the defense of equality.

In the Cornerstone Speech, to begin explaining the error that the Confederacy was correcting, Stephens confronts the legacy of Thomas Jefferson. The author of the Declaration of Independence never "fully comprehended the great truth" of human inequality.[5] Jefferson, like most of the Founders, grounded the republic in the idea that "all men are created equal"; but,

Stephens argues, new knowledge in science, political economy, even history and religion had proven that the opposite was true. In order to progress, self-governing republics—following the long example of monarchies and aristocracies—would have to recognize that human inequality is an insuperable reality and that accepting this prescriptive reality is necessary for civilization to prosper.

Preparing to dismiss Jefferson's assumptions about equality as a historical relic, Stephens summarizes the Founders' idealism:

> The prevailing ideas entertained by . . . most of the leading statesmen at the time of the formation of the old Constitution, were that the enslavement of the African was in violation of the laws of nature; that it was wrong in *principle*, socially, morally, and politically. It was an evil they knew not well how to deal with, but the general opinion of the men of that day was that, somehow or other in the order of providence, the institution would be evanescent and pass away.[6]

Though they did not know how to end it, many of the Founders had indeed conceded that slavery was an anachronistic holdover from less perfect times. In *Notes on the State of Virginia*, for example, Jefferson imagines the ancient origin of slavery in a way that assumes the inherent equality of slaves and masters.[7] He reels at the suppressed hatreds promoted by slave society: "With what execration should the statesman be loaded"? Jefferson challenges:

> Who, permitting one half [of his] citizens . . . to trample on the rights of the other, transforms those into despots, and these into enemies, destroys the morals of the one part, and the amor patriae of the other[?] For if a slave can have a country in this world, it must be any other in preference to that in which he is born to live and labor for another: in which he must lock up the faculties of his nature, contribute as far as depends on his individual endeavours to the envanishment of the human race, or entail his own miserable condition on the endless generations proceeding from him. . . . Can the liberties of a nation be thought secure when we have removed their only firm basis, a conviction in the minds of the people that these liberties are the gift of God?[8]

Writing in the early 1780s, and speaking as a slaveholder, slave trader, and master of a "substitute wife" with whom he would father seven children born into slavery, Jefferson sees the invention of slavery as the emergence of a universal civil war, a condition destructive to society and incompatible with his conception of the human being.⁹ Reaching back to a state of nature, he castigates the misguided "statesman" who first allowed one person to degrade another to the status of slave. Jefferson's gauzy but visceral complaint offers regret that slavery ever emerged, but it presents no measurable counterweight to the forces that had entrenched it in his society and in his home.

In the decades between Jefferson's and Alexander Stephens's careers, slavery, and the assumptions about human nature on which it was grounded, did not conveniently fade away through obsolescence. On the contrary, in the period between the Revolution and the Civil War, slavery expanded in both numbers and geography. In some parts of the country it was illegalized through gradual emancipation, but in others it expanded and grew even more dehumanizing. In the nineteenth century, several states were admitted to the United States in which slavery would be legal—including the giant-sized state of Texas. Most important for the broader assault on equality, the defense of slavery was the hub that held together all the spokes of a broad-based effort to discredit the idea of equality as either a personal value or a civic aspiration.

In the Cornerstone Speech, after dismissing the Founders as believers in anachronistic dogma, Stephens ticks off the newly affirmed truths on which the Confederate States of America would rest. The egalitarian ideals that were articles of faith for Jefferson and the "leading statesmen" of the Revolution

> were fundamentally wrong. They rested upon the assumption of the equality of the races. This was an error. . . .
>
> Our [Confederate] government is founded upon exactly the opposite idea; its foundations are laid, its corner-stone rests upon the great truth, that the negro is not equal to the white man; that slavery—subordination to the superior race—is his natural and normal condition.
>
> This, our new government, is the first, in the history of the world, based upon this great physical, philosophical, and moral truth.¹⁰

Stephens's defense of inequality is important not just as a statement of racist proslavery thought but also for the brazen self-assurance with which he summarizes the basic arguments that drove the assault on equality. He presents them here as if they were settled facts—which to his mind they were. He treats the debate over equality as a closed issue, at least within the Confederacy. Stephens's reference to newly articulated "physical, philosophical, and moral" truths was an intentional effort to erase Jefferson's "self-evident" truths by juxtaposing the abstractions of eighteenth-century moral philosophy against the concrete authority of modern empirical science. For Stephens, the Confederate States of America, by laying its cornerstone on the established fact of human inequality, had replaced a wrong idea with a right idea. Even more emphatically, by building its institutions on an ideal of inequality, the Confederacy would define a new stage in world civilization. The revised and updated nation would be a republic, but it would be a caste society that would create insuperable boundaries between many different types of people. In light of the truths established by the assault on equality, it strikes Stephens as madness to harbor Enlightenment ideals about equality. Those "who cling to these errors with a zeal above knowledge, we justly denominate fanatics." After all that humankind had learned, continued belief in universal equality was an "aberration of the mind," "a defect in reasoning," "a species of insanity."[11]

Ralph Waldo Emerson's public career was a lifelong effort to address the assault on equality that allowed Alexander Stephens to speak with such self-assurance. Stephens's confidence that he acts in the vanguard of history dramatizes just how successful the opponents of equality had been in making their case. The Confederacy's willingness to present itself openly to the world both as a modern society guided by reason *and* as a society committed to slavery and permanent inequality underscores just how narrowly equality was holding its ground and preventing the caste model from becoming the authoritative standard for American values. Between 1830 and the secession crisis of the late 1850s, an intense assault on equality had reversed momentum toward the general abolition of slavery. During this period, equality was at the center of a high-stakes debate over the nature and boundaries of human rights. New theories advanced the idea that inherent inequalities within the human race made slavery and other forms of domination moral, natural, and even necessary to the progress of civilization. Universal equality, rather than representing an original natural condition, a fact of divine creation, or even an aspirational civic ideal, was just a false idea that should be retired alongside alchemy and augury.

EMERSON
and the
DEFENSE
OF EQUALITY

Introduction
EMERSON AND THE
MEANINGS OF EQUALITY

The path that leads from Jefferson's claim that equality is a self-evident truth to the Confederate States' rejection of equality as false philosophy unfolds in a surprisingly brief time span and takes place in an environment where both equality and inequality were rapidly changing. As Jacksonian Americans took steps toward creating a more egalitarian society, organized opposition to equality was also intensifying. Nationwide, efforts to protect and expand slavery were gaining credibility through research in anthropology and history. In the South, slavery was becoming more deeply rooted. In the North, the expansion of factory production from the late 1810s onward was creating a concentrated proletariat in factory towns where owners and "hands" inhabited radically unequal worlds. The cotton boom that linked southern planters and northern mill owners created a class of magnates who marshaled wealth and influence which dwarfed that of the richest eighteenth-century landowners. In Congress, politicians such as Daniel Webster were arguing that the purpose of government was to protect property rights as a means of preserving a hierarchical social order, regardless of its implications for human rights. On a more subtle level, theorists of sex and gender such as Catharine Beecher were both assisting and subverting the assault on equality by advocating for women's empowerment within a social structure that accepted patriarchal domination as the context of a world sharply divided between men's and women's spheres. Antidemocratic, racist, and proto–social Darwinist ideas were creating powerful justifications for suspicion about the belief that all humans are equal in any sense whatsoever. These and other trends amplified inequalities and were being written permanently into landscapes as commercial, industrial, and residential areas began to separate and take on distinctive class identities. In this environment it was fully plausible to associate inequality with justice, nature, religion, and, above all, with a tradition-based social order ironically buttressed by new forms of knowledge.[1]

Nonetheless, with regard to progress toward a more equal society, the Jacksonian and antebellum years were periods of profound hope and very real change. The reform organizations and associations that formed to advocate for slaves, women, workers, and the poor reflect the sense of enfranchisement and the potential power that ordinary citizens believed they could wield. Reform movements of many types emerged, filled with activists who believed that ambitious goals were within reach. For example, though the pacifist Non-Resistance Societies are largely forgotten now, during Emerson's lifetime radical pacifism aimed to spearhead a global disarmament movement complete with international courts to settle disputes before wars broke out and a "Congress of Nations" to systematize global diplomacy. These global pacifists stood alongside and among women's rights reformers, antislavery organizers, and advocates of workers' rights. Edmund Quincy, for example, son of Josiah Quincy III, a relative of Abigail Adams, president of Harvard, and congressman, was a leader in both the antislavery and global pacifist movements. The dedication of activists committed to what we would now call social justice testifies to a widely held belief that social ills could be remedied by the collective action of free individuals speaking out and making the case for change.

This energy in the emergent culture of reform also reflects a foreboding sensitivity that was equally on the surface of antebellum society. Emerson was twenty-nine years old when he resigned from a prestigious position as senior pastor of a Unitarian church to enter the inchoate world of social reform. In an equally portentous act, just one year earlier, twenty-six-year-old William Lloyd Garrison began publishing his antislavery newspaper *The Liberator*. Though they differed greatly in style, they both embarked on paths that led to the same place: the defense of equality with opposition to slavery at its center. Even as the emergence of a broad-based culture of reform represented power and hope, its emergence underscores the pervasive sense that the whole social edifice was corrupt and brittle.

This book emphasizes Ralph Waldo Emerson's defense of equality within an environment where belief in equality was under extreme pressure. His thought about equality emerged as part of an ongoing debate and in direct response to the assault on equality that allowed Alexander Stephens to embrace a comprehensive anti-egalitarian worldview. While Emerson's name has become almost synonymous with the idea of individual freedom and is rarely associated with equality in anything other than an abstract spiritual sense, his theory of self-reliance is also a sustained rebuttal of the assault on equality. It is built around a theory of equality that took shape early in his career and remained remarkably stable through many tests and trials. Emerson's theory has three fundamental values: it is aspirational, it is universalizing, and it grows outward from the dignity people accord one another in acts of sincere communication. Throughout a long career advocating for liberty, Emerson argued again and again that freedom was a mockery if the society that promoted it did not also maintain high standards of equality among its members. The connection between freedom and equality in Emerson's thought begins in spirituality and runs through his attitude toward democratization, his thought about marriage and love, his response to scientific inquiry—especially racist anthropology—and his understandings of commerce and property rights.

In the face of sustained attacks on one of his core values, articulating the conviction that universal human equality is both the goal of human society and the necessary condition for individual freedom became a central mission of Emerson's public career. As an idealist and an optimist regarding the inevitability of moral progress, he believed that forces opposing the expansion of equality represent impermanent obstacles to be overcome as people hearken to the most aspiring and generous voices they hear in themselves and in the communities around them. Even as his idealism takes on pragmatic and even skeptical additions, Emerson never strays from the belief that what is most needful in the process of rising toward equality is the willingness to sweep aside the disabling institutions of the past and to rebuild relations on truthful and sincere acts of self-expression and communication.

Emerson's defense of equality was about sustaining the hard-won gains that had broken feudal and theocratic societies and facilitating the momentum of change toward a society in which individual self-respect presupposed recognition of every other person's equality. Since the values that bind all people into a single cosmopolitan community are universal and foundational, he believed they could be spoken by anyone, anywhere, and the individual need only unlock their "human doors," as he puts it in "The Poet," to liberate "a great public power" that would lift society toward a higher standard of equality (*CW* 3:16).

On a less soaring level of imagination, as he responded to various specific lines of argument that made up the assault on equality, his assumption that all people are equals in a universal Spirit was tested from multiple perspectives. Anthropological arguments that gave plausibility to statements like Alexander Stephens's rejection of racial equality or claims that women had more acute moral sense but were less capable of reasoning than men forced Emerson continually to plumb his own values and his own commitment to equality. In his lectures and journals he often wavers from position to position, and his thought about equality is rife with contradiction. On spiritual equality, Emerson was almost always unequivocal. But on equality as a normative value, or even as a historical and social possibility, he vacillated. He often expresses visceral prejudices—misogynist and racist. Over and over, however, and in contrast to the paths of influential public voices such his friend Louis Agassiz, an eminent scientist; Daniel Webster, the idol of his youth; and even fellow Transcendentalist Theodore Parker, Emerson resolves his ambivalences into public commitments to equality.

The debate over slavery was at the center of it all, and in regard to slavery and racial equality, Emerson concluded that the antislavery societies operating all around him represented a "moral revolution" that, if successful, would redefine what it meant to be human (*AW* 26). He concluded that for the United States to outlaw slavery as the British did in 1834 would signal the possibility of an actual, realized equality. Through emancipation in their West Indian colonies, the British had given the "immense fortification of a fact" to every egalitarian's dreaming, and the United States was shamed by Britain's example (*AW* 7). His own study of slavery and the slave trade, and then his participation in antislavery, sharpened his defense of equality.

In the late 1830s and the 1840s, Emerson's importance as a religious rebel made him an admired figure and a fellow traveler to activists in other reform movements. Sustained engagement with antislavery activists and friendships with women reformers, as well as personal observation of growing factory towns in Massachusetts, brought him to mount stronger and more comprehensive defenses of equality. His thought about the rights of laborers, contrary to his libertarian impulses, brought him to articulate a distinct position on the duties and responsibilities of government. It led him to conclude that "government exists to defend the weak and the poor and the injured party," and that all other acts of government, especially its bias toward property rights over human rights, functioned to oppress persons and to sustain existing inequalities (*AW* 26).

This repeating pattern in his thought, especially as it occurs in response to specific events in his society, makes Emerson as important in the history of equality as he is in the history of liberty. Further, his value as a theorist of equality is not only his real-time rebuttal of antiegalitarian arguments, but also in providing a detailed theory that presented equality as the condition that underpins individual liberty and makes it possible.

EMERSONIAN EQUALITY

Emerson's understanding of equality has its roots in spirituality. In the late 1820s, he began his long public life by working to change the way people experienced spirituality within the Unitarian Church. In the sermons he delivered as a minister, he asked listeners not to ground their faith in obedience to doctrine or tradition but to cultivate the values they found most true and to let those values define their words and actions. This integration of a self-reflective spirituality with action in the world encouraged each individual to craft an independent spiritual identity. It invited people to evaluate and judge conventional religious beliefs and to follow the spiritual signals that felt most truthful to them, even if it meant rejecting the "dear old doctrines of the church," as he puts it in "Self-Reliance" (*CW* 3:30). As his career progressed, he asked people to expand the range of self-reflective independence to include political democracy, friendship and marriage, racial equality, and property rights. This mode of "aversive thinking" encouraged each person to link individuality with a form of mental rebellion that allowed them to distinguish between their own values and the values they were feeling social pressure to accept.[2]

In Emerson's writing, equality adapts this process of self-culture to define a standard of authentic communication in both private and civil relationships. In a thumbnail creation myth that he articulates in "The Poet," Emerson defines interlocking values that shape his theory of equality: "The Universe has three children . . . which we will call here the Knower, the Sayer, and the Doer. These stand respectively for the love of truth, the love of good, and for the love of beauty. These three are equal" (*CW* 3:35). In Emerson's formulation, truth, goodness, and beauty are equal not because of similarity but because they are irreducible sympathies or values. In terms of Emerson's defense of equality, the two most important qualities to highlight about these values are, first, that as people live their lives, they are always *combining* them in thought, speech, and action. Eloquence without goodness is dangerous. Cynical eloquence is the demagogue's tool, whereas eloquence combined with goodness is the prophet's. Beauty without truth is attractive but frivolous.

Second, as an aspirational model, in Emerson's understanding of equality, combining these values involves a process of leveling up. Equality is a fact of Spirit, but in "the *divided*, or social state" it does not achieve itself. It is at the top of an aspirational ladder, not in the middle, like a mathematical mean or median. Unlike a mean or median, which divides something into two equal parts, Emersonian equality is at the very pinnacle, where the individual becomes equal to themself and equal to every other self. As he puts it in "The Poet," "Nature has a higher end, in the production of new individuals, than security, namely *ascension*, or the passage of the soul into higher forms" (*CW* 3:14). By facilitating the process of helping people ascend to their own individuality, he defines gifted rhetors as "liberating gods" who enable people to see themselves and the world more truthfully (*CW* 3:18).

In Emerson's thought, nothing comes down to equality; by its nature, people and societies must rise in order to achieve the condition of equals. Reaching equality in friendship, marriage, or citizenship marks the highest possible human achievement. In talking about Shakespeare in "Natural History of Intellect," for example, Emerson remarks that "Shakespeare astonishes by his equality in every play, act, scene, or line."[3] Equality, here, is almost synonymous with excellence. Emerson foregrounds the combination of substantive, contextual, and aesthetic elements to define Shakespeare's ability to unify various affects and write at the highest level of quality. To work at that level is to be equal.

The possibility of reform, growth, and improvement is built into Emerson's idea that equality is an aspirational standard. This recognition of realistic positive potential is crucial to Emerson's response to the assault on equality. Rather than accept popular and influential research that seemed to prove equality false, Emerson took the claims of anti-egalitarian research seriously but resisted the conclusions, working his way back to reconfirming equality as the valid universal ideal. In "The Divinity School Address," for example, shared ideals of virtue serve as correctives to the arrogance of educated religious elites by reminding each person "that he, equally with every man, is an inlet into the deeps of Reason" (*CW* 1:79). This foundational recognition of untapped potential, regardless of class or education, the sense that each person can be an "inlet" to truth, lies at the foundation of a more egalitarian society. Accepting one's own access to the highest truths denotes an aspirational standard of self-respect, but it also requires recognition and respect for others, since they too have access to the "deeps of Reason."

Using church attendance as a metaphor for the ties that bind a community together, he brings the potential for equality home to the audience of the address. Talking to the assembled faculty and graduates of Harvard Divinity School, Emerson ticks through a long list of reasons for the decline in church attendance. His critique of the church goes on for pages. But after pointing out all the reasons why people had walked away, he identifies a bedrock on which to rebuild. The new foundation will be not the eloquence or learning of the clergy, not doctrine, not even the promise of salvation. Rather, it will be the simple fact that congregants gather to acknowledge their shared spiritual equality: "What was once a mere circumstance" that "all should meet . . . in one house, in sign of an equal right in the soul,—has come to be a paramount motive for going [to church]" (*CW* 1:88). As much as "The Divinity School Address" was a call to spiritual individuality, it was also proposing a new standard of social and spiritual egalitarianism as a corrective to the intellectual and social elitism of the Unitarian ministry.

In addition to being an aspirational ethical standard for the way people should treat one another, Emersonian equality is universalizing. Emerson uses the word "equality" in ways similar to the way he uses the terms "union" and "unify" or "eternal." In his lexicon it implies universal recognition of all persons and things in a bond of equivalence that is either affirmed or violated by behavior. In *Nature* he writes, "Nature stretches out her arms to embrace men, only let his thoughts be of equal greatness." As in this case, where equality combines a universal embrace with an aspirational call, the idea extends beyond the purely personal—beyond being "equal" to a task or a responsibility. Reducing equality just to application in social settings, it asks each individual to recognize the vast, diverse world of individual persons and then to imagine them not in ranked order but organically united as equals. In "New England Reformers" he imagines this all-encompassing equality as a "congress of kings," a community in which each person acts as an independent sovereign meeting together with other sovereigns interested in reform. There, "each is proposing projects for the salvation of the world." In "Politics" he imagines it possible that "thousands of human beings might exercise toward each other the grandest and simplest sentiments, as well as a knot of friends, or a pair of lovers" (*CW* 3:129).

The universalizing aspect of Emerson's model of equality definitely has a mystical side. Since "the universe is the externisation of the soul," he writes in "The Poet," "all the facts of the animal economy, sex, nutriment, gestation, birth, growth, are symbols of the passage of the world into the soul of man, to suffer there a change and reappear a new and higher fact" (*CW* 3: 9,13). His universalizing mysticism allows him to occlude contradictions and loop together a unified whole, comprising an all-encompassing Spirit, external nature, and the authentic self-expression of every living person. In a crucial line at the very end of "Politics"—a line that most commentators tend to avoid—Emerson remarks that "the power of love, as the basis of the state, has never been tried" as a means of marking his aspirational merging of quotidian transactions like those of "the post-office, of the highway, of commerce and the exchange of property" with government through "the moral sentiment and a sufficient belief in the unity of things" (*CW* 3:128). For the purpose of detailing Emerson's thought about equality, his mystical universalizations obfuscate, but they also underpin his emphasis on integration and combination. In Emerson's thought, things want both to liberate or atomize themselves *and* to unify; they want to claim their freedom *and* to merge with their opposites. Emerson's preoccupation with this metaphysical churning provides a vital energy to his conception of progress toward a more genuine equality. For things to combine implies a deep sharing, a preexisting affinity that allows a literal connection.

Disparate things combining and recombining is the process of movement toward equality. While one's "thoughts" can be private and purely individual as they reach to be equal with Nature, the ethics Emerson builds into that aspiration are unavoidably social. Also in *Nature*, Emerson argues for parallelism between nature and society: "The axioms of physics translate the laws of ethics. Thus, ... reaction is equal to action" in politics and friendship equally with the motion of elements in nature (*CW* 1:21). The value of a proposition like "the smallest weight may be made to lift the greatest, the difference of weight being compensated by time," is true in both "an ethical as well as physical sense," so that propositions that explain the physical world "have a much more extensive and universal sense when applied to human life, than when confined to technical use" (*CW* 1:21–22).

Emerson's model of equality is grounded in the highest standard of sincerity in communication. Recognition of another is an act of spiritual trust. In "Self-Reliance" Emerson sets personal authenticity as a standard for achieving the equality that flows back and forth between others and oneself: "My life is for itself and not for a spectacle. I much prefer that it be of a lower strain, so it be genuine and equal, than that it should be glittering and unsteady" (*CW* 2:31). In "The Over-Soul" he connects equality in a social setting to sincerity in conversation. Sincerity in dialogue lifts all participants: "In groups where debate is earnest . . . the company becomes aware that the thought rises to an equal level in all bosoms, that all have a spiritual property in what was said, as well as the sayer" (*CW* 2:164). This level of reciprocal truthfulness "where debate is earnest" marks the most stringent demand of Emerson's framing of equality. The sincerity of the participants raises the whole group, giving each a share in a valuable "spiritual property." The sincerity is the point because it is the enactment of an internal demand and a sharing of intimate thought. Sincere expression represents self-affirmation for an individual as they *feel* they are equal to their gifts; and its success even among a small circle of friends gestures toward the possibility of a more equal society. The feeling this type of dialogue creates within the group is egalitarian recognition in action.

Emerson probes the connection between equality and sincerity most deeply in his thought about marriage and friendship, but the issue of sincerity in public speech is also central to his defense of equality. While he acknowledges that sincerity is difficult and causes even the most gifted speakers to stammer in their speech, the intentional insincerity of proslavery rhetoric is a very different thing. The cynical corruption of public discourse, which becomes one of Emerson's key targets in the 1850s, marked a central strategy in the assault on equality. His critique of proslavery rhetoric at that time was grounded in the belief that slavery's advocates were distorting language in ways that made sincere public dialogue more difficult. Sustained as a norm, this practice was becoming a potent threat to momentum toward a more equal society. As he puts it in his 1854 essay on the Fugitive Slave Law, "The habit of oppression cuts out the moral eyes, and though the intellect goes on simulating the moral as before, its sanity is invaded and gradually destroyed" (*AW* 85). The carving away of moral sight that allows slavery to be justified as a "positive good" brings forward the importance of sincere dialogue to Emerson's defense of equality. Equality for Emerson, is immanently social. It requires sharing and connection, is even incomprehensible without it, because when applied to persons, equality denotes the relationship between two or more individuals.[4]

After remarking that the habit of oppression "cuts out the moral eyes," Emerson offers a little scenario about communication: "If you have a nice question of right and wrong, you would not go with it to Louis Napoleon; or to a political hack; or to a slave-driver," because the conversation would surely be insincere. In that discussion, intellect could apologize for slavery, just as Daniel Webster had done in the crisis of 1850. But in this dialogue, "good" would be absent as the intellect goes "on simulating the moral." Without the combination of the "love of truth" and the "love of good," any conversation about a question of morality is sure to be guided by strategy rather than by sincerity. In his antislavery writings, Emerson argues that the assault on equality was conducted partly by promoting a general acceptance of hypocrisy. The rhetoric justifying slavery as benevolent, historical, and natural allowed the Fugitive Slave Act and the Kansas-Nebraska Act to shrink the geographic boundaries within which equality could even be discussed as a shared value. In his "Address to the Citizens of Concord on the Fugitive Slave Law," Emerson draws the realm of sincere dialogue very tight, just to the borders of Massachusetts, and even there it had failed. As he puts it, "The great game of government has been win the sanction of Massachusetts to the crime" (*AW* 71). But having been drawn into acceptance of slave hunting by their own senator, Emerson feels, the people are left "with all sense of self-respect and fair fame cut off, with the names of conscience and religion become bitter ironies." Public discourse had been so corrupted that any use of the word "liberty" becomes a "ghastly mockery." Preparing for the fight to come, Emerson exhorts his Concord townsmen to avoid complicity: "Here let there be no confusion in our ideas. Let us not lie, nor steal, nor help to steal; and let us not call stealing by any fine names such as 'Union' or 'Patriotism'" (*AW* 71).

Against the leveling down that encouraged his countrymen to slacken their attachment to equality, Emerson's model of egalitarian communication combines sincerity and aspiration to mark public dialogue as a high, generous, sincere form of sharing. Drawing out equality as aspirational, Emerson counterintuitively sees most individual achievements, especially those of politicians, as signs of people's *failure* to achieve equal relationships with their peers. In the 1844 essay "Politics," he remarks that most of us are "haunted" by a feeling that we should live with more "grandeur of character," but failing to live up to that ideal, we keep busy in the "strife of trade" to buy the "fig-leaf with which the shamed soul attempts to hide its nakedness" (*CW* 3:127). We each have some impressive skill, we "can do somewhat useful, or graceful, or formidable, or amusing, or lucrative. That we do, as an apology to others and to ourselves, for not reaching the mark of a good and equal life" (*CW*: 3:127). The contrast Emerson draws here is in the relationship between the visible achievements of the individual and the higher challenge of acquiring the discipline to treat other people as equals. In "Domestic Life," he applies this egalitarian idealism to the reform of domestic relations between husbands and wives. Domestic life is rife with rotten compromises, and this should be the starting place, the true incubator of equality: "Our social forms are very far from truth and equity. But the way to set the axe at the root of the tree is to raise our aim" (*CW* 7:59). Even in this most intimate relationship, justice within the household will require a complete reinvention of the way men and women talk to each other in the private realm. It will require a form of dialogue that acknowledges the truth and aims for equity.

The set of connections that underpins Emerson's thought about equality, its aspirational and universalizing quality, and its grounding in sincere dialogue does not change much over time. Late in his career, in "Natural History of Intellect," Emerson is still asserting that the simple fact of consciousness means that "all men are, in respect to this source of truth, on a certain footing of equality."[5] Or in "Worship," published as part of *The Conduct of Life* in the election year 1860, "the moral equalizes all: enriches, empowers all" (*CW* 6:124). Between the 1830s and the 1860s, the assault on equality put extreme pressure on Emerson's commitment to equality. Seemingly faced from all quarters with plausible claims against equality—some sincerely offered, some rankly cynical—he worked across a broad range of topics to address anti-egalitarian claims and to test them against the ideals that he believed drove history forward. For his society to accept terms of defeat or even to compromise in the debate over equality would simply yank the ground from under his commitments to liberty and self-reliance.

ANTEBELLUM EQUALITIES

In antebellum America the debate over equality was uniquely broad and intense. J. R. Pole, in an indispensable study, addresses four kinds of equality that he places at the center of *The Pursuit of Equality in American History*: political equality, equality before the law, equality of property, and equality of esteem or respect. In Pole's estimation, equality before the law is primary because it serves as the point of connection between earlier philosophical constructions of the human being and the political construction of civil society. He situates equality before the law at the roots of modernity, emphasizing its importance to early social contract theory and treating it as the necessary foundation for other forms of equality.

Pole frames equality before the law in antebellum America through the social contract theorists of the seventeenth century: "The egalitarianism of... Thomas Hobbes was that of total submission. All subjects of the Leviathan were subject equally to its laws and equally powerless; for this was the only way for humanity to extricate itself in safety from the terrible war of all against all that was its natural condition."[6] For Hobbes, Pole argues, the key issue is the maintenance of civil order through a universal requirement of submission to authority. In Hobbes's model, equality is valuable not because it is just but because it reflects the comprehensive power of the law.[7] Ultimately, for Hobbes, the Leviathan is there to sustain order; issues of justice and fairness are relevant but secondary to the idea that every person is governed under the same inescapable power. It is lawful and orderly; in its way, it is even equal. But it is just barely civil. Avoiding the "natural" human condition of unrestrained liberty, however, is the purpose of Hobbes's social contract.

John Locke, by contrast, revises Hobbes by ranking natural and civil law in a way that, Pole argues, launches the evolution of egalitarianism into the present, especially in relation to private property and political equality. Weighing natural law more heavily than Hobbes, Locke, in his amplification of natural law, is fundamental to Emerson's theory of equality, especially in its universalizing quality and in the way it relates to statute law. Emerson distinguishes between natural and statute law over and over. In reacting to the Kansas-Nebraska Act he echoes Locke, saying, "Laws do not make right, but are simply declaratory of a right which already existed" (*AW* 57). A certain limited standard of equality, for Locke, was written by God into the order of "Nature." "There being nothing more evident," Locke writes, "than that creatures of the same species and rank promiscuously born to all the same advantages of Nature, and [with] the use of the same faculties, should also be equal one amongst another without Subordination or subjection."[8] Locke here justifies civil equality among persons as a way of recognizing God's placement of humankind in the great chain of being that defines nature. For Locke, statute law had to reflect natural law because, as Pole paraphrases, "the function of civil law was to give security to already existing natural rights."[9]

Combining "protection for legally equal individuals" with the standard of consent of the governed as the test of legitimacy in Locke's transformed "leviathan" of civil society gave crucial momentum to claims for political equality and defines the root of modern democratic government. As Alexander Keyssar phrases it, "The idea that voting was a natural right or even a right at all was rhetorically powerful: it meshed well with the Lockean political theory that was popular in eighteenth-century America, it had a clear anti-monarchical thrust, and it had the virtue of simplicity."[10] As Pole concludes, participatory standards of political equality serve as the vehicle for reminding a democratic government that despite victory at the polls, elected officials always have to be wary of public opinion: "When dissatisfied individuals used the political or legal process to remind American governments of this obligation [to represent the people] they did not always succeed in their aims, but they had the satisfaction, however remote, of warning the government that its entire right to govern was founded on this commitment."[11] This legitimacy-check function of dissent expressed in elections codifies the egalitarian emergence of a long-present precursor to political equality as a standard for the legitimacy of political office. Ulrike Davy and Antje Flüchter give deep context to this often repressed foundation of democratic political values: "For centuries, at least in Christian Europe, social and political entities were conceptualized as being based on hierarchies of social status and rank. Yet to some extent, precursors of modern concepts of equality were present either in the context of spiritual movements or in the context of social uprisings."[12]

In contrast to the uniformity assumed in equality before the law, defining a model of other types of equality that would be flexible enough to acknowledge inequalities of talent, skill, and motivation is in many ways the necessary adjustment to the fact that equality denotes a relationship between things but has no explicit content within itself. In application, the fact that equality denotes a relationship also provides the justification for rejecting the validity of universal equality altogether. Many eighteenth-century liberal political theorists argued that unequal distribution of talent and skill justified a wide variety of inequalities, and that ensuring liberty required that many forms of inequality should not be mitigated. The churn in political priorities and the continual tendency toward inequality in different areas always posed a threat to liberty because as things change, some people come under the power of others. Making value judgments about the potential exploitative power of skill and property always has to be on the radar of a society that values equality. As Benjamin Rush, a signer of the Declaration of Independence and a Philadelphia physician, put it, even in an egalitarian republic, wealth will tend to accumulate, and as it concentrates, the wealthy will develop a "lust for dominion" that will threaten egalitarian values, at least in terms of economic opportunity and social mobility:

> It has often been said, that there is but one rank of men in America, and therefore, that there should be only one representation of them in a government. I agree, that we have no artificial distinctions of men into noblemen and commoners among us, but it ought to be remarked, that superior degrees of industry and capacity, and above all, commerce, have introduced inequality of property among us, and these have introduced natural distinctions of rank in Pennsylvania, as certain and general as the artificial distinctions of men in Europe. This will ever be the case while commerce exists in this country. The men of middling property and poor men can never be safe in a mixed representation with the men of over-grown property. Their liberties can only be secured by having exact bounds prescribed to their power, in the fundamental principles of the Constitution. By a representation of the men of middling fortunes in one house, their whole strength is collected against the influence of wealth. Without such a representation, the violent efforts of individuals to oppose it would be divided and broken, and would want that system, which alone would enable them to check that lust for dominion which is always connected with opulence.[13]

Debate over political equality was heated from the Revolutionary period onward, but in the world of Emerson's childhood, inequality was less troubling in economic relations because the opportunities available to enterprising men seemed so vast. As Noah Webster put it in 1793, in America "every man finds employment, and the road is open for the poorest citizen to amass wealth by labor and economy, and by his talent and virtue to raise himself to the highest offices of the State."[14] In Jacksonian America, equality of opportunity meant first and foremost economic freedom without domination by arbitrary powers. The titanic struggle over the Bank of the United States resonated so deeply among Jacksonian Democrats because the national bank symbolized a monopolistic power that rigged investment opportunity to the disadvantage of working people. At its core, the Jacksonian anti-bank stand was grounded in the belief that a venture capital market regulated by natural law rather than by a state-run bank would foster equality of opportunity and prevent an aristocratic elite from monopolizing access to capital.[15]

At the same time that Jacksonians fought for an unregulated market in the Bank War, workers' unions began to emerge to protect wages and negotiate safety, hours, and other work conditions. As factory towns such as Lowell and Lawrence, Massachusetts, re-created the poverty of European factory cities, it became increasingly difficult to believe that economic trends were promoting equality of opportunity or property. The deteriorating ability of workers to achieve economic independence through the labor market reduced the issue from a question of opportunity to a crisis of respect for workingmen.[16] In the free states, maintaining living standards for workingmen and resisting the centralization of production became a crucial front in the defense of equality. Even before the expansion of the franchise to white male non-freeholders, experiments in mass production were putting pressure on the ability of workers to believe that they had any chance to achieve economic independence. In New York in 1801, very early for this type of venture, when deep-pocketed investors tried to corner the market in bread by proposing to build a giant oven that could undersell the neighborhood bakeries, local workingmen saw the implication and joined with bakers in protest. A mechanic writing to the *New-York Gazette and General Advertiser* predicted that unless the new factory-sized bakehouse was stopped, its owners would "screw down wages to the last thread." Beaten down by poverty, "the independent spirit, so distinguished at present in our mechanics, and so useful in republics, will be entirely annihilated. The workmen will be servants and slaves." Shortly after it was finished, mysteriously, the industrial bakery burned to the ground and was never rebuilt.[17]

Glaring inequality in distributions of wealth lifted the relevance of issues of esteem and respect in discussions of the relationship between political and economic equality. As Pole phrases it, political equality stood "as a synonym for dignity and status, self-esteem as influenced by social esteem; it stood also for the rectification of unfair distribution of the rewards of industry, meaning in that sense *proportion* rather than real equality; and it stood for the old value of independence or personal control."[18] This idea above all, that equality meant having control over one's life, defined the deepest assumption that was being contested in the antebellum period. In economic terms, equality did not require radical redistribution of wealth—though there were robust egalitarian demands for that.[19] Rather, it required an economic environment in which those with little or no property could both avoid poverty and have a fair prospect of achieving economic independence. In political terms, it meant not just the vote but access to the public debates that would define the norms and values of the society. In terms of respect, it meant the ability to oppose the interests of wealth without fear of degrading or immiserating retaliation.

The move from an open to a secret ballot during the 1840s and 1850s marks a key point of intersection between economic equality, political equality, and equality of respect. During the early years of universal white male suffrage, many considered the secret ballot furtive and unmanly, but in a surprisingly short number of election cycles the secret ballot, and the right to keep one's voting private, came to reflect autonomy, independence, and an expression of the right to privacy.[20]

This popular awareness of layering among various forms of equality, each with significantly different consequences, is vividly represented in a well-known moment in the 1858 Lincoln–Douglas debates. Stephen Douglas, seeking to define Abraham Lincoln as a radical egalitarian, argued that Lincoln advocated comprehensive equality for African Americans. Lincoln replied to this charge neither by confirming nor by denying his egalitarianism, but by clarifying the one specific type of equality that he embraced and the types that he rejected. "I agree with Judge Douglas" in most of his racist judgments, said Lincoln, declaring that the African American "is not my equal in many respects—certainly not in color, perhaps not in moral and intellectual endowment. But in the right to eat the bread, without leave of anybody else, which his own hand earns, *he is my equal and the equal of Judge Douglas, and the equal of every living man.*"[21] Isolating the power to keep what one has earned through honest labor won Lincoln the cheers of the crowd that day. But what is important for my purpose is that Lincoln was able to assume that his audience had a subtle enough understanding of different types of equality that he could single out the equal right to personal liberty and the right freely to contract one's labor as inalienable, while excluding all other forms of equality from his ideal of civil justice.

As thin as his defense of equality is, Lincoln nonetheless assumes that some rights are universal and that there is thus a minimal standard of equality that civil society must defend. In Illinois, in 1858, a majority of voters disagreed and returned Stephen Douglas to the Senate. Lincoln, of course, won the presidency two years later at the top of the Republican ticket. But even then, he won a narrow plurality against his Whig and Democratic opponents. Not one of the slaveholding states was willing to accept even the narrow definition of equality that Lincoln campaigned on in his senatorial and presidential bids.[22] By that point, Lincoln's very limited egalitarianism was a minority opinion.

In this complex debate, the assault on equality was not confined to political propaganda from southern defenders of slavery. Its racist anti-egalitarianism had also become embedded in northern political discourse. As old-line Whigs were looking for a new political home after the formation of the Republican Party in 1854, Rufus Choate, a prominent constitutional lawyer who had taken Daniel Webster's seat in the Senate, rejected equality with a dismissive quip that was long quoted to sum up the realist's curt rebuttal to egalitarian idealism of the sort that Emerson championed. As the Republicans defined their platform and the Whigs disintegrated around the question of expanding slavery into the territories, Choate sent a letter to the battered Whig Party in Maine. Facing a new and treacherous political landscape, the stalwart rump of the party wanted Choate's advice on whom to support in the next election.

Choate's words make vivid just how successful three decades of concerted assault on the idea of universal human equality had been, even in Emerson's Massachusetts. Choate argues that the Republican insurgents' commitment to preventing the spread of slavery is self-destructive altruism: "To defeat and dissolve the new geographical party, calling itself Republican. This is our first duty." Casting the Republicans as a regional spoiler in the upcoming election, Choate adopts the posture of the national statesman. The question every patriot must ask himself is: "By what vote can I do most to prevent the madness of the times from working its maddest act,—the very ecstasy of its madness,—the permanent formation and the actual present triumph of a party which knows one-half of America only to hate and dread it." Of all things, he implores his readers to think of the insults that slaveholding honor had already suffered by the mere formation of a party publicly opposed to the spread of slavery. In dealing with the touchy feelings of the slaveholders, northern Whigs must allow "for passions, for pride, for infirmity, for the burning sense of even imaginary wrong" done to their slaveholding countrymen.[23]

As Alexander Stephens would do, Choate grounds his advice in the belief that the idea of universal human equality was a relic from an idealistic childhood. Equality still had many defenders, but it had been beaten so low that it had become a subject for mockery by United States senators. Even more cavalierly than Alexander Stephens, Choate waves away the Declaration of Independence as a jejune piece of wartime propaganda, a tract made up of empty slogans that no serious person could believe. The Republican Party was not viable because it was grounded in false principles: "The doctrines of human rights, which it gathers out of the Declaration of Independence—that passionate and eloquent manifesto of a revolutionary war—and adopts as its fundamental ideas, announce to any Southern apprehension a crusade of the government against slavery." If a party motivated by such principles were ever to take control of the national government, it would be "the beginning of the end" of the United States: "flushed by triumph, . . . its mission to inaugurate freedom and put down the oligarchy; its constitution the glittering and sounding generalities of natural right which make up the Declaration of Independence."[24] The pragmatic defenders of union in Maine thus had to decide whether the flagging Whigs, the hated Democrats, or the American Party would be a stronger bulwark against the discredited ideals of "natural right" voiced in the "glittering and sounding generalities" that expressed their opponents' naïve belief in equality.

Defending against this threatening political realignment would require, Choate assumes, rejecting equality as a glittering generality and accepting the realpolitik bargains that would enable all the states to continue to live under a single government. Choate's position echoes that which had been taken by his predecessor Daniel Webster ten years earlier, when he publicly mocked William Henry Seward's argument that there was a higher law than the United States Constitution.[25] Standing on a foundation of racist pseudoscience, distorted natural history, proslavery biblical criticism, and long traditions of political philosophy that assumed the presence of slavery, the Massachusetts senator's position in 1856 is virtually indistinguishable from that expressed by fellow Whig Alexander Stephens in defense of the cornerstone ideals of the Confederacy. For both the southern congressman and the New England senator, the idea that all human beings are created equal had been thoroughly discredited; it had become nothing more than a nostalgic generality expressing the innocence of early republican thought. The task of his generation, Choate assumes, was to adapt the virtues of republican society to the manifold facts proving that people of different races, sexes, and abilities had no claim to equality.

Through his participation in the debates of the antebellum culture wars, the principle of universal spiritual equality that drives Emerson's Transcendentalism hardened into a conviction that giving ground on the idea of equality meant giving up on the possibility that progress in civilization could also mean progress for each of its members. In the context of the debate over equality, this idealism stands in sharp contrast to arguments for a caste society that has a "mudsill" of slaves at its base and increasingly refined castes arrayed in hierarchical order above it.[26] Debate about the nature of human similarities and differences, always in process, but triggered in antebellum America as it has been at no other time in American history, is the immediate context of Emerson's defense of equality. As an integral part of his spirituality, the evolution of Emerson's thought about equality is a continual testing and reaffirmation not only of his belief in individual freedom but also of his even more fundamental belief that universal human equality is *the* condition that makes freedom possible.[27]

Seen in a longer perspective, the assault on equality and even the American Civil War was only one confrontation in a much longer debate about the legitimacy and value of the idea that all human beings should be thought of and treated as equals in any respect whatsoever. The establishment and ideological defense of the Confederate States of America mark one apogee of the power of anti-egalitarian ideas. Alexander Stephens's Cornerstone Speech draws together diverse strands to articulate the intent of the assault on equality: to legitimize a society that values liberty but rejects equality.

The debate over equality in the United States and the theories of nationalist and imperial exceptionalism that flourished contemporaneously in post-Napoleonic Europe are the precursors of the master race theories that underpin twentieth-century fascism and Nazism.[28] As Judith Shklar, herself a refugee from Nazism, argued, despite their defeat on the battlefield, those who would abandon equality as an American value may have prevailed ideologically. "In a way the South won the war of ideas," Shklar writes, because the "sociological fatalism" that southerners "developed to justify slavery remained strong long after the war, and in many ways grew even stronger for almost another century."[29] For generations, the strength of the assault on equality made the belief in universal human equality seem quaint and naïve. Even F. O. Matthiessen, writing as imperialism combined with a newer and more virulent breed of master race theory to hurtle the world into war, defined the American Renaissance as a rearguard action. The reform movements and literary achievements of the 1850s "marked the last struggle of the liberal spirit of the eighteenth century in conflict with the rising forces of exploitation."[30] A generation earlier, writing shortly after the end of World War I, the American historian Carl Becker also captured how hard it had become for even the most idealistic to sustain a philosophy that supported a belief in universal human rights. In the closing paragraph of his 1922 book on the Declaration of Independence, Becker pronounces the document dead. The faith that it expressed

> could not survive the harsh realities of the modern world. Throughout the nineteenth century the trend of action . . . gave an appearance of unreality to the favorite ideas of the age of enlightenment. Nationalism and industrialism, easily passing over into an aggressive imperialism, a more trenchant scientific criticism steadily dissolving its own "universal and eternal laws" into a multiplicity of incomplete and temporary hypotheses—these provided an atmosphere in which faith in Humanity could only gasp for breath.[31]

Each of the discourses to which Becker alludes chipped away at the egalitarian principles of Enlightenment thought. Emerging out of a religious tradition that preached each individual's right of access to the Divine, Ralph Waldo Emerson's intellectual life had its deepest roots in the idea of universal spiritual equality. Developing as a public intellectual in a world where the influence of religious authority was drowned out by the din of economic, political, and scientific spectacles, Emerson spent much of his career defending and adapting that egalitarian spirit as it was being battered by the anti-egalitarian hypotheses emerging from the disciplines Becker highlights. The assault on equality in the period leading up to the American Civil War is the great foil for Emerson's career. In his strenuous effort to sustain equality as a value, his defense of equality is far more important than his role as a religious reformer and equal in importance to his advocacy of nonconformist individuality. It required that he test his deepest beliefs and justify over and over again an idea that held the greatest promise for humankind but that has always needed relentless defense.

Chapter 1 of this book, on Emerson's effort to influence the meaning of democratic citizenship, addresses his response to the emergence of mass political parties in the 1830s. Despite his deep reservations about demagoguery and partisanship, Emerson believed that expanding the franchise was not simply a human right but would have positive implications for human dignity. As imperfect as Jacksonian politics was, "the Democracy," as Emerson and his contemporaries called it, was a huge step forward for equality and, therefore, for human dignity. If carried out properly, it would redefine citizenship by offering many more people the public recognition that had long been withheld by the elites of a more hierarchical society. He saw it as the culmination of a progressive history, a final blow to ancient delineations of rank that suppressed natural talents under invidious distinctions of wealth, education, and lineage.

Chapter 2 turns from politics and the civic sphere to domesticity and family life. Though it was difficult to talk about even within the reform community, during the 1840s and 1850s, marriage reform was especially important to antebellum women's rights activists. Emerson's interest in intimacy, friendship, and private relationships made him a vital ally in this project.

The trend toward hyper-gendered identities, amplified by the terms women were forced to accept within coverture marriage, impinged at least as much on women's ability to achieve individuality as the rise of mass political parties did for men. Though Emerson's thought has a clear masculinist bias, as early as 1836 the principle of universalization central to Emersonian equality was resonating with women such as Margaret Fuller and Lucy Stone, who would go on to build foundational arguments and organizations to advocate for women's equality. As theorists of women's empowerment through domesticity, Catharine Beecher and Sarah Josepha Hale, for example, argued that the path to a more just society was to demarcate social spaces according to gender, Emerson was leaning hard in the opposite direction. He argued that progress—not just for women but for all people—lay in allowing the values of sincerity, authenticity, and love to absorb and govern the public realms of the market and politics. By his thinking, the "revolution" that is to be achieved through "the gradual domestication of the idea of culture," as he puts it in "The American Scholar," is a millennia-long process through which the pursuit of domination in politics and markets will be transformed as they embrace the values of intimate friendship. The idealized norms of sincere dialogue and deeply personal self-expression that antebellum Americans associated with friendship, privacy, and the domestic sphere are crucial to Emerson's vision of egalitarian progress.

Chapter 3 addresses Emerson's thought about race and polygenetic theory, or the theory that God populated the earth with different types of humans at the Creation. The central project of the scientific assault on human equality was the effort to establish immutable racial hierarchy as a fact of science. This campaign began with natural historians such as Samuel George Morton and Louis Agassiz working in the Linnaean tradition to categorize and rank human races by genus, species, family, and so on. This "American School" of mid-nineteenth-century ethnologists had two goals: first, to define and stabilize race according to a ranked order that placed Anglo-Saxon European males at the pinnacle of creation; and second, to discredit emergent evolutionary theories This project of the polygenesists is where consequential arguments for the value of racial purity, or "purity of type," begin, and criticizing the idea of racial purity is a particular target in Emerson's defense of equality.

Thinking about topics that range from Cherokee men marrying their professors' daughters to the long history of ethnic assimilation that transformed the English from a Stone Age tribe into the preeminent nation of his century, Emerson reaches the following conclusion about the debate over mutability: those who were arguing for the immutability of species were wrong, and those who were arguing for evolution were right. For Emerson, this process of analyzing different theories explaining racial diversity marked a testing and confirmation of his deepest beliefs because polygenism challenged his conviction that Spirit is always seeking creative combination and transformation.

Chapter 4 focuses on the debate over the role that private property played in creating and sustaining inequality. Emerson's thought about property begins with a benign acceptance of the assumptions of eighteenth-century Common Sense philosophy that linked property, selfhood, and liberty. But it develops from there toward a strong critique of the coercive power of property rights and culminates in a surprisingly strong embrace of socialism. This change is most vivid in changes he made to his "Politics" lecture between 1837 and 1844. The revised version of "Politics" and a new essay, "The Young American," express strong sympathy for socialist movements. They also mark a change in his thought about law and the role of government. He suggests eliminating the legal protections that define property "rights." Since property seems to exert power regardless of human rules, Emerson reasons, then statute law should disregard property and focus exclusively on the protection of human rights, which are so often affected by the coercive powers of wealth.

This reversal is important to the debate over equality because it is part of a broad dispute about the relative roles of human rights and property rights in American society. Laws that were intended to disempower specific categories of people were built into property law in the same way that they were built into women's inequality in marriage. Many of the laws that defined property rights specifically excluded women from ownership. Further, any revaluation of justice that unambiguously gave human rights priority over property rights would make it impossible to maintain legal slavery.

This chapter completes the argument of *Emerson and the Defense of Equality*. Emerson's confrontation with property and commerce engages one of the most ancient sources for modern definitions of liberty and inequality. As strong as connections between property, liberty, and inequality have been in the development of American prosperity, and as fundamental as they remain today, it did not seem implausible in the mid-nineteenth century that a thorough reinvention of property rights was possible and even necessary in order to create a just society. Emerson, like those of his generation who embraced utopian socialism, saw establishing a foundational standard of material equality as the necessary prerequisite for a society that would allow all members the freedom, resources, and opportunity to achieve individuality.

The conclusion homes in on Emerson's long effort to present individuality as a universal human right that harmonizes liberty and equality. He tends to use metaphors of domesticity and intimacy to describe situations in which people communicate in personal terms, freely, and as equals. Sincerity in private conversation was Emerson's foundational model, but his defense of equality aims to advocate sincerity as the vital ethic of self-reliance on the public stage. He saw this standard met in an unexpected place. A series of meetings organized by radical reformers convened in a converted stable on Chardon Street, in Boston, to debate the future of American religion. Emerson found little in the content of the event worth passing on. But he was impressed with the way people treated one another there. He felt the participants had briefly created an authentic egalitarian community. This convention brought together ministers, atheists, men, women, Christians, Jews, white people, and black people, all to talk honestly and as equals about their most deeply held spiritual values. His response to the Chardon Street Convention offers a glimpse into Emerson's realized vision of what equality could mean to individuals who recognize it as a "promise to virtue" (*CW* 4:17).

Throughout his career Emerson was in the thick of debates about practical obstacles to a more equal society. As he participated in the cultural debates of antebellum society, he articulated a subtle, flexible, and influential concept of individual liberty, but he developed that discourse of freedom against a backdrop on which the companion idea of equality was under assault and was at risk of collapsing as a viable social value. His position, tested and reaffirmed over and over again, was that freedom is important, but that no person is free unless they also recognize that every other person is their equal.

I

POLITICAL EQUALITY AND THE "FURIOUS DEMOCRACY"

In 1834, when Andrew Jackson seemed indomitable and political conservatives felt power slipping away from them, the *Richmond Whig* lamented that the Democrats had "classified the rich and intelligent and denounced them as aristocrats[,] . . . they have caressed, soothed, and flattered the heavy class of the poor and ignorant, because *they* held the power which they wanted." As a result, "*the Republic has degenerated into a Democracy.*"[1] The newly formed Whig Party stood for cultural uplift, classical virtue, and respect for tradition. Even as late as 1845, the Whigs often treated democratic equality as a race to the bottom in terms of culture and values. In its introductory issue, the New York Whig journal *American Review* argued that the Democrats' success would level "all things" downward "to an equality of degradation and ruin."[2]

"The Democracy," as Emerson and his contemporaries called the movement that began with efforts to expand the right to vote in the early 1820s, which then coalesced into the Democratic Party at the end of the decade, is as fundamental a context for Emerson's writing as is the sectarian conflict that wracked New England Protestantism at the same time. But "the Democracy" is not synonymous with Andrew Jackson's Democratic Party.[3] It articulated the emergence of a new model of political representation, populist, even demotic, rather than self-consciously rooted in a classical ideal of virtue. When Emerson used the term, "the Democracy" signified an egalitarian impulse that was visceral, irrational, and populist, but that was also inconsistent with individuality. Its rise represented the interests and frustrations of many men who lived at the edges of political enfranchisement.

Holding deep reservations about the public rhetoric of mass politics and the forms of political organization that came with it, Emerson supported the Democracy because it was sweeping away arbitrary political distinctions that had long blocked progress toward equality. But he was ambivalent. Despite its risky implications for public life and the demagogues it hailed as heroes, the rise of the Democracy had the virtue of legitimizing broader access to the ballot box, and thus it had the potential to expand equality and raise the baseline standard of human dignity.

Though Emerson rejected the partisan organizations that were emerging to structure the enlarged electorate, as early as 1834 he grounded the independence that would become self-reliance not in a libertarian model of freedom from government but in the political equality of democracy. "Democracy," he writes, "has its roots in the sacred truth that every man hath in him the divine Reason or that though few men live according to the dictates of Reason, yet all men are created capable of so doing. That is the equality & the only equality of all men. To this truth, we look when we say 'Reverence thyself. Be true to thyself'" (*JMN* 4:357). Or, in a more directly political vein, he writes: "The root and seed of democracy is the doctrine, Judge for yourself. Reverence thyself. It is the inevitable effect of that doctrine, where it has any effect (which is rare), to insulate the partisan, to make each man a state" (*JMN* 4:342). He first announced it at the very end of his 1834 Phi Beta Kappa poem: "For, the true man, as long as earth shall stand, / Is to himself a state, a law, a land."[4] Here, in the image of the individual as a sovereign state, Emerson introduces his most basic metaphor for political identity. This ideal emerged as a consciously crafted alternative to the Democratic and Whig models of citizenship that were taking concrete form in the early 1830s and it says much about his effort to participate in the discourse that would defend equality in Jacksonian America.

The expanded franchise opened a broad new field of public involvement and political influence for hundreds of thousands of white male citizens.[5] By reforming the political structure so that every politically enfranchised citizen, regardless how humble, could see himself as an autonomous political agent analogous to a sovereign state acting in world affairs, "universal" suffrage raised the stature of each new citizen, enhancing his dignity as a human person.[6] The dignifying potential of the Democracy is central to Emerson's advocacy of political equality. At its best, whenever democracy genuinely "effects" a society, Emerson holds, it makes the citizen independent and pries the "partisan" free from the party line collective. The Democracy, by making each individual an independent political power, asks the individual to esteem himself highly enough to accept his own judgment as a source of political authority.

In his early writings Emerson validates the political equality promoted by the Democrats but also seeks to advance an alternative to the mass political parties. Especially in the two winter lecture series that he delivered between 1836 and 1838, Emerson develops a vision of history that emphasizes a slow and incremental liberation of the individual from arbitrary institutions of power. In his understanding of history, the emergence of democratic political equality stands alongside the Copernican revolution in science and the Protestant Reformation in religion as markers of the progress of civilization. In Emerson's eyes, the importance of each of these three revolutions lies in the way it repositions the human being in relation to the universe. For example, in assessing the impact of Copernicus's discoveries, he notes ironically that until astronomy swapped the solar system for Ptolemy's heliocentric model which had the Earth at the center of the universe, man "had esteemed himself the centre of beings and his globe the centre of nature. . . . Theologians did not hesitate to build their theory to suit and made this the stage of the Drama of Creation and of Doom. But Copernicus's plain tale put it all down and degraded our sphere from being a first rate globe in heaven to a diminutive speck utterly invisible from the nearest star." This discovery had terrible implications for what it meant to be human: "Man was like a deposed king from off whose back has been stripped the purple and from off whose head has been torn the crown, and who must henceforth owe his consideration not to office but to his personal character" (*EL* 2:184)." For philosophy, Emerson sees Copernicus's "plain tale" as a beneficial catastrophe. It regrounded philosophy on a foundation that forced recognition of a new relation between humans and nature. In the progress of liberal society, Copernican astronomy exemplifies the victory of reason over myth; in its religious parallel, Luther's Reformation ninety years later exemplifies the victory of faith over tradition. American democracy, the third great revolution in the progress of modern history, would achieve the victory of equality over hierarchy. Throughout this early period, Emerson's writing teems with images of potential power that is stifled or wasted by resigned or benighted subordination to ancient institutions.[7]

Referring to people's unused potential in *Nature*, for example, Emerson complains that "we are like travelers using the cinders of a volcano to roast their eggs" (*CW* 1:21). With each great advance in science, art, or politics, civilization incrementally moves away from tradition and toward the sovereignty of the individual. Copernicus, like Luther and the American Revolutionaries, plays a key role in this progressive narrative because even as the new astronomy moved the Earth out of the center of the cosmos, it moved the "personal character" of the individual toward the center. In his "Human Culture" lecture, Emerson situates this reversal as part of an unfolding power:

> In the eye of the philosopher, the individual has ceased to be regarded as a part, and has come to be regarded as a whole. He is the world. Man who has been—in how many tedious ages—esteemed an appendage to a fortune, to a trade, to an army, to a law, to a state, now discovers that property, trade, war, government, geography . . . are but counterparts of mighty faculties which dwell peacefully in his mind, and that it is a state of disease which makes him seem the servant of his auxiliaries and effects. (*EL* 2:215)

In "History" he links the emergence of democratic equality to the incremental progress of civilization: "Egypt, Greece, Rome, Gaul, Britain, America, lie folded already in the first man. Epoch after epoch, kingdom, empire, republic, democracy, are merely the application of this manifold Spirit to the manifold world" (*CW* 2:113). As broader recognition of equality emerges haltingly and clumsily across the vast span of history, progress is visible even in his immediate environment: "The Vote,—universal suffrage— . . . The furious democracy which in this country from the beginning of its history, has shown a wish, as the royal governors complained, to leave out men of mark and send illiterate and low persons as deputies . . . is only a perverse or as yet obstructed operation of the same instinct,—a stammering and stuttering out of impatience to articulate the awful words *I am*" (*EL* 2:213–14).

From early in his career, Emerson is unambiguous that democracy—and the political equality that it creates—defines the social context necessary to foster the sense of individual sovereignty that egalitarian self-reliance requires. At his moment in history, Emerson holds, a long trajectory of progressive social change had reached a point at which the idea of the individual had achieved a rough parity with the stature that institutions had long held in their imagination. The rise of American democracy, even a "furious democracy," marked a great progressive moment in human history.[8]

As he witnessed the rise of the Democracy, Emerson also recognized that the progress it denoted was tentative and obscure. Worse, a new threat, different from church or monarchy, was rising with it. In his view, the emergence of mass political parties threatened to make autonomy even more difficult to achieve. Yet rather than recoiling from the partisan drift of the political world, Emerson directly engages the rise of mass political parties in order to assert individuality as an alternative to partisan identity. Naming his model of citizenship "self-reliance," he seeks to describe the ways in which the expansion of political equality could facilitate the emergence of a society that combines the sovereignty of the individual we connect to political liberalism with the interest in the common good that we associate with civic republicanism.

LIBERALS, REPUBLICANS, AND THE ROOTS OF EMERSON'S POLITICS

Even before the constitutional era, Americans had been mediating between a liberal politics proposing that individuals should be free to pursue self-interest with minimal responsibilities to the collective and a more classically republican politics in which citizenship requires civic participation and implies an effort to bracket self-interest in the name of the general good. In important respects, the evolution of American political culture from Federalist republicanism through Jacksonian democracy marks a competitive push and pull between these two models of citizenship.

The tensions of this relationship between liberalism and republicanism are woven tightly into Emerson's thought about public life. For example, in his persistent effort to imagine a self radically unencumbered by civic obligations, Emerson offers a strong liberal construction of selfhood. But in his equally strong desire to envision the society as a single organic whole animated by a shared universal spirit, his idea of society evokes the republican ideal.[9]

Beginning his career as Jacksonian democracy was on the rise, Emerson joined the public debate during a time of structural reform in the meaning of citizenship, but he also joined a debate that had been going on for a long time. A generation earlier, in reaction to the forces propelling Thomas Jefferson toward reelection in 1804, John Adams compared the Jeffersonian democrat to novelist Samuel Richardson's consummate villain, Robert Lovelace, who, in the novel *Clarissa*, traps and rapes a young debutante. Adams complains in a letter to his friend William Cunningham that "Democracy is Lovelace, and the people are Clarissa. The artful villain will pursue the innocent lovely girl to her ruin and death."[10] Reading political change through a republican's paternal sense of stewardship over the interests of the people, Adams sees the democrat as an opportunistic rake who presents himself as a friend of the public even though his true motive is to advance a private agenda. As democratic equality competed with the deferential elitism of Federalist culture, the "people," whom Adams imagines as dependent, feminine, and manipulable, are doomed to be degraded by slick operators intent on picking their pockets and robbing them of their rights.

For Adams, broadening the political base meant that his countrymen were rejecting a natural hierarchy through which civic norms could be regulated by a class of men who had demonstrated the right to rule through a combination of economic independence and a record of public service. Economic independence guarantees that the citizen is not easily manipulated (as a contracted journeyman is by a master); public service proves a commitment to the common good (as opposed to the liberal's pursuit of self-interest). Gordon Wood referred to this republican standard as a system for the "filtration of talent" most likely to reveal qualified leaders. To the elder Adams, republican government need not be democracy. It should be *for* the people, but it should be *of* or *by* the people in only a very restricted sense.[11]

The assumptions that underpinned the republican model of political representation throughout the Revolutionary and Federal eras were coming under intense pressure just as Emerson was entering public life. About 1820—the year Emerson turned eighteen—as Mary Kupiec Cayton dates it, "an increasingly self-conscious middle class began to express openly the belief that government ought to represent the various interests of the town, not some vague conception of the common good."[12] In Emerson's Massachusetts, early advocates of this belief proposed that Boston stop electing selectmen to a town council made up entirely of what we would now call "at-large" members, and instead divide the town into geographical districts, each of which would have representation on the council.[13] This move away from a structure in which the "best men" gathered to represent an elusive "public good" fundamentally changed political representation. It marks the early emergence of interest-group liberalism. In place of the assumption that government would express an underlying consensus, political authority would now acknowledge that a plurality of interests compete against and compromise with one another in order to advance legislative agendas.[14] In the new political environment produced by this shift, political stability would derive not from the articulation of a universalized general will or an assumed harmony of interests between the people and their leaders, but from broad access to the ongoing dialogue among the conflicting values represented among the citizenry.[15]

The career of John Quincy Adams—John Adams's son—illustrates how the Federalists adapted to liberal pressure on the tradition of political representation that they inherited. Quincy Adams and Emerson knew each other, though not well. The second president's son entered public life as a Federalist working under his father's tutelage. Early in his career, just as he was entering politics, Quincy Adams faced the problem of partisan identification. He remarks in his diary: "I feel a strong temptation and have great provocation to plunge into political controversy . . . [but] a politician in the country must be the man of a party. I would fain be the man of my whole country."[16] He nonetheless decided to pick a side and joined the Jefferson party shortly before the War of 1812. This change in political affiliation not only meant pitching his tent in the camp of his father's archrival but also meant accepting the legitimacy of the political vision that was undermining the paternalistic public culture of Federalists like George Washington and his father. It was the right choice politically, though. In 1824 John Quincy Adams was elected president as a member of the short-lived National Republicans.

After serving one term and losing his reelection campaign to Andrew Jackson in 1828, Quincy Adams reentered politics as a Whig congressman, aggressively advocating free speech and opposing slavery. The crowning achievement of his late career was his successful campaign in 1834 to lift the gag rule on antislavery speech in the House of Representatives.[17] As the arc of John Quincy Adams's career demonstrates, the Whig model of citizenship that would serve as the starting point for Emerson's political values was more than just a revamped version of Federalist paternalism. The Federalist version of civic republicanism had been hammered into something new on the democratizing anvil of Jeffersonian liberalism. It emerged as an individualistic theory of democratic community based in civic dialogue and in an aspirational ideal of the virtuous citizen. The Whig voter appreciates pluralistic dialogue but also aspires to use politics to make the whole society better. In this era, union organizers like Ely Moore tended to be Democrats, while utopian socialists like George Ripley were likely to be Whigs. Abraham Lincoln, born six years after Emerson to a one-mule frontiersman, for example, remained a dedicated Whig until the formation of the Republican Party during the 1850s. He chose the Whigs largely because he favored their interest in public works projects over the Democrats' desire to leave things like ports, roads, and bridges to private enterprise.[18]

John Quincy Adams opposed the rising power of the Democratic Party not because he opposed democracy—as his father had—but because he felt that Jacksonian liberalism degraded political life. In his view, it cheapened public service by replacing rational deliberation with a form of bullhorn sloganeering that inflamed public opinion. Worse, it sought to exchange the neutrality of government for a political marketplace populated by blatantly self-interested, possessive individualists. Tension between liberalism's validation of a politics in which the private interests and convictions of individuals compete in a pluralistic marketplace of ideas and goods, and the republicans' ongoing desire to believe in common will, or at least in a "harmony of interests" that unites different identities in the society, explains much about Emerson's early political thought. He deeply believed in the idea that all human beings share a common, though ineffable, spirit. He expresses this fundamentally religious idea through highly contradictory images for the ideal of political society. On the one hand, Emerson held that the good society fosters each person's authority to speak from a position of individual sovereignty. Very liberal. But on the other hand, Emerson held that the test of public truth is its ability to echo with each and all, not as a personal or private utterance but as an expression of Spirit, equally true for all. Very republican.

EMERSON IN THE DEMOCRACY

Throughout the 1830s, and despite his radical religious opinions, Emerson leaned toward the conservative pole in politics. In 1834, when he was thirty-one years old, he spent the autumn in Manhattan preaching at a Unitarian church. While he was there, he witnessed a midterm congressional campaign. This election was a test of the newly formed political parties because it was the first time the emergent Whigs felt able to go toe to toe with the better-organized Democrats. For Whigs, it was a hopeful time. After their surprising success during local elections that spring, Emerson remarks cynically on the changing political winds: "There is a revolution in this county now, is There? Well, I am glad of it. But it don't convert nor punish the Jackson men nor reward the others" (*JMN* 4:287).

As he watched the campaign through October, he made his partisan preference clear. At times he even adopted the conservatives' pejorative slang "tory" for Jackson loyalists. Looking at the election paraphernalia passing by in the street, he admits that "on all the banners equally of Tory & Whig good professions are inscribed." The Democrats proclaimed their support for praiseworthy goals: "The Jackson flags say 'Down with Corruption!' 'We ask for nothing but our Right.' 'The Constitution, The Laws' and so on." These heartened Emerson so that, should "the Whig Party fail, which God avert!" the "latent i.e. deceived virtue which is contained within the Tory party" might prevent a descent into outright corruption. Nonetheless, he petulantly condemns the Democrats: "It is notorious that the Jackson party is the *Bad* party in the cities & in general." A few paragraphs later, he amplifies this judgment by accusing the Democrats of election fraud: "The Whigs can put in their own votes. But the Tories can do this & put them in again in another ward or bring a gang of forsworn gallows birds to boot, to elect the officers that are to hunt, try, imprison, & execute them" (*JMN* 4:333). Despite their embodiment of the "spirit of the beast," the Democrats' rhetoric proves that "they have not yet come to the depravity that says, 'Evil be thou my good'" (*JMN* 4:332). Twenty years later he would be accusing proslavery politicians of exactly that level of cynicism. In his commentary throughout the 1834 campaign, Emerson's point of view has much more in common with that of Horace Greeley, who at that time used his newspaper *The Constitution* to build up the Whig Party, than it does with the stance of Democrats such as Ely Moore, who in this election became the first workingman's union organizer to win a seat in Congress.[19]

Emerson even briefly plunged into the campaign scrum. A week before the three-day voting period began, Emerson went to a Whig rally that was among the largest get-out-the-vote efforts of the Jackson era. The *Niles' Register* report on the rally emphasizes the scale of the event and gives a vivid context to Emerson's criticism of the partisan political structure that was beginning to take shape:

> On Tuesday evening there was an immense gathering at the Masonic Hall to hear the report of the Whig nominating committee. A meeting was first organized in the great room, capable of holding about 5,000 persons—but that being instantly jammed, another meeting was organized in the long room on the first floor, and that also being found insufficient—an omnibus being drawn up, and chairs placed on its top

for the accommodation of the officers, a third meeting was organized in the street. This will shew what is doing[!] And at this meeting in resolution, recommending the mechanics to leave their shops and "give up the three days to the cause" was adopted. It was also ordered that the splendid steamboat *Ohio*, which plies on the Hudson, should be chartered to proceed to Albany, . . . saluting at each of the landing places, and firing two hundred guns at Albany, in "honor of the Whig victories in the state of Ohio."[20]

Emerson came away from this rally even more skeptical of the new party system which he had previously observed from a distance. "It is rather humiliating to attend a public meeting such as this New York Caucus," he writes, and see "what a low animal hope & fear patriotism is." The speakers had whipped up the gathered thousands with a "party-lie" designed to gain the "votes of that numerous class of indifferent, effeminate, stupid persons who in the absence of all internal strength obey whatever seems the voice of their street, their ward, their town, or whatever domineering strength will be at the trouble of civilly dictating to them" (*JMN* 4:327).

Despite his own sympathy with the Whigs, he indicts their speakers as demagogues and accuses them of sharing in the general failure to see the possibilities of individuality that lie in democratic equality. In a comment that treats the partisan demagogue almost as a "transparent eyeball," he describes a Whig orator who becomes "part and parcel" of the multitude he addresses: "Heard Mr. Maxwell at the Masonic Hall[,] a thoroughly public soul[,] the mere voice of the occasion & the hour. There are these persons into whom the general feeling enters & through whom it passes & finds never a hitch or hindrance; they express what is boiling in the bosoms of the whole multitude around them." They speak not as individuals but as windows into the impulses of the crowd. The problem with the fervent partisans, Emerson notes acidly, is that even though they have given up their claim on individual sovereignty, "their votes count like real ones" (*JMN* 4:334, 328). Far from prying citizens away from alienation, dignifying them, and asking each voter to see himself as king of a sovereign state, the expansion of political equality seemed to be incorporating people into a vast apparatus of partisan alienation.

As the voting began, Emerson notes: "Nov. 5. The elections . . . Noisy Election; flags, boy processions, placards, badges, medals, bannered coaches[—] everything to get the hurrah on our side" (*JMN* 4:332–34). Steeling himself for political exile after the defeat everyone had come to expect, he imagines the Whigs as a redemptive phoenix: "Let the worst come to the worst & the Whigs be crushed for a season & the Constitution be grossly violated, then you should see the weak Whig become irresistible. They would acquire the gloom & the might of fanaticism & redeem America as they once redeemed England & once aforetime planted & emancipated America" (*JMN* 4:334). Emerson's private gloom echoes the hysterics of the Whig press and parrots the cheap shots Whig politicians were taking at the Democrats. He even lets himself stoop so low as to record that "Mr. [Philip] H[one] says the Tories deserve to succeed, for they turn every stone with an Irishman under & pick him up" (*JMN* 4:333).[21] Succeed they did. The Whigs did better than expected, but the Democrats got more votes and sent their slate to Congress.

On returning home to Concord a few days after the election, Emerson decompresses by singing the praises of home and heritage: "Concord, 15 November, 1834. Hail to the quiet fields of my fathers! . . . Bless my purposes as they are simple and natural" (*JMN* 4:335). He takes some personal lessons and makes some resolutions based on what he had seen as a man on the street in the midst of the Democracy: "Henceforth I design not to utter any speech, poem, or book that is not entirely and peculiarly my work"; and he commits to speaking on "things which I have meditated for their own sake" rather than laboring on a lecture "to make a good appearance" at the scheduled gathering (*JMN* 4:335). Emerson's own clear identification with the Whigs notwithstanding, the lessons that he takes from the election are not ideological or partisan; rather, they address the formal relationship between public speakers and their audiences. He commits to a standard of public self-representation that he hopes will inoculate him from the appeals of partisanship.

Emerson's quarrel with Jacksonian politics is not with democracy, or even with the Democratic Party, but with the idea of mass parties as the structuring vehicle for political equality. In his eyes, to be a party man is a tragic failure because it eclipses the sovereignty explicit in democratic equality and suppresses the very dignity that expanded suffrage had conferred on so many people.

Coming out of a worm's-eye immersion in the politics of the new mass parties that characterized Jacksonian and antebellum political culture, Emerson homes in on the problem of developing individuality within the context of a large body of voters who had very quickly divided into titanic and impersonal parties.[22] In response to the Democracy, Emerson worked to define a standard for public speech that would allow for political engagement but that would also resist the pressure simply to articulate the tropes of a party machine. If he could fulfill this commitment to project the civic individuality democracy made possible, as he puts it in the closing words of "The American Scholar," each citizen would be able to walk on their own feet, work with their own hands, speak their own minds, and laugh off the charismatic attraction of partisan demagogues.

PUBLIC OPINION AND SPIRIT

The Democratic Party dominated politics in the 1830s by claiming to represent the interests of working people against the antidemocratic elites that had long withheld their rights from them. But in their rhetoric, the Democrats also asserted the authority of public opinion to determine the outcome of political debates. Far from being a metaphor for mindless parroting, to many serious political actors in Jacksonian America, the values expressed through public opinion represented a form of collective reason that is very similar to Emerson's definition of Spirit. Andrew Jackson, though complex and hypocritical in his relationship to democratization, consistently advocated the authority of public opinion and aggressively moved not just to disable elite centers of power (such as the Bank of the United States) but to move the republic as close as possible to a direct democracy. For example, rather than seeing government as a meritocracy in which high office was reserved for men with impeccable reputations and remarkable achievements, Jackson favored a government structured so that high officials could almost literally be chosen by a lottery. In his first message to Congress, he promoted rotation in office as a means of preventing government from becoming the exclusive province of bureaucrats with specialized skills: "The duties of public officers are, or at least admit of being made, so plain and simple that men of intelligence may readily qualify themselves for their performance." An effective policy of rotation in office would force agencies to keep the structures of government small and simple. If everybody, including officeholders, understood that tenure in office would be brief, and another "Johnny Raw" like themselves would soon be at the helm, the skills required for political appointment would have to stay accessible to the average citizen. This creative plan to deepen the democracy extends to other areas such as Jackson's strenuous but unsuccessful effort to eliminate the Electoral College in favor of a pure majoritarian standard for presidential elections.[23]

The struggle between meritocracy and democracy—each with its attendant forms of corruption—did much to shape thought about political equality. In Emerson's vocabulary, it is reflected in tension between the democratic equality of Spirit and the aspirational republican ideal epitomized in the idea of genius. In April 1835, Emerson recorded a line that links public and private opinion from an essay Thomas Carlyle had published in the *Edinburgh Review*: "Already my opinion has gained infinitely in force when another mind has adopted it" (*JMN* 5:29).[24] But this measure of the multiplier effect of some minds over others finds a corrective counterbalance in the universality of the Spirit. By the logic of Emersonian Transcendentalism, if an opinion is valid, it represents a truth that is already present in every other person's mind. In effect, the idea is asleep and the public speaker's words just awaken it so that it can be a conscious motivation. This is the task of the poet, scholar, and genius. Thoreau uses this metaphor extensively in *Walden*, culminating in the remark "If I were to meet a man who was truly awake, how could I look him in the eye?"[25] Conversely, by the l ogic of Emerson's Transcendentalism, if an opinion is invalid and it spreads anyway, then its promoters have seduced people *away* from truth, Spirit, and self-reliance. This is the threat posed by the demagogue: Napoleon or Andrew Jackson.[26]

Debate over thought about the value of public opinion in Jacksonian democracy mirrors Emerson's effort to popularize the idea of Spirit. As universalized sources of authority, the Transcendentalist Spirit and public opinion are closely related. Emerson even concedes that Spirit is sometimes disguised within public opinion, and he explicitly connects it to Jacksonian politics: "A man feels that his time is too precious[,] the objects within reach of his spirit too beautiful than that his attention should stoop to such disfigurements as Antimasonry or Convent riots or General Jackson & the Globe. Yet welcome would be to him the principle out of which these proceed, for all the laws of his being are beautiful" (*JMN* 5:29). Popular opinion—even in the form of conspiracy theories, mobbing, and demagoguery—though "disfigurements," will bear the trace of universal law. "At the source of things," Emerson writes in his 1837 lecture on politics, "before yet the question is encumbered with practical obstruction of personal or partial prejudices, there is no difference of opinion—no parties. In the mind's Republic there is neither Whig nor Tory; neither Radical nor Aristocrat and yet the necessity of the existence of these names may be foreseen and something of benevolent temper may arise in favor even of the other caucus" (*EL* 2:70). Partial and disfigured as public opinion is, it nonetheless reflects something of the "mind's Republic" and thus requires a delicate combination of opposition and reverence.

Disappointed that his model public man Daniel Webster, even at his best, seemed derivative of British originals, Emerson hopes that the raw and ill-mannered Democracy might actually be able to put a stake through the heart of Britain's aristocratic legacy: "We all lean on England[,] scarce a verse, a page, a newspaper but is writ in imitation of English forms." Emerson thinks that, perhaps, the "evil" of emulation "may be cured by this rank rabble party, the Jacksonism of the country. . . . [T]hey may root out the hollow dilettantism of our cultivation in the coarsest way & the new-born may begin again to frame their own world with greater advantage" (*JMN* 4:297). Even with his elitist Whig sympathies, Emerson saw the Democracy as a movement that expressed majority opinion—and he sees the rough beast of public opinion as a legitimate source of political authority. Seeing public opinion in this way was by no means uncommon among those reading the Jacksonian press.

Just after the extension of the franchise in the early 1820s, but before the organization of the national party system, Charles Stewart Daveis, a Maine lawyer and legislator, published a pamphlet that supported the sovereignty of public opinion. He describes its formation as a process of rational deliberation rather than the product of media-driven partisan manipulation: "By giving to public opinion an absolute and audible representation and by placing a more responsible and emphatic reliance upon the presiding sense of the community . . . that sense is quickened, corrected, cultivated, disciplined, caution and prudence are inspired, and all its faculties summoned in vindication of its principles." The maturation of public dialogue emerges through an organic process of germination. It appears in public only after "it has been working and striking its roots deep into the soil." The cultivation of public opinion slowly builds consensus as it works its way upward. The process "commences in the primary and internal principles of society, proceeding silently, ascending steadily up, invigorating the stock and entering with life into the branches." When it finally gains authentic expression, "its light advances like the day which first begins to illuminate the highest tops until it warms and fertilizes the earth and calls forth all its powers and luxuriance. Its influence is disseminated through the great mass of public sentiment until it thoroughly pervades the whole body of the community."[27] Daveis imagines public opinion as both organic and progressive. It moves authoritative political dialogue away from a classic structure of representation and regrounds it in a context rich in analogies to natural processes of fruition. As he defines it, however, the formation of consensus takes place without orators or geniuses. It is formed "silently," without the cacophony of partisan conflict.

This early argument for the authority of public opinion does not foresee the factionalism of mass democracy or the permanent state of conflict assumed by interest-group liberalism. In it, ideological struggle among political factions almost takes on the aspect of an individual conducting a private dialogue in their own head. Echoing the assumption Emerson will make in *Nature*, Daveis holds that the elimination of arbitrary processes of government will enable a new natural order to emerge as citizens practice self-government.

George Bancroft, the politician and historian who led the Democratic Party in Boston, defined public opinion in terms that bring it even closer to Emerson's model of Spirit.[28] In his 1835 essay "The Office of the People in Art, Government, and Religion," Bancroft argues that the formation of public opinion cultivates a universally shared spirit and then brings it onto the public stage. "There is a *spirit in man*," Bancroft writes, "not in the privileged few; not in those of us only who by the favor of Providence have been nursed in public schools: IT IS IN MAN: it is the attribute of the race. The spirit which is the guide to truth, is the gracious gift to each member of the human family. Reason exists within every breast."[29] But instead of advising self-reflection as the path to this *"spirit"* as Emerson does, Bancroft sees universal reason as an effect of public rather than private opinion: "If reason is a universal faculty, the universal decision is the nearest criterion of truth. The common mind winnows opinions; it is the sieve which separates error from certainty. The exercise by many of the same faculty on the same subject would naturally lead to the same conclusions." Thus, "the common mind is the true Parian marble, fit to be wrought into likeness to a God. The duty of America is to secure the culture and the happiness of the masses by their reliance on themselves."[30] More than just advocating the authority of mass opinion, Bancroft explicitly juxtaposes the individual and the mass in a progressive sequence that begins by subordinating individual opinion to public opinion, passes it through an intermediate stage of partisan strife, and resolves it by equating political consensus with the voice of God:

> Individuals are of limited sagacity; the common mind is infinite in its experience. Individuals are languid and blind; the many are ever wakeful. Individuals are corrupt; the race has been redeemed. Individuals

are time-serving; the masses are fearless. Individuals may be false; the masses are ingenious and sincere. Individuals claim the divine sanction of truth for the deceitful conceptions of their own fancies; the Spirit of God breathes through the combined intelligence of the people. Truth is not to be ascertained by the impulses of an individual; it emerges from the contradictions of personal opinion; it raises itself in majestic serenity above the strifes of parties and the conflict of sects; it acknowledges neither the solitary mind nor the separate faction as its oracle, but owns as its own faithful interpreter the dictates of pure reason itself, proclaimed by the general voice of mankind. The decrees of the universal conscience are the nearest approach to the presence of God in the soul of man.[31]

In this passage, Bancroft turns Emerson's understanding of "the dictates of pure reason" inside out. By Bancroft's thinking, the authority of democracy does not lie in its ability to dignify the individual as an autonomous sovereign state; democratic authority lies in the fact that democracy recognizes public opinion as "the nearest approach to the presence of God in the soul of man."

In Bancroft's model of political authority, conscience bridges individuality and universality in the same way that it does for Emerson. "Mind eludes the power of appropriation," Bancroft writes. "It exists only in its own individuality; it is a property which cannot be confiscated and cannot be torn away; it laughs at chains; it bursts from imprisonment; it defies monopoly. A government of equal rights must, therefore, rest upon mind; not wealth, not brute force, the sum of the moral intelligence of the community should rule the state." The difference is that in Bancroft's version of Spirit, "moral intelligence" is indistinguishable from public opinion: "The best government rests on the people and not the few, on persons and not on property, on the free development of public opinion and not on authority." Or "the exact measure of the progress of civilization is the degree to which the intelligence of the common mind has prevailed over wealth and brute force."[32] But, like Daveis, as Bancroft works to equate public opinion with political legitimacy, he simply tramples the individual. Bancroft imagines a public realm in which the purpose of political dialogue is to work toward consensus. As the process unfolds, individuals are incorporated into a common mind. The truth spreads like, in Daveis's terms, the sunrise spreading light across a landscape. For Emerson, by contrast, the primary purpose of political debate is to underscore the state-like sovereignty of each individual and to evoke from them the civic pride that goes with the freedom to speak as the king of a sovereign state in a society of other sovereign states.

Bancroft tries to authorize public opinion by infusing it with an aura of divine incorruptibility, and thus creates a model of public opinion that echoes Emerson's construction of a universal Spirit. He does so at the price of suppressing Emerson's libertarian emphasis on the individual. John L. O'Sullivan, by contrast, shares Emerson's libertarianism and literary nationalism but is a partisan of the Democratic Party and a political combatant against the Whig Party, to which Emerson was loosely allied. O'Sullivan addresses public debate as an explicitly secular political phenomenon and advocates the direct legislative authority of public opinion. But like Daveis, he projects an organic ideal of public discourse that emphasizes the removal of arbitrary barriers on the agency of individuals.

O'Sullivan, of course, coined the term "manifest destiny," and his brand of nationalism is central to the rhetoric of American exceptionalism, which promoted the conquest of Indian territories in the West. In his capacity as a public intellectual, he is equally important in defining the culture of the Democratic Party during the late 1830s and the 1840s. Also, unlike Duff Green, who acted as unofficial press secretary for the Jackson administration through his newspaper the *United States Telegraph*, O'Sullivan offered a vision of how public opinion should structure civil society far beyond the boundaries of politics.[33]

O'Sullivan's desire to treat public opinion as a source of political authority contrasts sharply with Emerson's effort to "smash" parties and release the individuals within them. Nonetheless, the two share many assumptions about the priority of culture over politics. Both O'Sullivan and Emerson held that government should be extremely limited and should function primarily as a judiciary. In the introductory essay to the first issue of the *United States Magazine and Democratic Review*, O'Sullivan defines the status of government in blunt terms: "All government is evil, and the parent of evil. A strong and active democratic *government*, in the common sense of the term, is an evil differing only in degree and mode of operation, and not in nature, from a strong despotism." In "Politics" Emerson condenses the same belief into a single line: "Every actual State is corrupt" (*CW* 3:122). O'Sullivan goes on to imagine government as an intrusive octopus and argues that as many limbs as possible should be lopped off: "Every instance in which the action of *government* can be simplified, and one of the hundred giant arms curtailed, with which it now stretches around its fatal protecting grasp over almost all the various interests of society," will foster democratic autonomy and prevent tyranny. In his view, the formal legislative procedures of government should be deliberative enough to prevent passage of "precipitate legislation," but "all should be dependent with equal directness and promptness on the influence of public opinion; the popular will should be equally the animating and moving spirit of all acts of government."[34]

Sharing a concern with Emerson and many Whigs, O'Sullivan links literary nationalism to the project of creating a sphere of dialogue that is egalitarian and indisputably American. "We are cowed by the mind of England," he writes. "We follow feebly and afar in the splendid track of a literature molded . . . by the ideas and feelings of an utterly anti-democratic social system." With the "young mind of our country so deeply tainted with anti-democratic sentiment," the advocate of "*democracy* occupies a position of defense," and "the attacking cause, [aristocracy,] ardent, restless, ingenious is far more attractive to the imagination of youth than that of defense." With democracy ever on the defensive against aristocracy and plutocracy, the intent of the *Democratic Review* is to vindicate "the true glory and greatness of the democratic principle, by infusing it into our literature, and by rallying the mind of the nation" away from the "splendid" foreign cultures that embody European aristocracy in order to inculcate reflexes that transfer sovereignty to public opinion.[35]

As constructed by Daveis, Bancroft, and O'Sullivan, public opinion denotes an informal process of democratic deliberation that is oriented toward consensus. It assumes the political equality of the participants and marks the replacement of an artificial structure of arbitrary powers with natural expressions of shared interest. All three assume that amplifying the authority of public opinion will vent tensions created by the violence with which arbitrary political power has repressed the voice of the people. Ultimately, in the view of all three, as majority opinion approaches universality, public opinion approximates divine authority.

In this model, far from representing the alienation of the individual in the mass, as Emerson believed was taking place, public opinion represented a kind of apotheosis of individual opinion into government by Spirit. In purely procedural terms, as a method of achieving universality, the Democrats' theory of public opinion is very similar to Emerson's belief that deep self-reflection combined with perfect verbal expression will result in a broad affirmation that brings people together as equals. As Emerson puts it at the beginning of "Self-Reliance": "To believe your own thought, to believe what is true for you in your private heart is true for all men—that is genius. Speak your latent conviction and it shall be universal sense; for the inmost in due time becomes the outmost." When we hear truths that we have repressed or avoided expressed in just the right words, "we recognize our own rejected thoughts; they come back to us with a certain alienated majesty" (*CW* 2:28). The Democrats' emphasis on allowing public dialogue to reach consensus without rigid institutional controls reaches toward the same organic authenticity in democratic deliberation as the processes of self-reflection, speaking, and listening do for Emersonian Transcendentalism.

When Emersonian self-reliance is viewed as a source of political rather than religious authority, the crucial difference between the Democrats' construction of public opinion and Emerson's theory of Spirit is that Daveis, Bancroft, and O'Sullivan are much less concerned with asserting the sovereignty of the individual. Where Emerson's antagonist is the alienation of the individual in the rise of the Democracy, as he characterizes it in "The Young American," the power of public opinion demonstrates that there is "more need of a withdrawal from the crowd, and a resort to the fountain of right, by the brave. The timidity of our public opinion, is our disease, or, shall I say, the publicness of opinion, the absence of private opinion" (*CW* 1:240). For these three other theorists of public opinion, though, the assumed antagonist is the delegated or virtual political representation that marks political inequality between representatives and constituents. The purpose of their defense of public opinion is to bring the dialogues that produce legislation as close to direct democracy as possible. O'Sullivan makes this objective explicit. "We cannot," he writes, "look with an eye of favor on any such forms of representation as, by length of tenure of delegated power, tend to weaken that universal and unrelaxing responsibility to the vigilance of public opinion which is the true conservative principle of our institutions."[36]

Having clawed political power out of the hands of the John Adamses of the world, the leading thinkers of the Democratic Party were much more focused on the goal of planting the idea of political equality deeply into the imaginations of the people than they were on the danger that newly enfranchised citizens would sell their souls to the party. But this blurring of the line between "the absence of private opinion" and the sanctification of public opinion is exactly where Emerson focused his effort to influence the way his countrymen understood the value of political equality.

INDIVIDUALITY AND THE DEMOCRACY

Democrats' effort to raise the stature of public opinion as a means of buttressing the Democracy provoked fear that political equality would undermine individuality. Not only were Democratic majorities able to run roughshod over the rights of minorities, but also the very idea that legitimate authority lies in the aggregated will of a majority threatened Emerson's ideal of citizenship. Political equality had the potential to dignify the individual by asking them to take their politics, civic commitments, and public voice more seriously; but the emerging political culture was driving toward yet another smothering conformity as individuals embraced partisan identities.[37] For Emerson, majoritarianism based on public opinion obviated the very purpose of democracy.

But that danger did not make it necessary to abandon political equality as an ideal. Rather, it required advocates of individuality to reimagine the public sphere. Commenting on the tactics of temperance activists in his 1837 lecture "Society," Emerson remarks:

> As long as they show me the evils of intemperance so long are they working directly to their end. They are satisfying me of that fact and turning me into a Temperance Agent, a Temperance Institution. But the moment they bring in any shape what they call Public Opinion to bear on me, to indulge me to sign a pledge, or join a society, they are thwarting their own design, for they are using numbers, that is, mobs and bodies, and disusing principles. They quit a spiritual for a material ally. If I yield to this force, I degrade myself. (EL 2:107)

The distinction Emerson makes here between substantive argumentation and organization building reflects the standard of sincere dialogue he envisions for democratic discourse. As a form of moral suasion, efforts at individual conversion are potentially dignifying. To take the care to show someone the substantive "evils of intemperance" recognizes that individual's rationality and personhood. It shows respect. Even if the reformer assumes their own moral superiority, to explain and try to convert another person recognizes the independence of the stranger who has given the reformer their attention, and thus the whole situation assumes that the two are equals as rational agents. In political terms, it embodies a dialogue between a "Temperance Institution" and a sovereign state. But when the conversation changes from self-culture to the building up of a mass organization, when the sovereign individual is invited to join a party, the whole situation changes. Instead of free and equal individuals meeting as temperance agent and independent citizen, Emerson sees a paid agent asking an independent citizen to embrace an ideological brand on the simple ground that many others have already done so.

This tension between the dignifying possibilities of democratic political dialogue and the alienating realities of majoritarian politics would continue to define Emerson's attitude toward the Democracy at least until 1850, when he campaigned for John Gorham Palfrey, the Free Soil candidate for the Fourth Congressional District of Massachusetts.[38] Though he never does "despair of the republic," as he puts it in his 1844 essay on politics, he grew deeply cynical about the potential of either the Whigs or the Democrats to promote a civic culture that would enhance the sovereignty of individuals. The Whig, he writes, "is merely defensive of property." He does not advance art or culture. Even though the Whig Party is "composed of the most moderate, able, and cultivated part of the population, . . . it aspires to no real good." The Democrat, by contrast, is "destructive only out of hatred and selfishness." His majority is "aimless" and marches toward "no ulterior and divine ends" (*CW* 3:123). Rather, the Democrats speak the language of envy and resentment.

To Emerson, the rise of the Democracy, and the amplified importance of public opinion that came with it, also marked a change in the relationship between individual character and the public stage. In Jackson's America, going public with your private opinion required a rare kind of bravery. In the lecture "Heroism" that he delivered in January 1838 as part of his "Human Culture" series, he offers antislavery martyr Elijah Lovejoy as a model of heroic individuality. Between 1834 and 1840, Americans endured (and perpetrated) a prolonged period of rioting, mobbing, and lynching. This civil unrest coincided with the growth of mass party politics and the rise of organized antislavery. For many, the killing of Lovejoy, an antislavery newspaper editor who was shot by a mob intent on destroying his printing press, symbolized a general breakdown in public order.[39] To Emerson, Lovejoy represented a model of political independence. His story both reflected the possibilities of political equality and revealed the frightening reflexes of Jacksonian democracy.

Posing the self-reliant hero against the mob, Emerson writes that heroism "is an obedience to a secret impulse of an individual character"; "it is the state of the soul at war" (*EL* 2:331–32). As the embodiment of a progressive truth, the hero stands alone against the mob. He (or she: it is a pretty rare occurrence in his writing, but in this essay Emerson explicitly admits women heroes) must be "self-collected, and neither defying nor dreading the thunder, let him take both reputation and life in his hand, and with perfect urbanity, dare the gibbet and the mob by the absolute truth of his speech and the rectitude of his behavior." Indeed, in a society where mobs spring up to terrorize unpopular newspaper editors, "the youth" who risks independent speech must ask "how fast he can fix his sense of duty" because "whatever outrages have happened to men, may befall a man again: and very easily in a republic. . . . Course slander, fire, tar and feathers, and the gibbet" might confront the hero "whenever it may please the next newspaper, and a sufficient number of his neighbors to pronounce his opinions incendiary" (*EL* 2:338). (Given the fact that Lovejoy's community wanted to destroy his press because they objected to his politics, it seems ironic that Emerson treats journalism as the flint for impulsive lynchings and riots.) But by describing heroism in terms of an ink-stained printer "baring his breast to the mob" as Lovejoy did, Emerson specifies his core objection to the Democrats' goal of investing public opinion with legislative authority. Public opinion articulates the lowest rather than the highest common denominator; it represents the most rather than the deepest. Instead of respecting each individual and his or her opinion, it implies a public discourse constantly looking into the crowd and claiming that authority lies with the visceral instinct of the mob rather than the high aspirations of egalitarian recognition.

Jason Frank, analyzing Emerson's idea of political speech, situates Emerson's view of political representation and self-representation in the "mandate-independence" debate among political theorists. This debate, focusing on the difference between representative and direct democracy, addresses the nature of a legislator's responsibility within representative democracy. "The mandate view," Frank explains, "reduces the representative to a mere agent of the represented acting only on the basis of their explicit instructions." Coming out of the American Revolutionaries' objection to the "virtual representation" of colonials in the House of Commons in London, this model of representation has deep roots in American political thought.[40]

In response to the emphasis that the Jacksonian Democrats placed on majoritarian public opinion, Whigs argued that representatives must have the independence to debate freely the long-term interest of the nation. As Joseph Story, the Whig-leaning Supreme Court justice who wrote the *Amistad* decision, phrased it in an 1834 essay in the *New England Magazine*, the statesman must "legislate for the future, when it is, as yet, but dimly seen; and he must put aside much, which might now win popular favor, in order to found systems of solid utility, whose results are indispensable for the safety, the glory, and the happiness of the country."[41] Toward this end, the Whigs emphasized character over interest to elect representatives who had the judgment to stand above the material interests of parties, or even the perceived interests of constituents. The legislator was not just a messenger; he was to be an aspirational figure in the broadest sense, an autonomous actor whose judgment exemplified civic virtue.

Frank reminds us that as political actors debated the authority of representatives in Jacksonian America, they were fully conscious of the contrast between the mandate and independence models. Edmund Burke, whom Emerson considered "a man who drawing from the fountainheads of wisdom and goodness, endeavored to make a little light in the dark and corrupt maze of politics" (*EL* 1:201), wrote in 1774, "Your representative owes to you, not his industry only, but his judgment; and he betrays instead of serving you, if he sacrifices it to your opinion." James Madison echoes Burke in the Federalist Papers, arguing that the deliberations of independent representatives will "refine and enlarge" public opinion because "the public voice pronounced by the elected representatives of the people will be more consonant to the public good, than if pronounced by the people themselves."[42] In Jacksonian America, sustaining this aspirational posture was an uphill struggle. As the Whig Party was working to maintain popularity, Robert McKinley Ormsby noted that any legislator who aspired to speak in a way that opposed public opinion found himself in an extremely frustrating position: "Let no man who desires to rise to high office in a popular government ever dare to express sentiments distasteful to popular prejudice." This stricture on speech that seeks to educate the public rather than simply to poll it and then articulate its will, he continues, is binding because "the theory of democratic governments, is that the people are always right, and that the statesman who shall advocate measures not in accordance with the popular opinion, must not be trusted or honored."[43] According to Whig ideals, as one historian of the party put it, the role of debate among elected representatives "was not merely to express the will of the people, it was to *refine* it."[44]

In terms of the independence of the citizen to speak in public, Emerson hoped to translate the idealistic civic republicanism that underpinned the Whig theory of representation into a model of ordinary public dialogue. What he saw in democratization was the possibility of a more genuine culture of self-representation. With his focus on the implications of democracy for individuality and for the way equals might communicate with one another, elections and even government are almost irrelevant in Emerson's political thought. His interest in democracy is focused on the transformation that political equality portended for citizens and their self-conception, not for the foundations of governmental authority. As O'Sullivan's introduction to the *Democratic Review* indicates, the Democrats tended toward the mandate view, treating deliberation as the responsibility of equal citizens working to define public opinion. The Whigs tended to prefer the independence model. Emerson's ideal of political equality combines the two. Emerson's Transcendental "Spirit" is similar to the Democrats' construction of public opinion. But his construction of individuality, especially of persons who attain public authority and influence through sincere self-representation—heroes, scholars, and ministers—more strongly resembles the Whigs' construction of the independent political representative.[45]

Emerson's effort to reconcile political equality as a necessary foundation for individuality with the emerging majoritarianism of American democracy is also an effort to adapt the independence model of political representation to the context of an expanding franchise. Emerson imagined all citizens seeing themselves as equals in an aspirational sense, and of each citizen taking that role seriously in both civic and personal contexts.

In terms of the ability of the newly enfranchised men to act as individuals, Emerson shared many of the reservations voiced by Alexis de Tocqueville. Remarking on the power of public opinion in Jacksonian democracy, Tocqueville warns of the same dangers that Emerson sees, but he also recognizes the opportunity that expanding political equality would create:

> I see clearly two tendencies in equality: one turns each man's attention to new thoughts, while the other would induce him freely to give up thinking at all.... There is matter for deep reflection here. I cannot say too often for all those who see freedom of the mind as something sacred and who hate not only despots but despotism. For myself, if I feel the hand of power heavy on my brow, I am little concerned to know who it is that oppresses me; I am no better inclined to pass my head under the yoke because a million men hold it for me.[46]

In his final comment on the 1834 election in New York, Emerson succumbs to the fears of mob rule that had marked John Adams's contempt for Jeffersonian democracy a generation earlier. Describing the expanded Democracy of 1834 New York in class terms as a site of repressed hatred and barely controlled violence, he closes his notes on the election by almost literally imagining rich patricians dining in luxury while misery riots in the street outside the window:

> It is a great step from the thought to the expression of the thought in action. Without horror I contemplate the envy, hatred, & lust that occupy the hearts of smiling well dressed men & women. [B]ut the simplest most natural expressions of the same thought in action astonish & dishearten me. If the wishes of the lowest class that suffer in these long streets should execute themselves, who can doubt that the city would topple in ruins. Do not trust man, Great God!, with more power until he has learned to use his little power better. (*JMN* 4:334–35)

Despite his hope that political equality will transform the identity of the citizen in the same way that Copernican science and Reformation theology had transformed the place of humanity in science and religion, Emerson cannot help but see majoritarian politics in terms of social and economic class. Like Tocqueville, he hopes expanding the franchise will "turn each man's attention to new thoughts." But the victorious Democrats still represent to Emerson a demotic force that he associates with mobs in the street, with suffering, and with an anarchy of "envy, hatred, & lust."

The contempt for mass partisanship he had expressed at the Whig rally in 1834 never really leaves, or even abates. As an election approached a few years later, Emerson overheard Cyrus Stowe, a Democratic organizer in Concord, doing his work and Emerson let off a bit of steam: "I passed by the shop and saw my spruce neighbor the dictator of our rural Jacobins teaching his little circle of villagers their political lessons. . . . I hate persons who are nothing but persons. I hate numbers. He cares for nothing but numbers and persons" (*JMN* 7:99). These two phenomena represent democracy at its worst: a democratic mob animated by envy; and a political operator snaring neighbors who are too self-interested to think of the common good and too egotistical to stand for an idea beyond their own personal interest.

INDIVIDUALITY AND DEMOCRATIC REPRESENTATION

The elected official, or "magistrate" as Emerson often called him, who both articulates his constituents' interests in public debates and exemplifies individuality is very similar to the identity Emerson envisions for the scholar or minister. The citizen is to be an idealized embodiment of individual character who serves as an aspirational example for all who hear them. As democracy reconfigured political life, the questions of intellectual independence and strength of character that are so central to Emerson's Transcendentalist thought parallel the terms of the debate about political representation in Jacksonian America. In his model of public selfhood, Emerson incorporates the Whig ideal of civic republicanism, but rather than situating the statesman in Congress, he adapts the independence model of representative authority by imagining him as an independent actor in civil society. This reimagining of political representation avoids both the partisan's alienation in public opinion and the citizen's disfranchisement from the consequential discussions that take place in actual legislatures.

The central interest in Emerson's thought about public representation is to imagine democratic equality as a context in which individuals can cultivate truthful standards of self-expression and sincere dialogue. As he thinks through the implications of political equality for community, he does not imagine new institutions such as utopian associations. Rather, he imagines the withering away of public institutions as improved standards of individual character redefines the way people interact with one another. His impulse to imagine self-government in terms so intimate that they moot public institutions leads, on the one hand, to images of organic unity among all the members of the society and, on the other hand, to images that collapse public institutions into intimate conversation in domestic spaces.

At the beginning of "The American Scholar," Emerson tells a story that evokes nostalgia for a lost world in which the society was analogous to a single person. He then silhouettes this organicism against an image of the pluralist liberalism that was taking hold in his own day: "The gods, in the beginning, divided Man into men, that he might be more helpful to himself; just as the hand was divided into fingers the better to answer its end." Over time, however, this organic division degraded into the "*divided* or social state" in which "functions are parceled out" in smaller and smaller portions until "the state of society is one in which the members have suffered amputation from the trunk." The "old fable" is a political analogue of Adam's Fall. In Genesis, Adam and Eve are cast out of the Garden and lose unmediated contact with divinity. In the political version, as the division of labor becomes finer and finer, citizens lose community with one another, and thus lose much of their contact with an all-encompassing organic Spirit that is larger than themselves:

> The old fable covers a doctrine ever new and sublime; that there is One Man—present to all particular men only partially, or through one faculty; and that you must take the whole society to find the whole man.... The fable implies that the individual, to possess himself must sometimes return from his own labor to embrace all the other laborers. But unfortunately, this original unit, this fountain of power, has been so distributed to multitudes, has been so minutely subdivided and pedaled out, that it is spilled into drops and cannot be gathered. (CW 1:53)

The "One Man" implies a paradox. He is both a noble savage in a pre-civil state, and he is a whole civil society in which the individual can be comprehended only through a ritualized assembly of the entire community—something like a church service or a town meeting. Emerson begins his lecture "Politics," also 1837, with a very similar image of an organic society. In this lecture, the goal or end state of civilization is already written in the human heart, and the problem of politics is the problem of harmonizing public policy with a universal moral sentiment. In its ideal form, government and conscience are indistinguishable. He opens by describing politics as a metaphor for utopian harmony:

> There is something grand in the idea of a state. It is a melting of many interests into one interest; of many millions of men as it were into one man, and this for good ends purely: for better defense, for better counsel, for better action. The common conscience of all the individuals becomes the law of the State and invisible as conscience is, envelops like a net, all the cities, villages, farms, over sea, over land to the farthest island colony of the people. (EL 2:69)

Just as in "The American Scholar," where Emerson uses the metaphor of "One Man" to project the image of an organically unified society, in the fabled origin to which the "One Man" alludes, all the "functions" of life are the responsibility of the individual, who must be hunter, architect, priest, and warrior. One can see the whole society in one man because the whole society *is* one man. Acting from this position of radical sovereignty, he approaches other people as one self-sufficient sovereign addressing another. No one is a countryman; nothing is communal. In political terms, everyone is a sovereign and everyone is equal in their sovereignty.

But the "One Man" of "The American Scholar" is only symbolically the noble savage in a pre-civil state. The "old fable" also describes a civil society. In this society, self-possession is contingent not on the radical independence of the sovereign state in international affairs, but on the individual's ability to recognize the equality of their own and every other person's labor. The fall from this organic unity-in-sovereignty occurs when members of the society cannot "embrace all the other laborers." They thereby lose the ability to validate the humanity of each other member. As a result, the community still functions, but it is diminished, and every member of it is diminished. When read as a response to the partisan culture promoted by the Democracy, the question of "The American Scholar" is: What kind of identity can achieve the paradoxical combination of individual sovereignty and organic social unity represented by the old fable?

Emerson begins to imagine a path toward this condition by proposing two revisions to the models of citizenship that were emerging in Jacksonian America. First, the scholar should stand and speak on conviction *as an individual* rather than as the representative of a scholarly or cultural tradition. Second, the functions of social institutions such as churches and governments should be internalized in what he characterizes as a "domestication" of culture.

Kenneth Sacks, in a richly contextualized reading of "The American Scholar," argues that this famous essay represents Emerson's response to the diminishing cultural authority of New England intellectuals. In Sacks's reading, Emerson asks his audience to turn away from classical models of culture and to take seriously the forms of popular and mass culture that were taking shape around them. This interpretation is useful for my purpose because Sacks's emphasis on popular culture and on Emerson's critique of cultural leadership represents an effort to reposition the scholar within the Democracy. The forum for this lecture, a meeting of the Phi Beta Kappa Society, made Emerson's iconoclasm stand out vividly. These annual addresses tended to reaffirm the cultural authority of Phi Beta Kappa members. But in his insistence that the scholar take the Democracy seriously, Emerson threads the needle between the Unitarian elite, who sought to arbitrate cultural standards, and the business elite, who sought to control the curricula of higher education. "Punctuating the oration with staccato-like bursts of intentional insult" to the scholars in his audience, Sacks writes, "Emerson questioned the very essence of the academic enterprise."[47]

Mocking the pedantry of classicist elitism in a world where Andrew Jackson defined politics and William Lloyd Garrison represented moral perfectionism, in "The American Scholar" Emerson argues that traditional forms of cultural leadership had become obsolete. Rather than sustaining a mandarin caste of scholars who see themselves as cultural and political arbiters, Emerson poses new questions for Phi Beta Kappa members to consider: "What would we really know the meaning of? The meal in the firkin; the milk in the pan; the ballad in the street." Orienting the scholar's eye away from elitist classicism and toward "the literature of the poor" and the "philosophy of the street," however, does not mean that he embraces public opinion as the legitimate means of cultural or political arbitration (*CW* 1:67). As Sacks puts it, with "The American Scholar," Emerson "not only defied the Unitarian call for elite leadership of American culture. He also refused to ally himself fully with those Transcendentalists who believed in popular sovereignty."[48]

Emerson's revision of the Phi Beta Kappa address is that his "American Scholar" emphasizes the importance of the scholar's intellectual independence and deemphasizes the scholar's role as the steward of a cultural standard. Rather than dutifully reiterating the tropes of republican deference and respect for the learned, Emerson urges scholars to discover the creative good that is implicit in the Democracy and to amplify it. Rather than articulating the virtues of a tradition, they should embody an aspirational ideal of egalitarian citizenship. This intervention into the implicit hierarchy of institutional authorities and deferential followers neutralizes a structure of domination and subordination by defining the scholar less as a leader and more as an example. Instead of standing as the representative of a classical structure of society by explaining its sacred texts to a rising generation, the scholar is to represent newly visible possibilities of democratic individuality. First and foremost, the scholar is to embody something higher than the carnal virtues of material greed and raw power over the lives of others. "Men, such as they are," Emerson remarks, "very naturally seek money or power; and power because it is as good as money—the 'spoils,' so called 'of office.' And why not? For they aspire to the highest, and this, in their sleep-walking, they dream is the highest" (*CW* 1:65). He doesn't blame or condemn anyone for seeking such goals. He just considers money and power to be dreamlike phantoms simulating values that have authentic merit. By his reasoning, the ambitious person who chases the pot of gold for the sake of the pot of gold is pitiable in the same way as the individual who allows a party or a leader to eclipse his or her own claims to political sovereignty:

> What a testimony, full of grandeur, full of pity, is borne to the demands of his own nature, by the poor clansman, the poor partisan, who rejoices in the glory of his chief. The poor and the low find some amends to their immense moral capacity, for their acquiescence in a political and social inferiority. They are content to be brushed like flies from the path of a great person, so that justice shall be done by him to that common nature which it is the dearest desire of all to see enlarged and glorified. (*CW* 1:65)

The scene of adulation is glorious, in Emerson's eyes, because in some sense the abject worshipers are recognizing the possibilities of human nature. But the scene is also "full of pity" because each person in the crowd contentedly acquiesces to their own inferiority. They are sleepwalkers and the "chief" is a mesmerist.

But when the hero is redefined to stand as a provocation and an example of a "common nature" rather than as a chief who accepts tribute, then he begins to fulfill the role of the scholar who awakens others to the possibilities of their own individuality. Should any person prove able to achieve influence without demanding the subordination of their followers, "the private life of one man shall be a more illustrious monarchy, more formidable to its enemy, more sweet and serene in its influence to its friends, than any kingdom in history. . . . Each philosopher, each bard, each actor has only done for me as by a delegate what one day I can do for myself" (*CW* 1:65–66). Unless the scholar's example overcomes the virtual representation of the republican model and thus equalizes citizen with scholar by liberating the would-be follower, they act as demagogues who usurp the individuality of each person caught in their orbit.

For Emerson, traditions and institutions have power in inverse proportion to the ability of individuals to enact the "immense moral capacity" of their "common nature." As "delegates," political institutions function like prosthetics, patching capabilities that individuals do not have in their own bodies. Whereas churches, governments, even schools are intended to improve society by empowering people or by regulating antisocial impulses, according to Emerson's progressive history they are necessary only in immature societies populated by immature people. Institutions emerge because, in their failure to live up to their moral capacity, the character of individuals has needed external restraints to compensate for their failings.

To exemplify how the achievement of a representative character can provoke the individuality of another, Emerson enlists the German philosopher Friedrich Schiller, whose transformation from Kantian rationalist to Romantic individualist symbolized the emergence of an individual out of the inertia of history: "I wish to acquaint myself with the genius of Schiller." But how to do so? Read "his Aesthetics? Oh no, that is his struggle with Kantean metaphysics from which by and by he cleared himself." What then? "His histories? His lectures? . . . All his writings were the fermentations by which his mind was working itself clear—the exercises by which he learned his skill, and the ultimate fruit of all is, Schiller himself" (*EL* 2:185). The ideological functions of parties and churches are analogous to the hurdles Schiller overcame in order to become Schiller. They are the exercises by which societies teach individuals to become themselves. But by Emerson's reasoning, the purpose of participating in institutions is to get clear of all of them and to emerge as a fully self-conscious individual. As character improves and people become sovereign over themselves, power slowly shifts away from institutions and toward individuals.

Extrapolating toward Emerson's liberal utopia, social institutions will wither away as individual character incorporates their virtues and makes them redundant. This "immense moral capacity" from which individuals are alienated underpins metaphors like Emerson's claim at the end of *Nature* that humankind is shrunk to a drop He sees that "the structure still fits him, but fits him colossally" (*CW* 1:42). It may seem that this quality of Emerson's language points away from the political and back toward the familiar ground of Emerson as a theorist of spirituality and selfhood. But through the metaphor of the individual as a sovereign state with responsibility to the entire society, Emersonian individuality also models citizenship and public dialogue. The incremental advance of civilization has less to do with society than it does with citizenship, with individuals acting as members of communities. As he puts it in the introductory lecture of the "Philosophy of History" series he delivered a few months before "The American Scholar," he proclaims that "progress belongs to the individual and consists in becoming universal" (*EL* 2:13–14). For one person, a chief, a Plato, or a Schiller, to reach their personal capacity is a heroic achievement, but it is not progress. It changes history only when the standard attained by the hero is universalized among the rest of their clansmen and partisans who, for now, are content to live pitifully in the shadow of their own proxies.

In the closing essay of the "Philosophy of History" series, titled "The Individual," Emerson describes the paradoxical isolation and universality that permit him to embrace democratic egalitarianism as a philosophical ideal: "Truly speaking, all history exists for the Individual. Each of us stands absolutely alone in nature, and the great events of history only colossally represent the tendencies, the emotions, and the faculties of one man. I look therefore at the result of all the great agencies we have looked at in [the lecture series] to be the education of the observer—of the private man. He takes them all up in his progress into himself" (*EL* 2:13–14). (By "agencies" Emerson refers to the topics of the lectures: science, art, politics, religion, work, and so on.) In this concluding statement, Emerson means something like the private man's progress *toward* himself, very much as if the perfection of character lies outward in time and humankind is walking *into* its own improvement.

The process of internalizing the "glory" of parties and clans, nations and churches as part of an individual's character represents the "domestication of the idea of culture" that will culminate in the organicism of the old fable. If people continue to live as sleepwalkers, they will always follow leaders and worship idols; but "wake them and they shall quit the false good and leap to the true, and leave government to clerks and desks. This revolution is to be wrought by the gradual domestication of the idea of Culture" (*CW* 1:65). The expansion of democracy, especially in its emphasis on the autonomy and political equality of every citizen, marked a very significant move forward in the long, slow "upbuilding of a man," as he puts it in "The American Scholar."

Provided his countrymen could resist the alienation of mass politics, democratization had prepared the ground for a civil society rooted in private rather than public life. He bookends the "Politics" lecture with images of a democratic society that has successfully domesticated culture by embedding the value of social institutions in the character of individuals. Once the "idea of culture" was thoroughly domesticated, what had long been necessary in the constitution of states would become constitutional to individuals. He introduces "Politics" with a poem that tracks the movement of civilization from Europe to an "Atlantic seat" where the "Muses" and the "Virtues" meet. In this new home, politics is conducted not in the grandeur of a senate but in the modesty of a firelit parlor. In Emerson's anticipatory vision, politics is equal to character:

> Where the statesman ploughs
> Furrow for the wheat;
> When the Church is social worth,
> When the perfect state is come,
> The republican at home. (*CW* 3:115)

In effect, in an ideal state, government vanishes and allows all its leaders to pursue their lives in a world where private and public interests are indistinguishable. Churches have ceased to compete over dogma and have been replaced by general benevolence. The perfect state assumes universal equality; and its democratic anarchy is possible because its citizens, like good republicans, always act in the public interest. The "Politics" essay closes with similar imagery, but this time, Emerson emphasizes sincerity of dialogue over the domestication of institutions. When politics is perfected, democratic public dialogue will be comparable to the pillow talk of lovers. Churches and senates will be unnecessary because "thousands of human beings might share and obey each with the other the grandest and truest sentiments, as well as a knot of friends, or a pair of lovers" (*CW* 3:129). These images of political community domesticated to a level of loverly sincerity represents an ideal of individual character as a mode of ordinary citizenship.

EMERSONIAN CITIZENSHIP IN MASS DEMOCRACY

In a moment of embarrassing hyperbole at the center of the 1844 "Politics" essay, Emerson describes the "wise man" as a sovereign state: "To educate the wise man the state exists and with the appearance of the wise man the state expires. The appearance of character makes the State unnecessary" (*CW* 3:126). But how do we know a person of character when we hear him? We will recognize him because

> he needs no army, fort, or navy,—he loves men too well; no bribe, or feast, or palace, to draw friends to him; no vantage ground, no favorable circumstance. He needs no library, for he has not done thinking; no

church, for he is a prophet; no statute book, for he has the lawgiver; no money, for he is value; no road, for he is at home where he is; no experience, for the life of the creator shoots through him, and looks from his eyes. He has no personal friends, for he who has the spell to draw the prayer and piety of all men unto him, needs not husband and educate a few, to share with him a select and poetic life. His relation to men is angelic; his memory is myrrh to them; his presence, frankincense and flowers. (*CW* 3:126–27)

Emerson offers this sketch not as the model of a political savior but as a model of ordinary citizenship. The wise man represents the perfection of character and the complete domestication of culture. The wise man has internalized the services and obligations of government and offers the insight of the transparent eyeball as the standard of citizenship for a society that needs no governing.

The highest standards of justice, decency, piety, and so on are inseparable from his character. In its absurdity, it makes vivid Emerson's desire to siphon authority away from social institutions and reground them in the individual. The wise man cancels out the military, schools, churches, judiciary, even treasury and transportation. All the functions of government and culture have been cultivated and domesticated into this one character. As impractical as it is, the wise man is an explicit alternative to the partisan citizen of the Jackson era. With both bitterness and sympathy, Emerson observes:

> Most persons of ability meet in society with a kind of tacit appeal. Each seems to say, "I am not all here." Senators and presidents have climbed so high with pain enough, not because they think the place especially agreeable, but as an apology for real worth.... If a man found himself so rich-natured that he could enter into strict relations with the best persons and make life serene around him by the dignity and sweetness of his behavior, could he afford to circumvent the favor of the caucus and the press, and covet relations so hollow and pompous as those of a politician? Surely nobody would be a charlatan who could afford to be sincere. (*CW* 3:127)

The traces of worth Emerson sees in politicians echo the juxtaposition of liberal autonomy and partisan servility that he rejects at the end of "The American Scholar." He begins the closing paragraph of that essay with an explicit reference to democratization: "Another sign of our times, also marked by an analogous political movement, is the new importance given to the single person." He then includes a revised version of the 1834 journal passage with which I began this chapter: "Everything that tends to insulate the individual—to surround him with barriers of natural respect, so that each man shall feel the world is his, and man shall treat with man as a sovereign state with a sovereign state—tends to true union as well as greatness" (*CW* 1:68).

In Emerson's version of democratic citizenship, political equality represents a stature that infuses the individual with "natural respect" equally for self and others.[49] But in the form it had taken, the Democracy produced neither the authentic individuality of the wise man nor the organic unity of the old fable: "Is it not the chief disgrace of the world . . . to be reckoned in the gross, in the hundred, or the thousand, of the party, the section, to which we belong; and our opinion predicted geographically, as the north, or the south." In place of this vision of partisan and sectional conflict, in the closing lines of the essay he makes yet another attempt at describing a democratic society that is egalitarian, that respects each individual as a type of nation with all the rights of sovereignty within its borders, and that is nonetheless organically united as a single society. When democratic equality authentically takes hold so that individuals count themselves at their true worth, then "the dread of man and the love of man shall be a wall of defense and a wreath of joy around all. A nation of men will for the first time exist, because each believes himself inspired by the Divine soul which also inspires all men" (*CW* 1:70).

The democratization that culminated in the election of Andrew Jackson in 1828 marked a fundamental redefinition in the foundations of political legitimacy as the United States moved toward a model of citizenship grounded more directly in liberal political assumptions. It had four effects that are especially important to Emerson's defense of equality. First, the official political sphere became not just a realm of elite self-representation but one in which a broad cross-section of the white male population could speak and act. In effect, it made the right of access to political discourse a basic criterion of civil equality. Second, as the political realm expanded, mass political parties emerged to structure the larger electorate. This emergent structure threatened to diminish and subordinate individuals to the machinery of parties. In the process, Emerson saw a door open and then close again. The rise of the Democracy, and of the two titanic parties with it, came to pose a serious intellectual challenge that did much to motivate his thought about citizenship. In theory, democratization allowed people to claim public power in unprecedented forms, but in practice it was producing a new machinery of alienation.

Emerson sought to level up the definition of citizenship in terms of struggle between partisan identity and individuality. Third, the rise of liberalism and the shift toward an effort to represent self-interest rather than the abstract common good of civic republicanism shaped Emerson's thought on universalization and on the spirit as a metaphor for shared interests. Fourth, the move away from an organic model of society and toward a pluralistic model that accepted factional conflict evoked a kind of nostalgia in which Emerson imagines a culture that is built around metaphors of sovereignty to capture an ideal of individual citizenship and metaphors of domesticity to capture an ideal of sincere, unaffected community.

In his ambivalent response to the rise of a democracy that was as brimming in idealism as it was in cynicism, Emerson struggled to understand the change that it could portend for the society as well as for the individual. As strong as his political bias toward the Whigs clearly is, the focus of his ambivalence is not the Democracy, or even the Democratic Party, but the implications of mass politics for the individual. Democracy offered so much dignity to each citizen because it defined the individual as *the* central and irreducible institution of politics. It opened the public forum in ways that would eventually expand to the boundaries of the nineteenth century's most radical thinkers. The Democracy also opened new fronts in struggles for other kinds of equality. But for Emerson, the most important change that it signified lay in its potential to help people see themselves as important, powerful, and responsible members of the society.

2

MARRIAGE, FRIENDSHIP, AND THE DOMESTICATION OF CULTURE

Money and illness were on the Emersons' minds in the years after Ralph Waldo completed divinity school in 1826. Dangerous signs of tuberculosis had been recurring among the Emerson brothers. During this period his older brother William was establishing himself as a lawyer in New York City. Waldo's younger brother Edward would have his legal training interrupted by both mental and physical ailments. Edward died of tuberculosis in Puerto Rico in 1834. Waldo Emerson got the news of his brother's death while he was working as a supply preacher in New York. His youngest brother, Charles, also a lawyer, was engaged to Elizabeth Hoar, a family friend whose father ran the law office Charles worked in. Charles would also be diagnosed with tuberculosis and would die in 1836, collapsing on his brother William's front steps in Manhattan.

As fraught with hazard as the time was, for these young men the world held almost unlimited prospects. Without family inheritance, but well educated and well connected, each of the brothers was in the process of finding a path in the world by settling on a profession and preparing for an independent family life. Waldo was the first to marry. Charles, learning of his brother's engagement to seventeen-year old Ellen Louisa Tucker in late 1828, writes of the news to their aunt Mary Moody Emerson: "Waldo's prosperity comes as you always predicted, *late*; Ellen is, we understand, for we do not see her till next week, a beautiful, sensible, religious, girl. She is rich too. Though this seems forgotten in her loveliness and excellence."[1] Propriety barely restrains

Charles's eagerness to report the wealth that would envelop Waldo upon his marriage to Ellen Tucker.

A month after his engagement, Waldo accepted the position of colleague, or junior, pastor at the Second Unitarian Church in Boston. It was understood that he would become senior pastor when Henry Ware Jr. retired. He was ordained in March 1829 and elevated to pastor that July. Waldo and Ellen married early in the fall. The young couple moved into Mrs. Keating's boardinghouse on Chardon Street in Boston. Ellen's sisters, mother, and stepfather also lived there. It seemed as though the major choices of his life were now made.

During the summer of 1829—between their engagement and wedding—Ellen began to show signs of tuberculosis. Six months into their marriage, Waldo and Ellen traveled to Philadelphia in the hope that the warmer temperatures would reverse her decline. By the end of 1830, Ellen was seriously ill, and Waldo's brother Edward was also struggling with bouts of tubercular coughing.[2] In early February 1831, one year and four months after their wedding, Ellen died. At the time of her death, Ellen was twenty and Waldo was twenty-seven years old. This brief marriage, as well as its emotional and material effects, would prove an important source for the roles of intimacy, friendship, and marriage in Emerson's model of equality.

In August 1830, as Ellen's symptoms were worsening, Waldo began to prepare for the blow she could receive and the grief that he might have to face. Simultaneously imagining Ellen's salvation and distancing himself from the kind of loving intimacy he had just embraced, he transcribes a line from Saint Matthew's gospel into his journal: "In the resurrection they neither marry nor are given in marriage" (*JMN* 3:193). During this phase of his life, however, fear for his wife's health wasn't Emerson's only concern. Under the laws of marriage, Emerson could be entitled to a significant portion of the Tucker family wealth. There can be little doubt that Emerson loved Ellen deeply; but there can be equally little doubt that the wealth he inherited through his first wife was a crucial enabling factor in the life he subsequently led. His role in the struggle for sexual and gender equality begins with the ambiguity of significant financial benefit overlaid on profound misery and anguish.

Both Ellen and Waldo had lost their fathers, and Ellen's older brother had also recently died of tuberculosis. Even during their courtship, Waldo and Ellen shared a fatalistic sensitivity that led to a mutual preoccupation with death. Waldo gave this morbid strain a practical and self-interested force by encouraging his seventeen-year-old fiancée to write a will that would ensure his claim to her portion of the Tucker wealth. By the time they married, Ellen had closed "the ugly subject," as she called it, by writing him into her will against the counsel of the uncle who served as her legal guardian. Though it took over three years before Emerson was able to claim her estate, the court had made an initial ruling in his favor before he provoked the crisis that led to his resignation from the pulpit of the Second Church. He cared about the money.[3]

He received over $11,000 in 1834 and another $11,000 in 1837. Managed properly, Ellen's wealth would provide him a regular income of over $1,000 a year, just slightly less than his starting salary as junior minister at the Second Church.

The loss of his young wife propelled him away from doctrinaire religion and faith in institutions of all kinds. It even put pretty sharp boundaries on what he thought marriage could mean in a person's life. Psychologically, it amplified the stoic sadness that casts a shadow of monastic isolation over self-reliance. "I who alone am," he would phrase this human condition in his essay "Friendship" (*CW* 2:120). In "Self-Reliance" and "Heroism," he talks about the ability to maintain the peace of solitude in a tumultuous crowd. His Transcendentalism emerged out of the solitude of a deeply private misery and is connected to broken dreams of love, intimate friendship, and family. In the struggle against despair that followed Ellen's death, we see emerge both the granite of Emerson's fatalism and the soaring spirituality that he wielded against it. Years later, it would bring him to define intimacy as a beautiful enemy.

By imagining spiritual life as a process through which individuals form closer relationships with other persons, Emerson presents sincere personal communication as the crucial provocation for Spirit. Whether it be through poetry, the hard words of street corner debate, or the pillow talk of lovers, Emerson's thought about equality has its deepest roots not in the "transparent eyeball" of *Nature* but in one person's effort to speak honestly to another. From the outset of his friendship with Margaret Fuller in summer 1836, Emerson's advocacy of every person's right to individuality and his attention to the repressive force of social institutions including marriage began to influence the thinking of early women's rights reformers, and he became an allied voice in their effort to win improvements in women's condition. Emerson's comments in his one lecture at a women's rights convention in 1855 show how far his personal recognition of universal equal rights extended. In regard to women's equality, he takes an extreme position on property, suffrage, and education. Women, Emerson agrees,

> have an unquestionable right to their own property. And if a woman demands votes, offices and political equality with men, as among the Shakers an Elder and Elderess are of equal power,—and among the Quakers,—it must not be refused. . . . Let the laws be purged of every barbarous remainder, every barbarous impediment to women. Let the public donations for education be equally shared by them, let them enter a school as freely as a church, let them have and hold and give their property as men do theirs. (*W* 11:354)

It is worth pointing out, though, that Emerson never self-consciously joined the movement for women's equality in the same way that he joined the antislavery movement. Although he occasionally expresses support for women's suffrage and more often points out the irony of arguments that ignorant or untrustworthy men put forward against it, these instances are rare enough that his writing did not significantly influence the suffrage side of the movement for equality between men and women. Where his writing *is* important, though, is in the emerging debate over women's unequal status in marriage and in his criticism of domesticity and the values associated with it.

As powerful forces in his society were driving the assault on equality by promoting models of gender that would clearly demarcate hierarchical inequalities between men and women, Emerson's expansive defense of each person's right to individuality articulated a mode of understanding universal human rights that echoed the most deeply held values of antebellum advocates for sexual equality. Even before the women's rights movement took a recognizable form, Lucy Stone, Elizabeth Cady Stanton, and Margaret Fuller heard their own aspirations for equality voiced in Emerson's essays.[4]

The most basic qualities that Emerson attributes to equality, especially its foundation in sincere communication, contrast sharply with the social order envisioned by people who wanted to demarcate gender spheres and define private dialogue in opposition to political debate. Whereas advocates of strictly defined gender spheres, such as Catharine Beecher, accepted the containment of women within domestic environments but then worked to enhance their authority by treating the management of domestic life as a profession that should command public respect, Emerson articulates a process of reform that subsumes the public sphere into the private realm, a reform that achieves the "domestication of the idea of culture" (*CW* 1:65). For Emerson, in his effort to link equality to a model of citizenship grounded in sincere communication, the most important measure of progress was the extent to which public debate expressed the sincerity that he associated with marriage and friendship. The contrast in style between Edward Everett's two-hour oration at Gettysburg and the expressive brevity of Abraham Lincoln's Gettysburg Address is perhaps the most vivid example of this "domestication" of public rhetoric. Where Everett was learned, Lincoln was sincere.

The debates over sexual equality and domesticity posed both political and rhetorical problems. Partly because it dealt with such intimate relationships, marriage reform was especially difficult to discuss in public venues such as newspapers and lyceum lectures. The idea of marriage as an irreversible union of souls created schools of thought about masculinity, femininity, and marriage that divided even the most single-minded allies in the women's rights movement.[5] As Jean Bethke Elshtain breaks down the alternatives, with the rise of Jacksonian democracy, there were only three rhetorical "options left open to women" seeking to subvert gendered distinctions and advance equality. Women could learn "to speak the public language of liberalism and to conceive of their entry into politics on those terms"; or, second, women might voluntarily accept consignment to the domestic realm and "speak, in private, the language of sentiment." (This language, however, Elshtain feels, was already losing its hard-won cultural influence. In the face of expanding male suffrage and the geographic separation of work and home life, the private language of sentiment had become, she finds, "increasingly cloying as it lost part of the force of the Christian ethic of caring and responsibility and was shorn of its power to beard power.") Third, women might extend "the language of sentiment" into public reform movements through existing church-connected benevolent societies. This path would bridge the public–private divide "to seek remedies to social ills," but it would also "define [women's] entrance into the public world along the lines of a frequently censorious moralism."[6]

As she surveys the rhetorical landscape, Elshtain distinguishes between masculine-identified public and feminine-identified private discourses. Taking the first avenue, that of appropriating the egalitarian principles of liberalism, women could claim, as reformers such as Sarah Grimké, Lucy Stone, and Susan B. Anthony did, a right to formal public equality by universalizing the principles of liberalism that were redefining the political status of propertyless white men. This path would point toward women's equality in civil rights, politics, and economic opportunity. In the process, public equality would come first, and private equality would follow. Alternatively, by moving the focus of reform toward the private sphere, women could ground equality in a rhetoric of "sentiment" that Elshtain connects to an "ethic of caring" rooted in domesticity. This path was advocated by public figures such as domesticity theorist and education reformer Catharine Beecher and Sarah Josepha Hale, editor of *Godey's Ladies Book*, both of whom advocated explicitly defined gender spheres to represent distinct types of cultural authority. Grounding women's authority in discourses of sentimental influence, this rhetoric of women's empowerment underpins the third, hybrid path by expanding and secularizing the public benevolent action women had long been performing through church organizations. Rather than marking a compromise between the type of civil rights liberalism that Lucy Stone advocated and religion-based benevolent organizations, this hybrid path marks a profound change in women's identities because its claim to cultural authority is grounded in assumptions about women's moral nature rather than in religious doctrine. Thus, its successes would be *women's* successes rather than the achievements of a reinvigorated Protestant Christianity. In its emergence, these rhetorical approaches are often intertwined as they are in Sarah Grimké's "Letters on the Province of Women" reprinted in *The Liberator* in early 1838. Grimké addresses issues of public equality but ultimately grounds her whole reform argument in marriage reform. She introduces the topic of redefining marriage toward equality from a Christian perspective thoroughly in her letter on the "relation of husband and wife."[7]

Both Catharine Beecher and Sarah Josepha Hale situate themselves as actors in this hybrid form that connects women's moral authority with renewed focus on the social value of domesticity and femininity. Both had stature as public intellectuals and moral arbiters, but their goal as influencers was relatively conservative: to project an orderly and slightly more egalitarian republic by bringing social values into conformity with "natural" talents defined by sex. Emerson's Transcendentalism aligns more with the classically liberal universalization of equality by rejecting rigid definitions of either masculinity or femininity. Instead, he emphasizes the priority of private life as the starting point for liberty from the constraints of normative institutions—and this includes critiques of marriage and family life.

More subtly, but also more pervasively, by treating communication between intimate friends as the model for public speech, Emerson's thought about equality is always gesturing toward domestic relationships in ways that minimize the boundaries between male/public and female/private spheres. This egalitarianism had important implications for the definition of domesticity and womanhood.

THE CONSERVATIVE EQUALITY OF DOMESTICITY

Catharine Beecher, in her 1841 *Treatise on Domestic Economy*, exemplifies the conservative claim that the path to women's empowerment lay not in achieving civil equality but in achieving a higher standard of respect for women in domestic and familial roles. In Beecher's functionalist view, nature would be more truly fulfilled, and womanhood better served, by amplifying differences between the genders than by eliding them in a public equality that, she believed, would always leave women at a disadvantage. Whereas racist anthropology and proslavery thought were very much part of an explicit assault on equality, antebellum conservative feminism is somewhat more ambiguous. Unlike the explicit demonization of women acting in public that characterized reactions against the Grimkés, Abby Kelley, and Lucy Stone, among others, moves to change the status of domestic womanhood were calibrated efforts at reform. Projects like Beecher's sought to advance equality even as they asked women to accept stark distinctions between the identities that men and women could cultivate for themselves.

In the opening chapter of her *Treatise on Domestic Economy*, titled "The Peculiar Responsibilities of American Women," Beecher argues for the importance of a gendered division of labor in democratic society. Citing Alexis de Tocqueville, she favors clear gender spheres over the ideal of gender-neutral civil equality, which she associates with a "European" mode of egalitarianism:

> There are people in Europe, who, confounding together the different characteristics of the sexes, . . . would mix them in all things,—their business, their occupations, their pleasures. . . . It is not this that the Americans understand [as] the species of democratic equality, which may be established between the sexes. . . . The Americans have applied to the sexes the great principle of political economy, which governs the

manufactories of our age, by carefully dividing the duties of man from those of women, in order that the great work of society may be better carried on.[8]

The home, on Beecher's formulation, is neither a sentimental refuge from the competitive efficiencies of the market nor a site of unencumbered individuality. Rather, it is a place where roles and identities are performed and reinforced as intensively as they are in any other arena. In it, identity is discovered not by the deeply expressive private communications that build trusting and intimate relationships, but by continually enacting and performing cultural standards similar to those that govern "the manufactories" of the age. *The Treatise on Domestic Economy* serves to make those standards explicit, much like a handbook that explains the responsibilities of a job.

In this articulation of gender spheres, American women willingly accept what Beecher calls a "peculiar" form of inequality:

> In this country, it is established, both by opinion and by practice, that women have an equal interest in all social and civil concerns; and that no domestic, civil, or political institution is right that sacrifices her interest to promote that of the other sex. But in order to secure her more firmly in all these privileges, it is decided, that, in the domestic relation, she take a subordinate station and that in civil and political concerns, her interests be intrusted to the other sex, without her taking any part in voting or in making and administering laws.[9]

This division of responsibilities, Beecher admits, requires that women accept an unequal status in public and forgo any claims to the right of participation in "civil and political concerns." She also concedes that even in the "domestic relation," women should accept "a subordinate station." Nonetheless, for Beecher, as "opinion and practice" recognize women's equal interest in all the affairs of the society, the renunciation of civil rights and domestic equality actually creates the context in which women can attain parity of power with men.

For Beecher, the home should be a professionalized space run by a professionally trained, highly skilled manager.[10] To emphasize its professionalism, Beecher rarely uses the word "wife," preferring "housekeeper" as her primary referent and using "mother" when necessary. Without addressing the fact that divorce was extremely difficult in antebellum America, she pushes the definition of housekeeper, implicitly also a wife, as the condition resulting from a free choice analogous to accepting a job offer:

> In a truly democratic state, each individual is allowed to choose for himself, who shall take the position of his superior. No woman is forced to obey any husband but the one she chooses for herself; nor is she obliged to take a husband, if she prefers to remain single. So every domestic, and every artisan or laborer . . . can choose the employer to whom he is to accord obedience, or, . . . he can remain without taking a subordinate place to any employer.[11]

In Beecher's definition of sexual equality, like any highly skilled professional, the prospective wife had the freedom of the market as a source of power. This is accurate as far as it goes, but once the contract is signed, the wife must accept that the husband is permanently in the "position of" her "superior."

Before she goes into chapters on preparing food, cleaning house, doing laundry, and raising children, Beecher devotes a chapter to the importance of professional training in housekeeping: "Domestic Economy as a Branch of Study."[12] Providing anecdotes about young women forced to take responsibility for "nursery, parlor, and kitchen" before they know how to handle them, Beecher makes the case for professionalizing the housekeeper's work:

> The eldest daughter of a family returned from school, on a visit, at sixteen years of age. But before her vacation had closed, her mother was laid in the grave; and such were her father's circumstances, that she was obliged to assume the cares and duties of her lost parent. The care of an infant, the management of young children, the superintendence of domestics, the charge of family expenses, the responsibility of entertaining company, and the many other cares of the family state, all at once came upon this young and inexperienced schoolgirl.[13]

The gap between the actual and the potential status of the home lies in the fact that the women who are required to maintain households are woefully unprepared for their responsibilities. This failure is, at root, a failure to recognize the importance of the domestic realm. In the first place, white middle-class girls had been trained to avoid physical exertion. Second, they were educated to attract husbands but not to manage households. For American women, "in consequence" of their enforced lassitude and poor preparation, "as soon as they are called to the responsibilities and trials of domestic life, their constitution fails, and their whole life is rendered a burden." Nevertheless, though unprepared in technical skills, they have an intuitive appreciation of the high office they will hold:

> No women on earth have a higher sense of their moral and religious responsibilities or better understand, not only what is demanded of them, as housekeepers, but all the claims that rest on them as wives, mothers, and members of a social community. An American woman, who is the mistress of a family, feels her obligations, in reference to her influence over her husband, and a still greater responsibility in rearing and educating her children. She feels, too, the claims that moral interests of her domestics have on her watchful care. In social life, she recognizes the claims of hospitality, and the demands of friendly visiting. Her responsibility, in reference to the institutions of benevolence and religion are deeply realized. The regular worship of the Lord's day, and all the various religious and benevolent societies that place so much dependence on female activity, she feels obligated to sustain, by her influence and example.[14]

Skillfully fulfilling these roles will require technical education in food preparation and hygiene, business sense to deal with expenses, leadership skills to manage an effective team of servants, and manners to stand among her peers in "social community." Emerson's daughter Ellen invokes these ideals as she recalls her own ramped-up participation in housekeeping as an adolescent. "When I took a share in the housekeeping I wished to take the whole," she writes, in order to experience "the glory of being a real housekeeper." But as she struggled with the work, she admits, "I needed a longer apprenticeship than I had supposed."[15]

In Beecher's vision of the household, sex and sexuality are completely avoided. In fact, the presence of grown men, as either husbands or fathers, seems incidental rather than pervasive. Although she acknowledges women's subordination, in her model the "domestic economy" of the nation is a realm of women's authority, control, performance, and fulfillment. With all its functions directed toward a greater good, as an institutional setting it is similar to a modern hospital or school, operating according to best practices, which means following mandatory protocols developed through and learned in an institute of professional housekeeping.

The parity she attributes to this model of domesticity is grounded in a basic civic-republican claim about the most fundamental criteria of adult personhood. With a censorious eye on Jacksonian materialism that Emerson would appreciate, Beecher places the formation of character at the center of her vision for the role of the home: "If the main object of this life were to make money, and secure those various gratifications of appetite and taste which money purchases," prioritizing politics and markets "might, to some extent, be justified," but since, "the main object of life, for ourselves and for others, is *to form character*," then "every man and every woman are under obligation to devote some portion of time to perpetuating and increasing family and neighborhood friendships, and to sustaining the various claims of domestic hospitality."[16] Entertaining guests and offering hospitality to strangers is a crucial method of tying the community together and projecting domestic values into the public realm. In this sense, Beecher sees home life in highly public terms, as an institution not just for the development of individuals but for the existence of a democratic society. Emerson is fully in accord with Beecher's prioritization both of character and of the domestic settings in which it is best nurtured.

The home, and the housekeeper's role in it, is important in terms of natural equality because it is nature's predetermined realm for women's fulfillment. "Every woman should imbibe," as Beecher puts is, "the impression that she is training for the discharge of the most important, the most difficult, and the most sacred and interesting duties that can possibly employ the highest intellect. She ought to feel that her station and responsibilities, in the great drama of life are second to none."[17]

Beecher's whole theory hinges on sharpening sex-identified spheres of life. She focuses so totally on womanhood as a gender-determined condition that nowhere in her large body of work does she stand and face relationships between men and women outside of their roles as wives, husbands, or parents. Perhaps paradoxically, her vision, while it defines a civic-republican model of an orderly society in which men and women can have a "peculiar" equality, it also lacks any real model of the individual subjectivity that is so central to Transcendentalism. Her thinking is deeply liberal in that it rates equality as a necessary value and that in its focus on the responsibilities of the individual, that unique quality of Romantic liberalism, the right to individuality is strikingly absent. It would empower the women who enact her model, but it would also leave them faceless. Her vision of parity based on gender identity refines one line in the assault on equality through its literally religious faith that the homes of wealthy white Protestants are the source of virtue and value for all other institutions. From these central locations, churches gain their energy and social value, business and politics are conducted with decency and honesty, propertyless laborers, "helps," and contractors are sustained and taught deference. The housekeepers at the center of these homes—properly credentialed and conscious of their importance—form an elite of professionals who move through the world as the equals of the high-status men who have parallel responsibilities in the institutions traditionally recognized as public or civic.

EMERSON'S "DOMESTIC LIFE"

In his one essay on domesticity, "Domestic Life," first read in March 1840 and then repeated frequently throughout that decade, Emerson engages the exact same context that Beecher addresses in her 1841 *Treatise on Domestic Economy*. Like Beecher, Emerson asserts the importance of home life to the formation of character. But unsurprisingly, and in sharp contrast to Beecher's thinking, Emerson's vision of the "household" is focused on the nurturing of boys and on the reform of the home to better articulate the individuality of the male head of household. He positions the domestic realm as a site of the first importance, but much of his essay is a straightforward critique of the model of domesticity that Beecher advocates. In it, Emerson often gestures toward women's labor, but just as much as Beecher, he totally erases women's subjectivity.

Contrasting the importance of public with private life, Emerson contends that "it is easier to count the census, or compute the square extent of a territory, to criticize its polity, books, art, than to come to the persons and dwellings of men, and read their character and hope in their way of life." But the predominance of public institutions inflates people's perception of their importance: "Is it not plain that not in senates or courts, or chambers of commerce, but in the dwelling-house must the true character and hope of the time be consulted" (*CW* 7:54–55). Further, he sees the "dwelling-house" neither as a place of anti-political community nor as a sacred realm of feminine moral authority, but as a site that should ideally be devoted to the "constitution," as he puts it, of masculine individuality: "If a man wishes to acquaint himself with the real history of the world, with the spirit of the age, he must not go first to the statehouse or the court room. The subtle spirit of life must be sought in facts nearer. It is what is done and suffered in the house, in the constitution, in the temperament, in the personal history, that has the profoundest interest for us" (*CW* 7:54). Here, in placing its focus on domestic life rather than on public deeds as a means of exploring the formation of masculine character, Emerson's essay embodies one of the vital difficulties that would confront the women's rights activists who prioritized marriage reform. For Emerson, to sit down and think about the meaning of "domestic life" does not elicit reflection on intimate relationships between men and women or connections between people of different generations. Nor does it bring the home into view as a place of women's labor, productivity, containment, or fulfillment. On the contrary, he denounces the bourgeois home as a conventionalized institution defined by norms that tyrannize and diminish all its inhabitants. In Emerson's essay, rather than the household's being the foundational site of women's claim to parity in a divided society, women are invisible *even in the home*. His image of domesticity minimizes the presence of women as thoroughly as Beecher's minimizes the presence of men.

Where Beecher actively seeks a highly conventional domestic realm as a means of professionalizing domestic labor, Emerson sees this goal as a threat to autonomy in general, and to masculine autonomy in particular. Rather than treating the home either as a haven made sacred by the moral authority of womanhood or as a site of authenticity and intimate dialogue, he treats it in much the same way that he treats the church—as a place where social convention stifles authentic self-reflection and makes sincere communication difficult. His most important metaphor of authentic political selfhood collapses political into private discourse so that senatorial speeches have the intimacy of dialogue between close friends, yet he represents existing domestic discourse in terms of stifling convention that reproduces the worst qualities he sees in politics, the church, and the schools. As he puts it, "The vice of government, the vice of education, the vice of religion, is one with that of private life" (*CW* 7:62). But seeking to push against the ideal of professionalizing the household, Emerson imagines a home that can produce what he calls a "domestic conqueror" who will "bravely and gracefully subdue this Gorgon of Convention and Fashion, and show men how to lead a clean, handsome and heroic life" (*CW* 7:68). In this familiar Emersonian gesture, he presents a vision of embattled masculinity as the catalyst for transformation.

To address the ills of home life, the would-be conqueror of domestic conformity faces manifold obstacles. "What idea predominates in our houses?"

Emerson asks. "Thrift first, then convenience and pleasure." If one were to "take off all the roofs," one would see not individualized habitations but rather a conformist domestic life defined by conspicuous consumption and emulation:

> The houses of the rich are confectioners' shops, where we get sweetmeats and wine; the houses of the poor are imitations of these to the extent of their ability. With these ends, housekeeping is not beautiful; it cheers and raises neither the husband nor the wife, nor the child; not the host nor the guest; it oppresses women. A house kept to the end of prudence is laborious without joy; a house kept to the end of display is impossible to all but a few women, and their success is dearly bought. (*CW* 7:56)

Emerson here offers an unvarnished view of married life, even acknowledging the influence of economic class and presenting the bourgeois home as an institution that "oppresses women." Whether housekeeping is built around thrift or display, it comes with costly trade-offs: "If the linens and hangings are clean and fine and the furniture good, the yard, the garden, and the fences are neglected." If everything in the house is "well attended, then must the master and mistress be studious of particulars at the cost of their own accomplishments and growth, or persons are treated as things" (*CW* 7:57).

Rather than serving as the locus of love, intimacy, and individuality, home marks the intrusion of compulsory conformity into a context that should be emphatically individual. It even reproduces the alienation of industrial labor in the way it exploits domestic help. Conventional wisdom argues, Emerson reports, "'Give us wealth, and the good household shall exist'" (*CW* 7:59). A wealthy householder can simply hire enough skilled help to complete all necessary tasks. But this conventional wisdom, Emerson observes, ignores the economic caste system that undermines equality in the domestic sphere. The conventional approach to good housekeeping "is vicious, and leaves the whole difficulty untouched." Degraded domesticity cannot be eliminated simply by increasing the household budget. Another, more egalitarian age, he goes on,

> may divide the manual labor of the world more equally on all the members of society, and so make the labors of a few hours avail to the wants and add to the vigor of man. But the reform that applies itself to the household must not be partial. It must correct the whole system of our social living, it must come with plain living and high thinking; it must break up caste, and put domestic service on another foundation. (*CW* 7:59)

It is worth noting that at the time he wrote this essay, the Emersons had both a live-in cook and local farm girls who worked as daytime helps around the house.

Although Emerson shows a modest recognition of the way domestic life oppresses women and creates exploitative wage labor relationships, his real objection to the trends that Beecher was trying to amplify is the effect that domestic life could have on masculine character. To say "*Give us wealth and the home shall exist*" even undermines, in Emerson's eyes, the very idea of masculinity. "Men are not born rich," he continues, and "in getting wealth the man is generally sacrificed, and often sacrificed without acquiring wealth at last. Besides . . . there are objections to wealth. Wealth is a shift. The wise man angles with himself only, and with no meaner bait" (*CW* 7:58).

The conventional household, like so many other institutions, Emerson sees as an obstacle to masculine self-reliance, and in this masculinist focus, the ideal of domestic life he expresses later in the essay effaces womanhood, even in the private sphere of the home: "There should be nothing confounding and conventional in [domestic] economy, but genius and love of the man so conspicuously marked in his estate that the eye that knew him should read his character in his property, in his grounds, in his ornaments, in every expense" (*CW* 7:55). Emerson, thinking of homes built around the expression of masculine individuality, wants each household to be private, unique, and idiosyncratic. He wants each home to be an extension of personality that allows its owner both to live with authenticity and to present visitors with a sensory embodiment of his character when they enter.

"Domestic Life" is not a paean to the home as an idealized and feminized place of virtue or safety, but it is a call to reform the meaning and purpose of home life. No refuge from the competitive public sphere, the households he sees around him are in a cutthroat competition to embody the conventions of the moment. In these same conventions that Emerson sees as stifling, Beecher sees a vehicle for giving womanhood the kind of professional status she saw in ministers, lawyers, and judges. Rather than threatening to create alienated housekeepers trapped in a dehumanizing structure of mass-culture discipline, Beecher saw the possibility of domesticating industrial bureaucratization to women's advantage by combining expert stature with moral authority. The difference between Beecher's and Emerson's visions marks the terms of an emerging debate about the potential meanings of marriage, family life, and domestic privacy within the struggle to defend equality.

Beecher and Emerson describe almost the exact same setting, but they see in it radically different implications for equality. Beecher sees a towering new ideal of womanhood, one that combines attributes of the minister with those of the business executive. In the *Treatise*, Beecher effectively, as Emerson suggests, "take[s] off all the roofs from street to street" of prosperous homes and aims to make their operations transparent, efficient, and professional (*CW* 7:56). The bourgeois home would become, in effect, a public institution, defended through an official ideology that would also define an asymmetrical, but real, equality between men of property and the housekeeper-wives who run the households. The standards kept there would set behavioral standards for the whole society.

These parallel visions of domestic life reflect intertwined understandings of marriage and equality. Both Beecher and Emerson imagine the married couple living in a private home as the central institution of society. Both also see domesticity in paradoxically politicized terms. For Beecher, this paradox lies in the ideological ascendance of the idea that the home orbits around the skill and character of the housekeeper, and that all other social institutions should be understood to revolve around the home. For Emerson, this paradox lies in the effort simultaneously to see domestic life as a place of authentic self-expression and from there to imagine the emergence of religious and political practices that have the same standards of authenticity. The essay "Domestic Life" makes a similar gesture in relation to domesticity to that which "The American Scholar" makes in relation to democratization. "The American Scholar" juxtaposes classical learning against popular culture and then argues for the importance of popular culture to the scholar's vocation. In "Domestic Life," Emerson juxtaposes bourgeois conventionality against idiosyncratic self-expression and then argues for the importance of idiosyncratic self-expression. In doing so he also juxtaposes private against public life and asserts the primacy of the domestic realm as the site of authentic *masculine* rather than feminine fulfillment.

With the universal right to individuality and the priority of private over public life as critical elements of his argument for egalitarian liberalism, Emerson creates an important counternarrative to the codification of gender spheres. Even if marriage is a private matter, the private life, including the norms of day-to-day conjugal life, would have to be central in any egalitarian reform agenda because private relationships are where individuality and the equality that authenticates it is best nurtured and cultivated. By Emerson's reasoning, equality has to begin at home because the foundation of equality and individuality is sincere self-expression. His failure as a theorist of private life is that despite his iconoclasm, his nonconformity, and even his willingness to be the "devil's child," Emerson's vision of domesticity is grounded in the head of household's character rather than in the relationships that domestic life can foster.

Emerson's construction of equality as a universal right to individuality combined with his strong sense of difference between the sexes makes his value to sexual egalitarianism very ambiguous. In his thought about race, we can see him voicing a deeply ingrained white supremacy and then resisting that reflex in order to validate a universalized, cosmopolitan model of human personhood. In his thought about gender, the pattern is reversed. He occasionally offers soaring validations of the equality of the sexes, but more frequently he asserts an instrumental right to civil and legal equality but then reconfirms his belief in essential differences in character and temperament between men and women. His deepest contribution to antebellum arguments for gender equality lies in the priority he attributes to private life in any person's ability to achieve individuality. Conventional coverture marriage defined private life in his society, but it also worked against the attainment of individuality for either men or women.

WOMEN'S EQUALITY AND THE PROBLEM OF MARRIAGE

Although in the *Treatise on Domestic Economy* and in "Domestic Life" neither Beecher nor Emerson acknowledges the fact, both assume that marriage defines adult life. As antebellum Americans debated various trends that were reshaping gender, they were also beginning to grapple with long-standing assumptions about marriage. Advocates for women's equality were trying to find ways to discuss issues ranging from property rights to child rearing, from spiritual obligations to divorce. Reformers with the bravery to address the "marriage question," however, struggled to define a language subtle enough to carry the issue of women's sexual, economic, and psychological lives within marriage onto the public stage. The issue is publicized tentatively in the 1848 Declaration of the Seneca Falls Convention, concluding that, in marriage, "the law, in all cases, going upon a false supposition of the supremacy of man," gives "all power into his hands." But the whole topic remained fraught throughout the antebellum period. At an 1860 convention, when Elizabeth Cady Stanton sought to discuss divorce and Antoinette B. Blackwell objected, Wendell Phillips tried to declare the whole topic out of order, shouting, "This convention is no marriage convention!"[18] As many women's rights reformers recognized early on, advocating for political and civil equality, or even for moral authority in the home, was the corollary to an even more fundamental institutional transformation.

In both religious and legal terms, as nineteenth-century Americans experienced it, marriage revolved around the idea of unification. The issue of unification of souls is important to Emerson's defense of equality because achieving equality within marriage would be crucial to achieving the equal right of each person also to achieve individuality. In the Christian New Testament, marriage is explicitly defined as unification by both Mark (10:9) and Matthew (19:6). As Matthew puts it, husband and wife "are no longer two, but one flesh." He then defines the marriage tie as indissoluble. Husband and wife are merged into a single body, and "therefore what God has joined together, let no one separate." The idea of unification into one indissoluble spiritual being had long been a powerful denotation of the marriage tie; and despite the fact that marriage was criticized for its similarity to chattel property relations, divorce was often unattainable and remained controversial even among many of the staunchest advocates of equality.[19] After the Civil War, for example, Lucy Stone broke away from Elizabeth Cady Stanton because Stone could not advocate a women's rights platform that included divorce.

As a legal tradition, the doctrine of marital unity that erased women's right to individuality has its roots in Anglo-Norman law. "Coverture" marriage began as a contract of exchange between two men—the father of the bride and the husband. In the resulting legal relation between husband and wife, the bride's identity was subsumed into that of the husband. As William Blackstone phrased it in his *Commentaries* (1765): "By marriage the husband and wife are one person in law; that is, the very being or legal existence of the woman is suspended during the marriage, or at least is incorporated and consolidated into that of the husband; under whose wing, protection and cover, she performs everything; . . . her condition during the marriage is called her *coverture*." Blackstone recognizes the asymmetry of coverture and justifies the doctrine of marital unity as a model of respect rather than degradation. Setting aside the stately cadence of his commentary, he enthuses, "Even the disabilities which the wife lies under are for the most part intended for her protection and benefit: so great a favorite is the female sex of the laws of England."[20] But in practice, coverture had always been about subordination rather than unification. One American commentator in 1845 glossed these lines by quipping, "Such politeness on the part of the law is like amiability from a hyena."[21] John Stuart Mill sums up the economic and legal asymmetry coverture created in *On the Subjection of Women*. On the relation of husband to wife Mill writes, "What is yours is mine, but what is mine is not yours."[22]

The reform that would most profoundly contribute to equality of the sexes was for women to achieve equal rights within marriage. But attaining this goal was going to require a redefinition of conjugal ties far beyond the property relationship Mill highlights. It would mean redefining the power to control sexual relations, plan pregnancy, resist domestic violence, expand access to divorce, and gain custody rights of children. To achieve these ends, the very idea of marriage would have to be transformed so that it ceased to signify an act of unification in which two identities were inseparably joined and began to denote a loving partnership between two free and equal individuals. Emerson's thought about this topic stands at the beginning of a process that has resulted in changes as radical as those in any other institution of American life.

To reimagine the interior world of marriage was different from advocating for civil change. More than just a relationship between two independent persons, marriage bridged the public, private, and personal realms. It linked couples together with prescriptive standards that began in public ceremony but extended deeply into intimate physical and spiritual experiences. In addition to offering sanction for sexual relations, marital norms even prescribed the psychological affects men and women were to adopt during sexual intercourse. On a spiritual level, for those who believed marriage was a holy sacrament, God was bonding two souls in a permanent union that raised the conjugal link above all other human connections, even those between parent and child. Its social repercussion was to ground the identity of husband and wife in a metaphysics that dictates gender roles and defines the meaning of a faithful life.

But through coverture, the sexual duty marriage imposed on women put wives in a position of self-abasing abjection. So many other reforms had been contested in public dialogue, but this one was different. The rhetorical hurdle of taking women's sense of sexual degradation public, of seeking redress for a condition so rife with humiliation or shame and so profoundly personal as the defenselessness of one's own body created visceral anger. Margaret Fuller, despite her optimism that change was within reach, does not gloss over the issue of mandatory sexual submissiveness in marriage. In *Woman in the Nineteenth Century* she addresses it frankly, beginning clinically and ending with scathing sarcasm. "It has been inculcated on women for centuries," Fuller writes, "that men have not only stronger passions than they, but of a sort that it would be shameful for them to share or even understand. . . . That the least appearance of coldness or withdrawal, from whatever cause, in the wife is wicked, because liable to turn her husband's thought to illicit indulgences; for a man is so constituted that he must indulge his passions or die!" Unmistakably addressing the expectation of sexual submissiveness here, Fuller places this aspect of coverture as the poison at the root of marriage in the nineteenth century. Fuller's *Woman* is above all a critique of marriage in which she argues for a reinvention that demands husbands and wives accept a "religious recognition of equality" as their crucial marital vow.[23] This reform, in Fuller's view, would change the nature of gender, sex, and sexuality. It would transform womanhood as a human condition more profoundly than any other reform.

Efforts to raise the profile of marriage reform caused friction within the women's rights movement. At a convention in 1852, Elizabeth Cady Stanton gave a groundbreaking speech linking divorce to temperance. She argued that women should be able to divorce alcoholic husbands. Hotly criticized, even by peers within the movement, Stanton defended her breach of the taboo.[24] Writing to Susan B. Anthony in early 1853, she explains her conviction that

> it is in vain to look for the elevation of woman, so long as she is degraded in marriage. I say it is a sin, an outrage on our holiest feelings to pretend that anything but deep, fervent love and sympathy constitutes marriage. The right idea of marriage is at the foundation of all reforms. . . . Man in his lust has regulated this whole question of sexual intercourse long enough. Let the mother of mankind whose prerogative it is to set bonds on his indulgence rouse up and give this whole question a thorough fearless examination. . . . I feel this whole question of woman's rights turns on the point of the marriage relation, and sooner or later it will be the question for discussion. I would not hurry it on, neither would I avoid it.[25]

In 1857 Stanton expands on the implications of women's position within marriage, also in a letter to Susan B. Anthony, in terms perfectly aligned with the central link between liberty and equality to which Emerson was so deeply connected: "So long as our present false marriage relation continues, which in most cases is nothing more nor less than legalized prostitution, woman can have no self-respect, and of course man will have none for her; for the world estimates us according to the value we put on ourselves." This claim leads immediately to the concentric contexts that reinforce women's inequality: "Personal freedom is the first right to be proclaimed, and that does not now and cannot now belong to the relation of wife, to the mistress of the isolated home, to the financial dependent."[26] Lucy Stone, one of Stanton's early allies, who waged one of the first recorded campaigns for pay equity, made similar remarks about the constraints faced by married women. Shortly after her own wedding in 1855, Stone writes in a letter to her sister-in-law Antoinette Brown, an ordained minister in western New York:

> Paulina Davis has written me, that she wants the marriage question to come up at the national convention . . . [but] it seems to me that we are not ready for it. I saw at Philadelphia, by private conversations. No two of us think alike about it. And yet it is clear to me, that question underlies, this whole movement and all our little skirmishing for better laws, and the right to vote, will yet be swallowed up, in the real question, viz, has woman, as a wife, the right to herself? It is very little to me to have the right to vote, to own property &c, if I may not keep my body and its uses, in my absolute right. Not one wife in a thousand can do that now, & so long as she suffers this bondage, all other rights will not help her to her true position—
> This question will *force* itself upon us some day, but it seems to me it is *un*timely now—[27]

Stone's own courtship reveals much about the psychological pressure that turning custody of her body over to a husband placed on a woman. Stone was from Massachusetts but moved west on her own to attend Oberlin College. As a student, she bonded with classmate Antoinette Brown over Emerson's essays.[28] After graduating, Stone decided to eschew marriage and become a professional lecturer on women's rights. Earning her living by speaking on antislavery and women's rights, Stone became one of the first professional reformers in antebellum America. A few months before discussing her thoughts on marriage with Brown, however, Stone had married reformer and businessman Henry Browne Blackwell.[29] Their marriage became a kind of touchstone in the emerging debate over women's rights within marriage. After years of patient courtship, Stone decided that with clearly defined standards of equality, she could gain the psychological intimacy she craved, explore sexuality in new ways, and even become a parent.[30]

Lucy Stone's correspondence with Henry Blackwell is a study in mediating the change in identity marriage would create. She was wounded by the idea that marriage entailed such a one-sided sacrifice. She was also torn between her seething anger at the idea that she would be *a wife* and her desire to trust her beloved friend. Even if Henry Blackwell was a better man than the institution assumed, marriage was still defined by a long tradition of women's legal erasure under the rules of coverture. If she entered it, she would be a wife in fact and a wife in the eyes of the law. She would probably not even be able to use her own surname on legal papers. She was also ambivalent about sexual intercourse and expresses herself clearly enough that Blackwell felt compelled to assure her he would never abuse the power over her body that was granted to him by law and custom.[31]

Despite the importance of the Transcendentalists to most reform movements connected to liberal ideals of equality, with the exception of Margaret Fuller, they addressed marriage relatively rarely. It is the topic of Emerson's essay "Love," it is relevant to "Domestic Life," and he discusses it in the "Swedenborg" chapter of *Representative Men*. In "Swedenborg" (1850), he virtually endorses divorce. As early as 1841 he treats women's equality in property and voting rights as so self-evident that it is hardly worth debating. The topic of marriage virtually never comes up in Thoreau's writing. As difficult as rigorous application of liberal philosophical principles makes it to exclude women from equality, as Moira Gatens explains, from the start, the social contract philosophers

> were able to treat man's political possibilities without (explicit) reference to sexuality, reproduction, the family, and the domestic sphere because these matters were assumed to fall outside the public realm of politics. Certainly, the political body assumes the private sphere, which underpins public life, but this sphere is taken to be the natural base of political life. Any consideration of women's access to or place in the public sphere necessarily raises the question of their role in the private sphere.

Restricting their thought to the affairs of public life, for the most part classical liberal thinkers accepted medieval marital norms just as Blackstone did, allowing them to extend fundamentally unchanged into the nineteenth century.³² As part of the broader assault on equality, the mid-nineteenth century saw strenuous efforts to regulate sexual identity by codifying ideas about temperament and capabilities into sharply defined sex and gender roles rooted in natural law, religion, and empirical science. As Americans continued to grapple with the egalitarian principles of their own liberalism, conservative views of woman's nature and of the stabilizing role of femininity, marriage, and domesticity served as moral counterweights to the fear that natural law made commercial life a cutthroat free-for-all governed only by the heartless amorality of economic law. Indeed, scientific racism and sexism, so often linked to religion, coalesced in the assault on equality by offering a providential design that negated the philosophical demand that liberal-egalitarian standards be applied equally to men and women. In effect, just as Alexander Stephens would do with race, the ideology of gender spheres treated equality as a fool's errand because the author of natural law had created insuperable differences in the capabilities of men and women. Both Catharine Beecher and Ralph Waldo Emerson had no choice but to think about womanhood, marriage, and relationships between men and women in the context of this debate.

Emerson's role in this struggle was to provide a generation-long critique of institutions that imposed conformity and stifled individuality. In its place, he advocated a universal standard of equality for *all* institutions. The only vertical hierarchy he would recognize reflected individual character, and equality in respect to character changed only when one free and equal person chose to admire the character of another. This flexibility in intimate relationships—the freedom to admire and then to change one's mind—is enjoyed by all people. It is not specific to women. As Jeffrey Steele first observed, by and large, Emerson associated masculinity with Spirit and femininity with the material on which Spirit acts.³³ Considering masculinity and femininity to be expressions of Spirit rather than essential sex-determined expressions of the human body, Emerson's understanding of gender has a flexibility very much at odds with efforts to sharpen binary sex identities. Emerson's household and his own long second marriage were a paradox in this respect. He accepted gendered deference within his household and made little effort to redefine family relations even while he was advocating radical movements away from doctrine in religion and away from partisanship in politics.

WALDO AND LYDIA

Well before Emerson joined hands with the antislavery movement, committed antislavery was part of daily life in the Emerson household, and it was primarily voiced by his wife, Lidian, and her women visitors.[34] Assessing norms of dialogue within Bush, the Emerson family home, Phyllis Cole highlights the accessibility and expressive authenticity she sees among members of the family. "My reading of the Emerson family," Cole writes, "substitutes the openness of conversation for the pathology of schizophrenia" that could emerge in sharply defined male-female households, "and I discover moments of contact as well as resistance between genders and styles."[35] Cole argues that Emerson was embedded in a domestic realm in which women had political commitments that put pressure on his own impulse to stay out of topical politics. These commitments, especially his wife's, drew him into reform politics and both motivated his involvement in the 1837 Cherokee removals debate and defined the timing of his entry into the antislavery movement in 1844.

It may be that the "openness of conversation" experienced in his own home served as Emerson's antetype for egalitarian public speech. The atmosphere at Bush seems to have been supportive, but it was also multifaceted, and the family that created it combined social radicalism with very conventional class and gender relationships. Lidian, formerly Lydia Jackson, married Emerson four years after Ellen's death. On moving to Concord, she took up the household obligations that came with her marriage as a serious responsibility. These involved marketing and ordering household supplies, managing the household budget, and supervising helps. But domesticity did not preclude political engagement.

From the mid-1830s onward, Emerson's radical views on spirituality made him both a religious apostate and a public voice of continually growing importance. Among the members of his household, however, his wife was the most political and had the most radical political views.[36] In 1837 Lidian hosted the abolitionist Grimké sisters—Sarah and Angelina—when they lectured in Concord. After a meeting at Bush, where the Grimkés "dined and took tea," Lidian wrote to her sister, "I think I shall not turn away my attention from the abolition cause till I have found whether there is not something personally for me to do."[37] That fall, Waldo addressed antislavery in a speech at the Second Church. But it was a one-off. Lidian, in contrast, responded to the Grimkés' lecture tour in a persistent way, by becoming a founding member of the Concord Female Anti-Slavery Society.[38]

Lidian's activism was neither anomalous nor unprecedented by Massachusetts standards. She was deeply grounded in a supportive environment of female activists, many of whom were members of prominent families. The gap in Lidian's and Waldo's commitments to antislavery lasted for quite a long time. Only in 1844, when Emerson gave an address on emancipation in the British West Indies to the antislavery organization of which his wife was a founding member, did the two begin to speak the same antislavery language. Even in that speech he vacillates, occasionally echoing tropes promoted by the scientific racists. Yet by the time of the rendition in 1854 of Anthony Burns back to slavery in Virginia after he had escaped to Boston, Waldo Emerson's rhetoric was sounding like the fierce abolitionism he had probably been hearing at home since the late 1830s. Sandra Herbert Petrulionis situates Emerson amidst a group of organized women activists. He was, she writes, "encircled by the antislavery fervor of the many women sharing his home." At the time Petrulionis refers to here, the later 1830s, Emerson is in the high Transcendentalist phase of his career. It is the period of *Nature*, "The Divinity School Address," and "The American Scholar." As Petrulionis characterizes his rough indifference to his wife's, aunt's, and neighbors' intensifying antislavery activism, she concludes, "Emerson simply did not comprehend that the women could transform their sentiments into effective political action, although this is exactly what they were doing."[39] Beyond her own household, Lidian worked with her neighbor Mary Brooks on antislavery throughout the 1840s and 1850s. As Ann Bigelow, whose Concord house served as a harbor for escaped slaves, remarks on the Mary Brooks–Lidian Emerson connection, as well as on the gendered sensibilities that influenced antislavery activism in Concord, "Mr. Nathan Brooks & Mr. Ralph Waldo Emerson were always afraid of commital—we women never—they must obey the law."[40] Active members of the Anti-Slavery Society chapter that Lidian helped to found included Henry David Thoreau's mother, Cynthia, and his two sisters, Helen and Sophia. It also included an African American woman, Susan Garrison, and her daughter Ellen.

Lidian and Waldo's domestic relationship is difficult to capture.[41] They hardly knew each other at the time of their engagement and were not long-term friends when they married. Indeed, they had met only once, after

Emerson gave a lecture in Plymouth, her hometown. They nonetheless quite quickly created a rich, bustling, and complex home. Emerson proposed marriage in a letter dated January 24, 1835, and then a few days later the two had what seems like a formal interview in which Lidian, thirty-two years old and never married, assessed Waldo's seriousness as a suitor. As their daughter Ellen would later report, Lidian remembered Waldo's proposal as a sort of mystical experience. After hearing him lecture, Lidian briefly had a vision of the two of them together in wedding attire but "banished the thought and forgot it." Then "on the 26th of January a Sunday evening, she beheld Father's face, very beautiful, close, gazing at her, just for a moment. Then it was gone." The next day Lidian received Emerson's letter proposing marriage: "She was utterly amazed. How could he condescend to [marry] her? And then how little he knew her!"—or she him![42] After the meeting in Plymouth two days later, they agreed to marry. Then Emerson returned to Concord because he had to work.

On February 1 he sent a letter to Lidian that gives a sense of exactly how little they knew each other and how awkward their relationship was at that point. He seems embarrassed and self-conscious, noting that on his visit he "went & came without one vehement word—or one passionate sign." Sensing that this might make him seem cold at heart, he tries to explain but takes one verbal pratfall after another. His restraint "was nothing of design," he explains. "I merely surrendered myself to the hour & to the facts. I find a sort of grandeur in the modulated expressions of a love in which the individuals, & what might seem even reasonable personal expectations, are steadily postponed to a regard for truth & the universal love." He then immediately takes back this squishy confession by affirming his concrete masculinity: "Do not think me a metaphysical lover. I am a man & hate & suspect the over refiners, and do sympathize with the homeliest pleasures & attractions by which our good foster mother Nature draws her children together." Opaque as this statement is, doesn't it have to be a reference to domesticity, sexual desire, and even the children through which nature may draw married couples together? Changing tone to comically warn Lidian what she has signed on for as an Emerson, he reports that when he told his mother about her, he had to confess that he didn't know the most basic things about his betrothed. Reporting that he was now engaged to be married, he couldn't tell his mother whether her new daughter could "sing, or read French, or Latin, or where you have lived, & much more. So you see there is nothing for it but that you should come here

& on the Battle-Ground stand the fire of her catechism," just as he had withstood Lidian's a few days earlier (*L* 1:434). Emerson's mother, Ruth Haskins Emerson, would move in with them immediately after they set up house in Concord. She lived with them until her death eighteen years later.

In temperament, Lydia Jackson and Waldo Emerson were well matched. Like Waldo, she was able to maintain an aloofness that belied the intensity of her feelings and that observers found cold. Ellen adds to her description of her mother's engagement that "the tremendous manner in which she loved Father was always astonishing to me as the coolness with which she treated him." Many years into their marriage, when all the children but Ellen had left the nest, Ellen records her mother and father figuring out how to transfer luggage from the train to the hotel where they would meet up. Waldo says: "The best way will be for me to send a carriage to meet you at the train. I'll do that." Lidian objects, "But how will the driver know me?" To which Waldo replies, "I can tell him to look for a tall thin lady, dressed in black, with a white face and her eyes fixed on the distant future."[43]

Margaret Fuller stresses Waldo's remote manner in recounting an embarrassing moment at lunch while she was visiting the Emersons in 1842. Fuller had been a frequent guest at Bush since first coming for a two-week stay in 1836. At the time of the 1842 visit, the death of their firstborn child, Waldo, at the age of five, was just a few months in the past. Ellen was a toddler and Edith was an infant. Within a few months, at age thirty-nine, Lidian would be pregnant with their youngest child, Edward. Fuller was worried that she had hurt Lidian's feelings by not spending enough time with her over the prior few days. As they all sat down to eat together, Lidian asked Margaret, "I have not yet been out, will you be my guide for a little walk this afternoon[?]" Fuller replied:

> "I am engaged to walk with Mr. E but"—(I was going to say I will walk with you first,) when L. burst into tears. The family were all present, they looked at their plates. Waldo looked on the ground, but soft & serene as ever.... I hardly knew what to say, but insisted on going with her, & then she insisted on going so I might return in time for my other walk. Waldo said not a word: he retained his sweetness of look, but never offered to do the least thing.[44]

The misunderstanding here is complicated. It is partly about connection to Waldo, but it is also, and more directly, about the friendship between Lidian and Margaret Fuller. Fuller fears that she has broken an unspoken equal-time rule in her relationships with her host and hostess. There is also a deeply self-reflexive dimension to this meditation. Throughout the journal entry, Fuller is acutely aware of her own awkward position as a guest and an outsider in a household that is grieving and that also has two babies to care for.

Fuller's review of the incident says much about the way women of Fuller's and Lidian's class understood their options in life.[45] It causes her to meditate on the terms of intimacy in the Emerson marriage, as well as her own situation as a single woman without similar family ties. During the walk that followed, Fuller says, "I felt reassured," but nonetheless, "I think she will always have these pains because she has always a lurking hope that Waldo's character will alter, and that he will be capable of an intimate [sic]; now I feel convinced that it will never be more perfect between them two." The marriage will never grow closer because "he don't believe in anything better." While she judges that Waldo and Lidian's intimacy had reached a limit, she also judges that it will never diminish, either, because "where he loved her first, he loves her always." Seeking intimacy that she too had not yet achieved, Fuller admits that she is not up to the grinding disappointment that would come with marriage to Waldo Emerson: "I don't know that I could have fortitude for it. . . . Yet nothing could be nobler, nor more consoling than to be his wife, if one's mind were only thoroughly made up to the truth."[46] Through the whole entry, Fuller also recognizes the fundamental differences in social position—for good and ill—that distinguish her from the wives and housekeepers of her class.

Why couldn't the three of them simply go for a walk together? Why didn't Waldo suggest it? Why did he just sit there staring at his shoes as his wife cried and his guest stammered? With this in mind, Fuller gets to her deepest reading of the incident. She grieves as she acknowledges the intellectual intimacy she had achieved with Waldo but that Lidian couldn't, and she feels the sting as she recognizes that women in Lidian's position will never understand the insecurity that single women like herself must come to terms with on a daily basis:

> I suppose the whole amount of the feeling is that women cant bear to be left out of the question. And they don't see the whole truth about one like me, if they did they would understand why the brow of Muse or Priestess must wear a shade of sadness. On my side I dont remember them enough. They have so much that I have not, I cant conceive of their

wishing for what I have. (*enjoying* is not the word: these I know are too generous for that) But when Waldo's wife & the mother of that child that is gone thinks me the most privileged of women, & that E[lizabeth]. H[oar]. was happy because her love was snatched away for a lifelong separation, & thus she can know none but ideal love: it does seem a little too insulting at first blush—and yet they are not altogether wrong.[47]

The record of this incident has cemented an impression of Lidian as a fragile hypochondriac who spent much of her time in isolation. It does seem that a combination of depression and health anxieties affected Lidian's participation in family and social activities, but in trying to see into the Emerson marriage, it is more important to recognize that Lidian was a dominant figure and a shaping presence at Bush. From her earliest years she had an aptitude and a pleasure in verbal debate, and this trait characterized her throughout life. Ellen records that before her mother married, everybody in Plymouth knew that she had a "skill in repartee" that made it "simply impossible to catch her at disadvantage." This trait was central to her personality and also underscores the kind of obliviousness that she shared with her husband: "She loved to argue and there was a funny incapacity about her of seeing when she was worsted. When her adversary after a telling blow looked to see her brought low he always found her advancing against him with a cheerful confidence and brandishing a sword." In her memoir of her mother, Ellen introduces Emerson's aunt Mary Moody by noting that "all her relations were more or less afraid of her" but that her mother was not the least intimidated: "Father & Grandma [Ruth Haskins] trembled when mother answered her back and enjoyed the combat." Lidian and Aunt Mary clashed as "diamond cut diamond" such that "the earth shook under them." There are no descriptions of the content of the debates, but Ellen recalls "several set-tos," with "Aunt Mary growing more and more violent, and Mother, undismayed and laughing at her shafts." Describing an incident that took place after she and her brother were grown, Ellen records the persistence of Lidian's pleasure in argumentation. After church one Sunday, Lidian was discussing the mixing of politics and religion with a neighbor. They began to argue: "This was the first light I had on two points 1st that Edward hated arguing and 2d that mother loved it better than any other amusement."[48]

The early years of their marriage were a time of particular contentment for both Waldo and Lidian. But beginning in about 1839, things became more difficult. Lidian might have been able to pursue a career similar to that of Elizabeth Cady Stanton, who married a prominent lawyer and prospered as the Erie Canal made western New York a rapidly growing population center. But despite the radical politics that grew out of her empathetic morality, Lidian hewed to a very conventional sense of duty in her roles as wife and housekeeper. The cult of domesticity attributed high moral rewards to a wife's patient deference to the lifestyle priorities of the male head of household. This standard was both a curse and an affirmative identity for Lidian Emerson.

Being a housekeeper, in the high sense that Catharine Beecher defines, was the primary outward-facing identity for Lidian and, later, for her daughter Ellen. The period between 1839 and 1843 saw particularly heavy traffic in and out of Bush, and this came with intensified domestic work for Lidian and the help. Ellen confirms this hostelry phase through her mother's grocery records. The ingredients for recipes "are all three times the quantity that we have cooked since I had charge" of the housekeeping, Ellen writes.[49]

Lidian Emerson's ideal of herself as a housekeeper is very similar to the identity that Catharine Beecher defines in her *Treatise on Domestic Economy*. She was more a household manager than a cook or house cleaner. In this role, Lidian worked to get the most out of every household object, often creating complex tasks for hired workers. Almira Flint, the daughter of a local farmer who was employed in the Emerson house as a seamstress and maid of all work, told Ellen that Lidian "taught her to do many things by telling her how, and simply expecting her to do it; she made her a carpenteress, an upholsterer, a paper-hanger, a dress-maker." In lines that echo Beecher's ideal, Ellen characterizes her mother's standards: "Her house must be handsome and her children must be well dressed, these were necessities to Mother's mind while Father considered both as less important."[50] At its core, Ellen is describing a kind of difference in values around the way domestic resources would be used, but more importantly, she is describing the way Lidian projected her own character in the Emerson's shared domestic life. Her housekeeping standards mark a complex and ambivalent realization of her husband's words in "Domestic Life": "There should be nothing confounding and conventional in economy, but genius and love of the man so conspicuously marked in his estate that the eye that knew him should read his character in his property, in his grounds, in his ornaments, in every expense." In the midst of the Panic of 1837, for example, Emerson vetoed his wife's desire to have a velvet hat made for their infant son on the grounds that it might show up their neighbors.

Notwithstanding the frictions of family life and his own incapacity to show affection that met his wife's wishes, in his theory of equality, an ideal of sincere intimacy among family, friends, and neighbors marks the standard against which Emerson measures personal connections, both private and public.

"LOVE" AND MARRIAGE

Even if Emerson felt constrained in his home life, it is not a consistent theme in his journals or letters. There is playful sarcasm in many of his letters to Lidian, but they read as if these jabs were the back-and-forth of a shared journey rather than passive-aggressive acts of intimidation. In contrast to his call for a hypermasculine "conqueror" strong enough to wrench domesticity away from emulation and conformity, Emerson's marriage with Lidian was highly conventional, and they both seem to have been conventionally happy as part of it. In his writing, Emerson virtually never extends himself to imagine a world where heterosexual marriage was not the norm for adults; and while he acknowledged the justice of recognizing women's right to suffrage and other civil liberties, he was ambivalent about a public sphere in which women acted as the equals of men. Nonetheless, marriage plays crucial roles in Emerson's theory of history and in his thought about equality. Like Lydia Maria Child, Emerson envisioned the medieval ideal of chivalrous monogamous marriage as a crucial progressive innovation in the history of civilization. Monogamous marriage, especially as a *permanent* one-to-one relationship, is one half of Emerson's model for egalitarian universalism. The other half is friendship, to which he attributes a different kind of intimacy and an even higher standard of sharing. He carries the intimacy of these two models as exemplars into other, less permanent and intimate relationships.

If done properly, Emerson believed, marriage could allow for an equality to emerge that would break down the boundary between the private and the public realms, because private relationships are the setting in which the "domestication of the idea of culture" must occur before it can be valid anywhere else. In his essays "Love" and "Friendship," published in that order in the first series of *Essays*, Emerson addresses both conjugal love as a permanent relationship and friendship as a contrasting relationship built around the demands of absolute sincerity. In marriage, Emerson assumes permanence, which, over the long haul, creates an oddly universalizing egalitarian spirit as a couple's life together lasts longer and longer. In friendship, the exacting demands of total and constant sincerity make the connection fragile, resulting in what Emerson describes as constant events of gender reversal and constant acts of divorce and remarriage.

The essay "Love" could easily be titled "Marriage." It is an essay on the changing forms of attraction and love during courtship and marriage. As he summarizes at the very beginning of the essay:

> The introduction to this felicity is in a private and tender relation of one to one, which is the enchantment of human life; which, like a certain divine rage and enthusiasm, seizes on man at one period and works a revolution in his mind and body; unites him to his race, pledges him to the domestic and civic relations, carries him with new sympathy into nature, enhances the power of the senses, opens the imagination, adds to his character heroic and sacred attributes, establishes marriage, and gives permanence to human society. (*CW* 2:99)

He immediately goes on to link all of these qualities with sexual desire: "The natural association of the sentiment of love with the heyday of the blood seems to require that in order to portray it in vivid tints, which every youth and maid should confess to be true to their throbbing experience, one must not be too old." Indeed, Emerson goes on, "the delicious fancies of youth reject the least savor of a mature philosophy, as chilling with age and pedantry their purple bloom" (*CW* 2:99). He is not interested, however, in exploring the connection between love and sexuality very deeply, though in an essay on love in marriage, he may have felt he had to address it in some way or another.

Although he acknowledges its connection to sexuality, along with socialization, domestication, and maturity, he defines love as a spontaneous spiritual force that compels a man to recognize the equality and individuality of a woman. By asking individuals to imagine how things feel or appear to another, youthful love marks progress toward equality because it chastens self-involved egotism. In Emerson's logic, developing a love relationship compels people to appreciate vistas that they otherwise would ignore, to read books they otherwise would not, and to imagine the feeling that shared experiences might provoke. Love is the beginning of "the domestication of the idea of culture." As he puts it, romantic love "is the dawn of civility and grace in the coarse and rustic." He imagines its beginnings in a schoolyard, during the first steps of courtship: "Among the throng of girls," a boy "runs rudely enough, but one alone distances him; and these two little neighbors, that were so close just now, have learned to respect each other's personality." As the attraction to this other "personality" develops, "the passion rebuilds the world for the youth. It makes all things alive and significant. Nature grows conscious" (*CW* 2:101).

But the awakening of love can also be a kind of trap. If "from too much conversing with material objects, the soul was gross, and misplaced its satisfaction in the body," then the lover will reap "nothing but sorrow." Should attraction based on sensuality lead to marriage, once the two have been tied together for life, middle-aged lovers will have to face the estrangement and alienation of an indissoluble marriage in a relationship that locks them down rather than opening doors for growth. The danger is greater for the woman: "When this sensualism intrudes into the education of young women, and withers the hope and affection of human nature by teaching that marriage signifies nothing but a housewife's thrift, and that woman's life has no other aim," every woman's spirit risks being crushed by a low idea of domesticity even before courtship begins (*CW* 2:102).

At its best, though, this danger can be avoided if the "heyday of the blood" passes and allows Spirit or soul to move into the foreground. Focused on nonphysical elements such as "discourses and actions," the lovers, now a married couple, can turn the "purple bloom" of sexual fulfillment into forms of mutual growth. If "the soul passes through the body and falls to admire strokes of character, the lovers contemplate one another in their discourses and actions, then they pass to the true palace of beauty, more and more inflame their love of it, and by this love extinguishing the base affection, as the sun puts out the fire by shining on the hearth, they become pure and hallowed" (*CW* 2:106). Emerson uses a noteworthy metaphor here. If one builds a fire in the hearth to brighten a dim and rainy day, but then the clouds clear and sunshine fills the room, the little fire becomes invisible behind the brighter sunshine. In effect, "the sun puts out the fire by shining on the hearth." By analogy, conjugal love may—even should—have its origin in sexual attraction; but in Emerson's view, as love grows more intimate, "character" must eclipse "body" in a way that allows a different kind of love to emerge.

In Emerson's thinking, as intimacy between spouses grows, it also becomes more universal.[51] In this respect, the image of the sun on the hearth also alludes to Plato's allegory of the cave and represents the pinnacle of married love as a condition that allows the individual to leave the cave and enter the realm of real sunlight. In his revision of Plato's allegory, the first attractions, including those of the body, are like the shadows in the cave. But if the condition of permanent marriage deepens intimacy, love shifts toward "discourses and actions" which serve as the gateway to appreciation of the universal Spirit or soul. By Emerson's reasoning, in a successful marriage, "even love, which is the deification of persons, must become more impersonal every day" (CW 2:107).

Assuming that marriage was indissoluble, as it was for most people, Emerson treats a deepening intimacy between married couples as a high-stakes spiritual wrestling match with one's own feeling of love. One's spouse, man or woman, is inevitably flawed. The sensual union will not eclipse other feelings forever. It is a "temporary state. Not always can flowers, pearls, poetry, protestations, nor even home in another heart, content the awful soul that dwells in clay. The soul which is in the soul of each, craving a perfect beatitude, detects incongruities, defects and disproportion in the behavior of the other. Hence arises surprise, expostulation and pain." The surprise of wakening to a spouse's failings marks both an invitation and a fall. One's partner is seen more truthfully, even though that truth pierces a bubble of infatuation. At this point, the challenge of "Love" becomes sustaining growth despite the fact that no spouse can live up to the ideal, and neither partner can leave the marriage to seek a new spouse. Chastened in their mutual recognition that they are still solitary, yet seeking fulfillment of the "awful soul," spouses become to each other representative of the impossibility of sustaining a unification of souls. As married "life wears on, it proves a game of permutation and combination of all possible positions of the parties, to employ all the resources of each and acquaint each with the strength and weakness of the other. For it is the nature and end of this relation, that they should represent the human race to each other" (CW 2:107–8).

As he almost always does, even in this essay on the longest and most intimate relationship most people ever experience, Emerson positions the most important site of spiritual and emotional life in an amorphous middle zone between dialogue and imagination. Each of "the lovers" learns to "contemplate" the other in ways that open the doors to the "true palace of beauty." In effect, a mature conjugal love, in which "the soul passes through the body," becomes a heuristic for the transcendent unities that equalize all things in Spirit. Flowing both ways, this strange Platonic dialogue creates a love that is both unique to a single individual *and* impersonal, universal, and tantamount to love for every other human person because they are discrete individuals just like one's spouse. On a most basic level, Emerson's universalizing and impersonal model of mature married love reaches an outward-facing posture that says, "If I can put up with all the gross things my spouse does on a daily basis, then I can at least try to see the best in every stranger I encounter." By appreciating the universal similarity of the human condition alongside the particular character that they found hidden under physical attraction, the lovers move toward a universalized, egalitarian appreciation of the good: "At last they discover that all which at first drew them together ... was deciduous ... and the purification of the intellect and the heart from year to year is the real marriage." Through conjugal love, the mature lover "by conversation with that which is in itself excellent, magnanimous, lowly, and just, the lover comes to a warmer love of these nobilities. . . . Then he passes from loving them in one to loving them in all, and so is the one beautiful soul only the door through which he enters to the society of all true and pure souls" (*CW* 2:109).

In the end, then, Emerson circles back to marriage as an act of unification, but its object is not the isolated unity of two partners; rather, love in an authentic marriage is a doorway through which one seeks "the society" of multitudes of souls (*CW* 2:109). In the entire essay about individual growth within marriage, Emerson does not distinguish gender roles beyond the first moment of courtship. The function of the permanence of marriage is to compel a kind of uplifting close-quarters wrestling match in which "a game of permutation and combination of all possible positions" causes conjugal love to become both an intimate personal relationship and a vehicle for the universalizing recognition of what it means to share your humanity as an equal with an equal. "Thus," he writes at the end, "we are put in training for a love which knows not sex, nor person, nor partiality, but which seeks virtue and wisdom everywhere, to the end of increasing virtue and wisdom" (*CW* 2:108). Married love is Emerson's training ground for understanding equality as an aspirational ideal.

In his essay on Swedenborg, published in 1850 as part of *Representative Men*, Emerson expands his allusion to Plato's allegory of the cave by analyzing Swedenborg's idealistic theory of marriage. He is drawn to this theme because Swedenborg treats marriage as an ideal and transcendental institution that characterizes even heaven. He is also drawn to it, however, because in Swedenborg's analysis gender is fluid and marriage is neither permanent nor monogamous. As Emerson puts it, Swedenborg's is "a fine Platonic development of the science of marriage; teaching that sex is universal, and not local;

virility in the male qualifying every organ, act, and thought; and the feminine in woman" (*CW* 4:71). These essences, universal to nature, not local to individuals, imbue all aspects of the world with virtues that are fluid in the sense that femininity and masculinity are spirits accessible to all bodies, not physical traits or physiologies inseparable from specific bodies. This construction of gender, for Emerson, liberates the individual to experience progressive forms of self-recognition. It allows the individual to leave the boundaries of male-husband and female-wife and imagine spiritual growth that transforms individual gender, and even implies an ongoing series of marriages and divorces.

In a line of thought that had been even more important to Margaret Fuller, Emerson sees the idea of "ideal" or "Platonic" marriage—not in the sense of nonsexual, but in the sense of marriage as a Platonic ideal—as a relationship that expands far beyond the connections that married partners create. Endorsing Swedenborg's model, Emerson writes: "In the real or spiritual world, the nuptial union is not momentary, but incessant and total; and chastity not a local, but a universal virtue; unchastity being discovered as much in the trading, or planting, or speaking or philosophizing, as in generation; and that though the virgins he saw in heaven were beautiful, the wives were incomparably more beautiful, and went on increasing in beauty evermore" (*CW* 4:71–72). The chastity of wives, in this context, replicates the ideas of movement toward the perfection of character that he identifies with mature conjugal love in his essay "Love." In this sense, chastity is connected to the authenticity of the love relationship with no reference to the physicality of the "nuptial union."[52] Emerson appreciated this aspect of Swedenborg's thought, that chastity represents the idea of aspirational equality in a broad, fluid sense. Shooting the gulf, or transformation into one's next perfect form, is to chasten or purify one's self. In Swedenborg's idealized heavenly marriage, Emerson sees the imagery of relationships that links interpersonal intimacy to a mutable and equalizing process of spiritual growth.

In the theoretical and idealistic context of "Swedenborg," Emerson remains within a binary model, but he frees himself from conventionalities of gender identity and from the unity of souls and the permanence of marriage. In the "real or spiritual world," marriage, like all personal relationships, must be temporary because the self's paramount duty is to grow in spirit. In rejecting conventional boundaries on the liberty of individuals to free themselves from the constraining ties of biological sex, Emerson is willing to push farther than his model. Swedenborg, Emerson concludes, "exaggerates the circumstances of marriage" because "of progressive souls, all loves and friendships are momentary. *Do you love me?* Means, Do you see the same truth? If you do, we are happy with the same happiness; but presently one of us passes into the perception of new truth;—we are divorced, and no tension in nature can hold us to each other" (CW 4:71–72). The idea of a permanent marriage strikes Emerson as simply babyish: "I know how delicious is this cup of love,—I existing for you, you existing for me; but it is a child's clinging to his toy; an attempt to eternize the fireside and nuptial chamber; to keep the picture-alphabet through which our first lessons are prettily conveyed" (CW 4:72). Sex, marriage, even domestic life are all entry-level starter kits for the soul that seeks Spirit.

Further adapting Swedenborg, Emerson integrates an idea of marriage into salvation. The final progress of the soul in Swedenborg's heaven leads not to an ideal conjugal union between two persons, or even souls, but toward a transcendent authenticity in communication. Emerson expands:

> Perhaps the true subject of the "Conjugal Union" is *conversation*, whose laws are profoundly illuminated. It is false, if literally applied to marriage. For God is the bride or bridegroom of the soul. Heaven is not the pairing of two, but the communion of all souls. We meet, and dwell an instant under the temple of one thought, and part as though we parted not, to join another thought in other fellowships of joy. So far from there being anything divine in the low and proprietary sense of, Do you love me? It is only when you leave and lose me, by casting yourself on a sentiment which is higher than both of us, that I draw near, and find myself at your side; and I am repelled, if you fix your eye on me, and demand love. In fact, in the spiritual world, we change sexes every moment. You love the worth in me; then I am your husband, but it is not me, but the worth, that fixes the love; and that worth is a drop of the ocean of worth that is beyond me. Meantime, I adore the greater worth in another, and so become his wife. He aspires to a higher worth in another spirit, and is wife or receiver of that influence. (CW 4:72–73)

Emerson here is unambiguously assuming static gendered categories. Masculinity is the recognition of a higher spiritual ideal, and femininity represents the aspirant seeking growth. But he equally unambiguously detaches these roles from bodies in a way that would encourage persons freely, and frequently, to see themselves move from feminine to masculine and then back to feminine "every moment."

This mutability takes Emerson back to the foundational tenet of his egalitarianism. He translates the idea of marriage in the world of experience into "conversation" as the analogous relationship in the spiritual world. In the movement toward "the communion of all souls," he imagines marriage as the sharing of a single thought. This equal sharing represents the highest intimacy. But this marriage is necessarily temporary, and it allows both parties to the conversation to leave at any moment. Indeed, it is crudely shattered if it materializes in property, in "a proprietary sense of, Do you love me?" Whether it is legally dissolved or not, the marriage ends the instant one spouse's journey hooks "on a sentiment which is higher than both of us."

Thus in Emerson's thought, marriage is a gendered process of leading and following, but the process works by turning away from particular persons and toward ideas, thought, or sentiments. The spiritual initiative of this turning and leaving is literally magnetic. "It is only when you leave or lose me," Emerson writes, "that I draw near, and find myself at your side." The medium of this spiritual process is intimate conversation such that in "Swedenborg" Emerson gives marriage a different connection to equality than he had in the earlier essay "Love." Whereas his assumptions about the terms of conjugal love restrict his ability to see indissoluble and monogamous marriage as a path to permanent spiritual intimacy, it allows each spouse to see the other and their relationship as *the* equal and universal representation of the human condition. He makes no gendered distinctions between spouses who achieve this "love which knows not sex, nor person, nor partiality, but which seeks virtue and wisdom everywhere," because it has sustained fervor through every test of a shared life. Against this universalizing and aspirational equality, in the imaginary marriages he spins out of Swedenborg's *Conjugal Union*, gender, the roles of husband and wife, and status of married or divorced can all change in an instant as the yearning individual follows their spiritual path.

The process of aspiring to equality by connecting, sharing, leaving, and reconnecting is the driving force of Emerson's theory of friendship. In "Friendship," the counterpart essay to "Love" in the first series of *Essays*, Emerson seems to assume that the topic is male friendship, but in contrast to the essay on marriage, he also assumes that friendship is something a person can and will enter and leave often over the course of a lifetime. In "Friendship," equality is as central an issue as is the liberty to leave. Emerson also sees the relationship as a means of progressive ascension toward universality, with its ultimate goal being the same as the goal of "Love": "There can never be deep peace between two spirits, never mutual respect, until in their dialogue each stands for the whole world." But whereas the assumed context of "Love" is heterosexual, monogamous, indissoluble marriage, in "Friendship" Emerson treats the annihilation of individual personhood that was explicit in coverture marriage as the most dangerous threat that connection poses to individuality. Equality is his remedy for this threat. Emerson holds that there are two "sovereign" elements in the "composition of friendship": truth and tenderness (*CW* 2:124, 119). By truth, he means sincerity or truthfulness in communication. By tenderness, he means a sympathetic attentiveness that wholeheartedly accepts the friend's words and acts without judging them in conventional moral terms.

The fullest achievement of friendship is marked by a sharing that can be achieved through the intimacy of two people only. Groups create a short-lived "social soul exactly co-extensive with the several consciousnesses there." This "social soul" of a conversation circle is rare and desirable, but nonetheless it always "destroys the high freedom of great conversation, which requires an absolute running of two souls into one" (*CW* 2:122). It reflects more of a following of the same stream of thought, or a revolving around the same issue or question before leaving it and "casting" yourself on another. The "freedom of great conversation," though, also has a very threatening and unstable power dynamic. It never meets expectations and it is always subject to collapse. The briefest moment of insincerity crashes conversation, and may corrupt a whole friendship. Worse, any perceived act of domination or un-tender superiority humiliates the friend and has gross consequences. Adopting the stance of high sovereignty that he associates with individuality, Emerson sees friendship as a test of poise: "I ought to be equal to every relation. It makes no difference how many friends I have and what content I can find in conversing with each, if there be one to whom I am not equal. If I have shrunk unequal from one contest, the joy I find in all the rest becomes mean and cowardly" (*CW* 2:118). Equality here represents the courage to be truthful:

> A friend is a person with whom I may be sincere. Before him I may think aloud. I am arrived at last in the presence of a man so real and equal, that I may drop even those undermost garments of dissimulation, courtesy, and second thought, which men never put off, and may deal with him with the simplicity and wholeness with which one chemical atom meets another. Sincerity is the luxury allowed, like diadems and authority, only to the highest rank, *that* being permitted to speak truth,

as having none above it to court or conform unto. Every man alone is sincere. At the entrance of a second person, hypocrisy begins. We parry and fend the approach of our fellow-man by compliments, by gossip, by amusements, by affairs. We cover up our thought from him under a hundred folds. (*CW* 2:119)

Emphasizing Emerson's metaphors of stripping down social forms to a kind of vulnerable but demanding self-exposure, George Kateb describes Emersonian friendship as a physical stripping of social manners. Friendship is the effort to reach a "mutual intellectual nakedness" in which a person can allow unfiltered self-expression. As a physical comparison, Kateb's analogy even draws mutual nakedness toward the language of sexual intimacy. Conventions of behavior require that we avoid staring at each other's bodies, especially naked bodies. But in friendship, we are invited to reveal and to see up close, to leave nothing covered or unexplored.[53]

Emerson links the deep intimacy of equalizing mutual nakedness to the grand pageantry of meetings between sovereign monarchs. To return to his controlling metaphor for the sovereignty of the individual, Emersonian friends meet like kings, having no one above them "to court or conform unto." The sincerity of friends is the luxury of the "highest rank," robed in "diadems and authority." Emerson casts friendship as perfect egalitarianism crowned by mutual recognition of the king-like autonomy of each individual person. This peculiar metaphor of egalitarian friendship as a pair of kings talking themselves naked is one of Emerson's most extreme images of the "domestication" of culture.

Despite this strange aspirational standard for equality, one is drawn to a friend by an odd lack of self-confidence. Their "goodness seems better than our goodness." Even "our own thought sounds new and larger from his mouth" (*CW* 2:115). This lamb-eyed admiration threatens the equality necessary to friendship. Or, conversely, it threatens to undermine one's own self-respect: "We seek our friend not sacredly, but by an adulterate passion which would appropriate him to ourselves" (*CW* 2:117). It is connected to adultery because it is almost a betrayal of one's own equality. Friendship, in Emerson's ideal, both must be and yet cannot be a leader–follower situation. Branka Arsić develops a deep reading of this collision of the spiritual and visceral in Emerson's thought about equality in conversation. The conversation "Emerson has in mind," Arsić writes, "is less informative than transformational."

She compares Emersonian conversation to going into "bad company," into a psychological space that "destabilizes" and challenges basic "principles." It can't just be an intellectual attraction; it has to be physically exhilarating too. The challenge it poses is that to be authentic, to be a worthy and equal friend, you have to be just as much bad company as your friend is.[54]

The fraught instability of unguarded self-revelation combined with the transformative hero worship of friendship risks subsuming and canceling out one's own individuality. In the complex demand for equality in vulnerability, a friend is at best what Emerson calls a "beautiful enemy" with whom encounters are "mutually feared." Given the legal bonds marriage places on people, friendship is the highest possible relationship any person can attain, even higher than married love. Friendship, "that select and sacred relation which is a kind of absolute, and which even leaves the language of love suspicious and common, so much is this purer, and nothing is so much divine" (*CW* 2:118). Or, in a sentence that illustrates the impossibility of sustaining the standard: "Friendship requires that rare mean betwixt likeness and unlikeness, that piques each with the presence of power and of consent in the other party. Let me be alone to the end of the world, rather than that my friend should overstep, by a word or a look his real sympathy. I am equally balked by antagonism and by compliance" (*CW* 2:122). By its nature, Emerson sees friendship as a highly idealized competition in authenticity, a means of recognizing and affirming universal equality through utter, naked sincerity. This can be achieved only through brave personality that is accepted with a kind of sacralizing tenderness for what is shared. Any who would become "a candidate for that covenant" of friendship, approaches, "like an Olympian, to the great games where the first-born of the world are the competitors." His or her efforts are opposed by pitfalls that are legion, and "he alone is victor who has truth enough in his constitution to preserve the delicacy of his beauty from the wear and tear of all these" (*CW* 2:119). Suspicion, second-guessing, caring if one is judged, hedging words—these are all shields against the self-exposure that friendship requires.

This exacting model of communication marks the grounding condition of Emerson's thought about equality. In those moments of rare and ideal conversation, each is fully exposed and perfectly equal. It is a counterpart to the solitude of the invisible eyeball because it allows "the Deity in me and in them" to deride and cancel "the thick walls of individual character, relation, age, sex, circumstance . . . and now makes many one" (*CW* 2:115). In the image of a friend, the conundrum of the philosophical isolation that self-reliance requires and the radically universalized egalitarianism that anchors Emerson's spirituality reaches its fullest expression: "A friend, therefore is a sort of paradox in nature. I who alone am, I who see nothing in nature whose existence I can affirm with equal evidence to my own, behold now the semblance of my being in all its height, variety and curiosity, reiterated in a foreign form; so that a friend may well be reckoned the masterpiece of nature" (*CW* 2:120). Rather than a unification, friendship represents an encounter with something simultaneously foreign and identical. As a "kind of absolute," it is the relationship in which Emerson pushes furthest the idea of equality emerging from communicative sincerity.

This grounding for equality emerges through his critique of domesticity as a place of convention that creates incentives for conformity. In this respect, Emerson's reaction to the cult of domesticity is a counterpart to his critique of the Democracy as a missed opportunity to emphasize sincere self-expression over partisan polarization. In his analysis of domestic life, he criticizes home life by stressing its similarity to the conventionality of churches and schools. He denounces this stifling quality, and though he reads it partially in gendered terms, he primarily sees it as a broad cultural trend that has swept up both men and women, impelling them voluntarily to give up their independence. In his analysis of marriage as an intimate and enduring relationship between two people, he barely remarks on gendered identity and does not advocate adherence to gendered behaviors. On the contrary, against the married couple's journey toward equality as universalized representatives of the human condition, Emerson aims to find equalizing grounds that allow each person to share not through a masculine or feminine identification, but through a perspective that universalizes love with no regard to sex whatsoever. When he reaches beyond the boundaries of existing coverture relationships by entering the landscape of Swedenborgian mysticism, rather than recoiling and reasserting gender, Emerson pushes further, releasing masculinity and femininity from specific bodies and imagining people flowing freely back and forth as the Spirit moves them.

In the idea of friendship, Emerson pushes even harder toward the intimacy that anchors his theory of equality. In this relationship, he transfers the physical sexuality of the marriage connection into a metaphor for independent people baring their souls to each other. More than an act of communication, the function of this sharing is to model equality. While marriage, in its long-enduring movement toward an affirming universalization, becomes the metaphor for a society of equals connected by domesticated cosmopolitan love, and thus expresses equality in its universality, Emerson sees friendship more in aspirational terms, like the momentariness of the transparent eyeball. The connection it achieves, the self-exposure, mutual trust, and loving recognition, is the momentary achievement of equality.

3

EMERSON'S COSMOPOLITAN ANTHROPOLOGY AND THE POLYGENESIS DEBATE

Arguing against the theory of evolution in 1874, fifteen years after Charles Darwin published *On the Origin of Species* in 1859, Louis Agassiz accuses Darwin of practicing sloppy science. Agassiz, whose theory of the "ice age" made him the most eminent scientist in America, argues that Darwin had skipped crucial steps in the process of verifying his data. He "frequently overstepped the boundaries of actual knowledge and allowed his imagination to supply the links which science does not furnish." If Darwin had used a different method, "it might be said that he treated his subject according to the best scientific methods." But, Agassiz held, since Darwin's methods were flawed, his theory of random selection should be rejected.[1]

More hung in the balance than rivalry between two eminent scientists. Darwin and Agassiz were promoting contrasting models for the order of nature and, consequently, for the place that human beings hold in it. Emerson followed the debate closely, not only because it was relevant to the status of equality, but also because it engaged the most basic assumptions linking the spiritual and material worlds. For Emerson, what was at stake was the possibility of transformation and, consequently, of progress. Agassiz, who lent his voice to the assault on equality, promoted a theory of nature that drew impassable boundaries between races. His version of nature justified slavery, apartheid, racism, and caste societies of all sorts. Further, in the 1850s, Agassiz's high standing in the scientific community added the weight of leading-edge scientific authority to long-standing claims that people of different races are made unequal not by historical circumstance but by divine design. If Agassiz's position had prevailed, belief in racial hierarchy would have become even more firmly embedded in Americans' understanding of the order of nature. It would become the concrete foundation that supported all the other projects of the assault on equality.

Darwin, in *On the Origin of Species*, did not argue for equality; but he did argue that creatures passed on minute but consequential changes. Generation over generation, organisms may present a pattern of incremental change through which the traits of a species are constantly tweaked in an ongoing process of mutation and cross-fertilization. When these random tweaks converge and become normal through biological reproduction, a new species has come into being. If Darwin's evolutionary theory prevailed, the whole study of nature would move away from a focus on explaining a static structure that was originally established by God. It would move toward a study of nature that sought to explain ongoing transformation, even progress, as species slowly and subtly changed. In anthropology, or "ethnology," as Emerson's generation termed the study of human culture, it would mean that every species, even the human race, was in flux, and that combinations of diverse races, not purity of blood, was the order of nature.

One of the alarming implications of the new theory was that Darwinian random selection seemed to offer little inherent dignity to the human being. If true, it would be as traumatic as the Copernican revolution. Rather than standing near the angels in a hierarchical chain of being, the species *Homo sapiens sapiens* is merely a moment in an ongoing process of random adaptive change. The existence, let alone the relative status, of any animal species is purely a by-product of chance. Humankind is *not* the perfection of God's work. Man, woman, African, European, Eskimo stand in no intentional relationship to one another and define no orderly hierarchy: the similarities and differences between them represent momentary stopping points in an endless sequence of chance mutations that reaches back through all the eons of animal life and forward into an unpredictable future.

Darwin endorsed the randomness of mutation, but he was ambivalent about divine design and progress.[2] Louis Agassiz rejected the possibility that mutation could create new species, but he wholeheartedly embraced intelligent design and argued that self-correcting mechanisms made nature essentially static. In his defense of equality, Emerson created a bricolage out of both positions. He embraced evolutionary change and rejected stasis, but he also assumed that the world was working toward a cohesive and progressive spiritual consciousness. In Emerson's thought, progress is necessary by design and is not arbitrary. The possibility of biological mutation confirmed one of his basic assumptions about freedom: that we are fated to live in a material world, but that the material of nature must ultimately take the shape that Spirit "antagonizes" it into. As he describes this confrontation in the essay "Fate":

> Though fate is immense, so is [human] power, which is the other fact in the dual world, immense. If fate follows and limits power, power attends and antagonizes fate. We must respect fate as natural history, but there is more than natural history.... He [man] betrays his relation to what is below him, thick-skulled, small-brained, fishy, quadrumanous, quadruped ill-disguised, hardly escaped into biped and has paid for the new powers by loss of some of the old ones. But lightning which explodes and fashions planets, maker of planets and suns is in him. On one side, elemental order, sandstone, granite, rock-ledges, peat bog, forest, sea and shore; and, on the other part, thought, the spirit which composes and decomposes nature[;] here they are, side by side, god and devil, mind and matter, king and conspirator, belt and spasm, riding peacefully together in the eye and brain of everyman.... To hazard the contradiction, freedom is necessary. If you plant yourself on the side of fate, and say, fate is all; then, we say, a part of fate is the freedom of man. (*CW* 6:12)

As he struggled to come to terms with conflicting theories of natural history during the two decades leading up to the Civil War, Emerson increasingly saw antislavery as a transformative power, as a version of the "lightning which explodes and fashions planets." The claims of reformers of all kinds, beginning with himself in religion and extending through Margaret Fuller's and Lucy Stone's efforts to read women's equality into the language of reform, to the antislavery and non-resistance radicals who were then coalescing around William Lloyd Garrison, were forcing Emerson to connect natural history and the new field of ethnology to religion and his own commitments to thought, Spirit, God, mind, and, above all, to "the freedom of man." The status of different people, he concluded, follows the evolutionary progress of the Spirit toward the domestication of culture and the equality of all people. In this sense, social reform and science made common cause, permitting him to believe not just that racial equality was the *destined* and necessary objective of Spirit, but that Spirit sought the universal equality of all people.

CITIZENSHIP, RACE, AND THE CHEROKEE REMOVALS

As Emerson was composing "The American Scholar" in the spring of 1837, the fate of the Cherokee Indians living in Georgia and Tennessee was very much on the minds of his countrymen. On its surface, the removals debate focused on questions of property rights and issues of Indigenous sovereignty, but it was also about ethnic assimilation. In their justification of ethnic cleansing, advocates of removal laid the groundwork for much of the racist jurisprudence that characterized the assault on racial equality during the 1840s and 1850s.[3]

Removals were a question of general concern at two points during the 1830s. The question first rose to national attention during the debate over the Indian Removal Act, a proposal to force the Cherokee to move from their homeland in the Smoky Mountains to the newly designated "Indian Territory" in Oklahoma.[4] It reemerged several years later when President Martin Van Buren ordered federal troops to drive the Cherokee from their homes and onto what would become known as the Trail of Tears. As Emerson was drafting "The American Scholar," Congress was debating whether or not the government should enforce the treaty that the national council of the Cherokee had explicitly repudiated.[5] As the removals were looming, the Cherokee crisis provoked a national debate over the alternatives of assimilation and expulsion. The prominent place the removals held in the newspapers is relevant to the cultural nationalism of "The American Scholar" because, while a debate involving the moral standing of American national identity was being conducted in Congress and the press, Emerson was working on an essay that has long been cited as an important expression of literary nationalism. The expected theme of the annual Phi Beta Kappa address at Harvard, the occasion for which the essay was written, was to reinforce the self-congratulatory belief that the highest civic duty of the scholar was to define the contours of an American ethnicity that rising generations could emulate.[6]

In his "American Scholar" address, the instrumental mastery that Americans were extending over nature in both science and invention is the intellectual counterpart to the legalistic and military conquest of Native American nations. In both cases, the expansion of power over nature and geography articulated the growing strength of the young United States. Americans were inventing tools ranging from early refrigeration machines to the telegraph to the "lock-stitch" or two-thread sewing machine. Since Emerson's birth, the

Union had added ten states, with Michigan entering on the first of January 1837. Just as science and scholarship were bringing more and more of nature under the control of reason and pushing the United States into new intellectual territories by rolling onward the frontiers of knowledge, the incorporation of Indian lands was bringing more and more of the continent under the control of the US government. This analogy, in which the work of the scientist Emerson describes in "The American Scholar" unifies "refractory facts" to achieve an instrumental end, mirrors the political work of incorporating diverse immigrant and Indigenous peoples into a more or less homogeneous United States. In this sense, competing policies of removal and assimilation anticipate the debate between Agassiz and Darwin over intelligent design and evolution. On the one hand, Indian "removals" would put their lands in the hands of full-blooded "Americans" and sustain an order that affirms domination by resisting racial mixing of either property or bloodlines.[7] Assimilation, on the other hand, would recognize Native American individuals as human equals and, potentially, as civil equals.

In a study of the litigation that legalized the Cherokee removals, Priscilla Wald details how making a case for ethnic cleansing compelled removal advocates to sharpen racial definitions of American identity. The Cherokee cases, Wald writes, "call attention to the symbolic processes through which the United States constitutes subjects: how Americans are made." In order to justify removal, the courts had to define the justifications that could supersede the Cherokee's claim to property rights over their ancestral homelands.[8]

The nationalist interest in exploring how various courses of action could define a collective American identity reflects the point of view from which Emerson entered the removals debate and does much to clarify the defense of racial equality that early theories of evolutionary science made possible. Though he was ostensibly speaking out to defend the Indians, Emerson's primary concern was the implications of the removal policy for a model of citizenship grounded in an aspirational ideal that pushed equality further and further. In effect, he asks: What does the removal policy mean for *my* ability to identify as an American? According to his preferred construction of citizenship, "American" identity is underpinned by assumptions that subsume the national into a cosmopolitan universalism. The public letter he wrote to President Martin Van Buren lays out the evolution of many New Englanders' understanding of the Cherokee crisis and explains why he sees the removal policy as a rejection of the assimilationist practices that he believed enhanced the dignity of both the Cherokee and the citizens of the United States. He begins by describing the Cherokee's progress toward assimilation in terms of a willing transformation of identity that will "redeem their race" from primitivism:

> Even to our distant State, some good rumour of their worth and civility has arrived. We have learned with joy their improvement in the social arts. We have read their newspapers. We have seen some of them in our schools and colleges. In common with the great body of the American People, we have witnessed with sympathy the painful endeavors of these red men to redeem their race from the doom of eternal inferiority, and to borrow and domesticate in the tribe the inventions and customs of the Caucasian race. (*AW* 2)

Despite the Cherokee's commitment to redefining their identities so that they resembled those of "Caucasian" Americans, the government was pushing ahead with the removals. Emerson continues, remarking in a bewildered tone that "the President and his Cabinet . . . are contracting to put this nation into carts and boats and drag them over mountains and rivers to a wilderness at a vast distance beyond the Mississippi." At this point he reframes the issue to underscore the way removal disrupts identity within the "great body of the American people." He does not say that most Americans supported the assimilationist policy, but he does say that he thinks most Americans have "sympathy" for the Cherokee's efforts to adapt. This observation implies an openness to prioritizing cultural transformation over racial difference.[9] He then asks the president, "Sir, does the government think that the people of the United States are become savage and mad? . . . We only state the fact, that a crime is projected that confounds our understanding by its magnitude—a crime that really deprives us as well as the Cherokee of a country" (*AW* 2). In Emerson's view, the removal policy will not just be a disaster for the Cherokee and consequently a blight on the reputation of the United States; it will also disrupt national membership from within by causing many citizens to resist self-identification as Americans. Emerson was never a "come-outer" in the Garrisonian sense of repudiating citizenship in the political nation as a gesture of self-purification. But here he implies that government policy is doing the reverse, propelling him out of the ranks of citizens through its own anti-American actions. Thoreau will repeat this gesture almost exactly in "Slavery in Massachusetts," written in response to the rendition of Anthony Burns back to enslavement in Virginia. He had been feeling "a vast and indefinite loss," Thoreau says, which, when explored, led him to realize "that what I had lost was a country."[10]

As the crisis was coming to a head, the Cherokee hoped for some kind of miraculous reprieve and did not follow orders to vacate their homes. The president responded by giving General Winfield Scott an army of eight thousand soldiers and instructions to force the Cherokee westward.[11]

A remark that Emerson made in his journal shortly after publishing his letter to Van Buren underscores the pressure the ethnic cleansing policy put on his sense of citizenship. Following a trip to New York, where he had visited William Cullen Bryant, Orville Dewey, and some of the other bright lights of New York society, Emerson explicitly juxtaposes his highest and lowest images of American identity. The vibrant combination of cultural aspiration and democratic politics that he had seen in New York leads him to write: "I begin to have hopes of the Republic. Then is this disaster of Cherokees brought to me by a sad friend to blacken my days & nights. I can do nothing. Why shriek? Why strike ineffectual blows?" (*JMN* 5:475). His letter, in the end, as he implicitly recognized, was less about opposing the Cherokee removals than it was about speaking up for a concept of citizenship that embraces the "painful endeavors" of the Cherokee to "domesticate" Anglo-American customs and thereby to progress, as he sees it, in "worth and civility."

In regard to his representation of racial inequality, it is important to note that Emerson does not disqualify the Cherokee from political and social equality on the grounds of inherent racial inferiority. Though he uses the racial signifiers "red men" and "Caucasian race," which imply inferior and superior positions, he represents the difference in cultural rather than biological terms. Equally important, he simply assumes that assimilation can be real and not a form of mimicry that is destined to die out as the regressive power of race overwhelms the progressive forces of culture. He even inverts the hierarchy, asking the president if his nation of white supremacist Americans has reverted to a "savage" state by refusing to recognize the Cherokee's effort to achieve similarity. He presents assimilation as a process of the domestication of culture, much the way he imagined an ideal of democratic citizenship as the domestication of an equality that could cultivate self-reflective individuality. The Cherokee had worked to "domesticate in the tribe . . . inventions and customs" such as European farming techniques, permanent settlements, constitutional government, and written texts. He alludes positively to the controversial practice of educating Cherokee men in New England schools. This detail deserves some attention because it directly evokes the history of intermarriage and miscegenation between whites and Indians. Two high-profile instances involving Cherokee men educated in New England, Elias Boudinot and John Ridge, caused significant racist backlash in the 1820s when both married the white daughters of their professors.[12]

Yet despite his cosmopolitan assumptions about racial equality, Emerson's equally strong convictions about the progress of civilization are unambiguously ethnocentric rather than pluralist. In his letter to Van Buren, Emerson never questions the premise that the proper goal of federal policy should be to foster assimilation as the lifestyles of the Cherokee become more and more like those of their white neighbors. By grounding his support for the rights of the Cherokee in their progress toward assimilation into the culture of recent Caucasian settlers, Emerson's letter is typical of anti-removal rhetoric. Rather than valuing a multicultural society or recognizing ethnic pluralism as a condition of democratic equality, Emerson affirms a universalized identity that acknowledges equality but that also subsumes race into a narrative of cultural progress. The result is dismissive of Cherokee culture, even as it defends the right of equal recognition to each individual Cherokee person.

It is nonetheless hard to see Emerson's assimilationist bias as a narrowly racist expression. His criteria for membership are grounded in an affiliative model of citizenship that accepts racial pluralism even as it foresees the Cherokee abandoning their ancestral culture in favor of the "inventions and customs of the Caucasian race." Far from being a threat to the United States or to the identity of the Americans, as Emerson presents it, the assimilation of "red men" is virtually a tribute to the excellence of their "Caucasian" overlords. He thus advocates a high standard for equality of opportunity by validating the Cherokee's right of access to the public goods of American society. Further, as he would also do in the debate over slavery in the late 1850s, Emerson proves quite willing to stake his sense of national membership on an aspirational ideal of citizenship that emphasizes combination as a vehicle of progress. Just as social life seeks a "domestication of the idea of culture" that will permit individuals to maintain civil societies grounded in the "character" of individuals, the progress of civilization must be designed to cultivate the equality of all people through civil, peaceful assimilation, regardless of race.

A few years previously, Alexis de Tocqueville had articulated a similar critique of ethnic cleansing after he witnessed the removal of the Creek Indians in 1832. Tocqueville contrasts the viciousness of Spanish conquest in Central and South America with the fastidious legal apparatus that the Americans had constructed to legitimize removals. He sharply distinguishes "United States Americans" from Indigenous people:

> The Spaniards let their dogs loose on the Indians as if they were wild beasts . . . but one cannot destroy everything, and frenzy has a limit; the remnant of the Indian population, which escaped the massacres, in the end mixed with the conquerors and adopted their religion and mores.
>
> On the other hand, the conduct of the United States Americans toward the natives was inspired by the most chaste affections for legal formalities. . . . The Spaniards, by unparalleled atrocities which brand them with indelible shame, did not succeed in exterminating the Indian race and could not even prevent them from sharing their rights; the United States Americans have attained both these results with wonderful ease, quickly, legally, and philanthropically, without spilling blood and without violating a single one of the great principles of morality in the eyes of the world. It is impossible to destroy men with more respect to the laws of humanity.[13]

The terms of Tocqueville's indictment will resonate throughout Emerson's thought on the relationship between race and civil society. The hypocrisy of the government's "chaste" legalism and the ironic contrast between a vicious conquest that resolves into the pluralism of Spanish America and a chaste legal process that is successfully "exterminating the Indian race" animate both Emerson's and Tocqueville's responses. Tocqueville's contempt for the hypocrisy of the "United States Americans" is the Frenchman's counterpart to the alienation from citizenship that Emerson communicates when he says the removals represent "a crime that really deprives us as well as the Cherokee of a country." As he takes this stand, Emerson seems no more concerned than Tocqueville by the idea that Indians might become "mixed" with Anglo-Americans, "sharing their rights" as equals.[14]

POLYGENESIS AND RACIAL PURITY

By the time Emerson wrote his letter to President Van Buren and delivered "The American Scholar," the assault on equality had eroded eighteenth-century cosmopolitanism enough that the few remaining traces of racial egalitarianism could no longer support policies for the assimilation of either African Americans or Native Americans.[15] As Louis Agassiz's work exemplifies, scientists in natural history and the related field of ethnology were developing a new vocabulary and a new set of procedures for the definition of racial identity. This vocabulary moved away from the assumption that racial difference was an environmental adaptation and began to assert that racial differences could be explained only by the introduction of multiple types of humankind at the original biblical Creation. In the polygenesists' argument, race was equivalent to species, and the presence of different species of humans was written into the order of nature as part of God's original design.[16]

Scientific polygenesis not only did much to justify race-based slavery but also changed the meaning of miscegenation. If God's original population included multiple races, then each human race is perfect only in its pure, original form. From this emerging perspective, race mixing represented a perversion of God's will, a degradation of type in and of itself. Racial purity, or "purity of type," as Agassiz termed it, now had a new, scientific justification that could be written into law and rationalized as a qualification for civil rights and opportunities.[17] He concludes his essay "The Diversity of Origin of the Human Races" with the remark: "We entertain not the slightest doubt that human affairs with reference to the colored races would be far more judiciously conducted, if, in our intercourse with them, we were guided by a full consciousness of the real difference between us and them and a desire to foster those dispositions that are eminently marked in them, rather than by treating them on terms of equality."[18]

From early in his career, Emerson paid close attention to developments in natural history. His interest is not surprising, given the depth of the Unitarian commitment to reconciling Enlightenment empiricism with Christian theology. Between the publication of Samuel George Morton's *Crania Americana* in 1839 and Darwin's publication of *On the Origin of Species* twenty years later, American scientists conducted an intensive debate on the implications of polygenesis. On one side were those working in the Enlightenment tradition who assumed that all humans were descendants of a single stock and that racial variations were somehow the effect of environmental factors. With its roots in Christian mythology buttressed by Enlightenment cosmopolitanism, this is the strain of anthropology that is most consistent with the Unitarianism of Emerson's background. These monogenesists, in defending the unity of the races, advocated the idea of adaptive change in order to explain racial diversity. For example, writing in 1859, the same year that Darwin published *Origin of Species*, Lewis Henry Morgan, a monogenesist anthropologist and railroad lawyer who published extensively on the Haudenosaunee people (formerly, Iroquois Federation), distinguishes between biology and culture to define the "human genus" very broadly:

> Man, indeed, progresses in knowledge from generation to generation, but yet the limits of human understanding have not been advanced one hair's breadth within man's historical period. All the capacities of the entire race of man existed potentially in the first human pair. . . . Notwithstanding portions of the other portions, as the Bushman and the Hottentot, still sit in the darkness of ignorance and intellectual imbecility. The Bushman, however, is of the human genus; and logically, the point of comparison between man and the species next below him, commences with the Bushman just as legitimately as with the European.[19]

Morgan distinguishes cultural difference from biological identity. He links the "first human pair" to the most advanced cultures, and the Bushman to the European, as identical in terms of their inherent "capacities." Though the European has progressed the furthest in technology and civility, the Hottentot and the Bushman equally embody all "the capacities of the entire race of man." All humankind is a single race. Environment defines the only difference between the Hottentot and Morgan himself.

Among those advancing polygenesis to undermine equality were Philadelphia physician Samuel George Morton, his followers Egyptologist George R. Gliddon and surgeon Josiah Nott of Mississippi, and eventually Louis Agassiz, who joined them in the 1840s and gave a new level of scientific credibility to their assault on the possibility of racial equality. All three worked within the recognized methodological bounds of legitimate life sciences, primarily by distinguishing between categories and arranging them in hierarchical scales according to Linnaean categories of order, family, genus, and species.[20]

Arguing that God populated the earth with several races and that differences between them were inherent, immutable, and hierarchical, the polygenesists raised questions about all efforts to promote equality between members of different races. Efforts to educate or even evangelize people like the Native Americans or Africans were, to the polygenesist, a waste of time because their primitivism was a product of race rather than culture. By the logic of the polygenesists, even Christian missionary work was pointless because God's grace was beyond the reach of non-Caucasian human species. In fact, religious conversion and cultural assimilation were downright harmful because bringing the races closer together diluted pure bloodlines, degraded the Caucasian race, and created people who defied orderly classification.

In the 1854 edition of Nott and Gliddon's *Types of Mankind*, published to memorialize the career of Samuel Morton, Agassiz contributed an essay titled "Sketch of Natural Provinces of the Animal World and Their Relation to the Different Types of Man." This long essay, accompanied by a geographical map showing the "natural range" of various human types, offers Agassiz's version of polygenetic theory. He emphasizes the connection between specific races and geography:

> There is one feature in the physical history of mankind which has been entirely neglected by those who have studied this subject viz., the natural relations between the different types of man and the animals and plants inhabiting the same regions. The sketch here presented is intended to supply this deficiency, as far as it is possible in a mere outline delineation, and to show that *the boundaries, within which the different natural combinations of animals are known to be circumscribed upon the surface of the earth, coincided with the natural range of distinct types of man.*

The Arctic, for example, has a particular type of human created to prosper in it. Describing the fauna, Agassiz continues:

> The coasts of the continents and of the numerous islands in the arctic seas are peopled by clouds of gannets, of cormorants, of penguins, of petrels, of ducks, of geese, of mergoniers, and of gulls, some of which are as large as eagles and like them live on prey. No reptile is known in this zone. Fishes are, however, very numerous, and the rivers especially swarm with a variety of species of the salmon family. A number of representatives of the inferior classes of worms, of crustaceans, of mollusks, of echinoderms, and of medusae are also found here.
>
> Within the limits of this fauna we meet a peculiar race of men, known in America under the name of Esquimaux, and under the names of Laplanders, Samojedes, and Tchuktahes in the north of Asia. . . . The uniformity of their character along the whole range of the arctic seas forms one of the most striking resemblances which these people exhibit to the fauna with which they are so closely connected.[21]

The humans originally designed to inhabit the Arctic are uniform from continent to continent and match the uniformity of flora and fauna in the Arctic zone.

With the globe divided among pure types situated in particular settings, even the far-flung European has an original ecological home "It cannot escape the attention of the careful observer," writes Agassiz, "that the European zoological realm is circumscribed within exactly the same limits as the so-called white race of man. . . . We exclude, of course, modern migrations [such as European emigration to the Americas] and historical changes of habitation from this assertion." Agassiz briefly interrupts his sketch to make an aside that underscores the polygenesists' assumption that all parts of the world were populated by appropriate species of humans at the Creation. In respect to the expansive travels of the European, "there is a singular fact, which historians seem not to have sufficiently appreciated, that the earliest migrations recorded, in any form, show us man meeting man, wherever he moves upon the inhabitable surfaces of the globe."[22]

Mixing these different types of humans will disrupt the order of nature by violating the harmony of creation. "Nobody can deny," Agassiz continues, "that the offspring of different races is always a half-breed, as between animals of different species, and not a child like either its mother or its father."[23] The racially pure offspring is a "child," whereas the mixed-race offspring is a half-something, less than either of its parents.[24] Agassiz concludes that the perfection of the original order means that no pure type of human can intermingle without degradation. "For I maintain distinctly," he continues, "that the differences observed among the races of men are of the same kind and even greater than those upon which the anthropoid monkeys are considered as distinct species." To interpret this diversity, Agassiz frames the claims of the monogenesists and polygenesists as two irreconcilable understandings of nature:

> Now, there are only two alternatives before us at present:—
>
> 1st. Either mankind originated from a common stock, and all the different races with their peculiarities, in their present distribution, are to be ascribed to subsequent changes—an assumption for which there is no evidence whatever, and that leads at once to the admission that the diversity among animals is not an original one, nor their distribution determined by a general plan, established in the beginning of the Creation;—or,

> 2nd. We must acknowledge that the diversity among animals is a fact determined by the will of the Creator, and their geographical distribution part of the general plan which unites all organized beings into one great organic conception: when it follows that what are called human races, down to their specialization as nations, are distinct primordial forms of the type of man.[25]

Agassiz's rhetoric here shows both the grounds of Emerson's intellectual sympathy with him and the grounds on which he rejected Agassiz's insistence on the fixity of type.

The fecundity and diversity of nature are central fascinations for both Emerson and Agassiz. At the heart of Agassiz's theory of nature is a diffuse but harmonious system of organisms and environments that embody a transcendent creativity. Scientific research—both cosmic, like Alexander von Humboldt's, and microscopic, like Agassiz's own study of jellyfish—is a form of theology; it reveals the acts of a conscious God.[26] In the view of Louis Agassiz, nature embodies an almost infinitely complex world, but its guiding principle is equilibrium or stasis rather than transformation or evolution. He conceded the point that plants and animals could mutate, but he also argued that when they did mutate, the change was an aberration, even a vaguely blasphemous distortion of a sacred design in which each animal's habitat was formed as a perfect, unchanging home that was literally made for it in the divine workshop. As he put it, "The laws which regulate the diversity of animals . . . apply equally to man, *within the same limits and in the same degree*; and . . . all our liberty and moral responsibility, however spontaneous, are yet instinctively directed by the All-wise and Omnipotent, to fulfill the great harmonies established in Nature."[27] In the "great harmonies" between species and habitat that God has established in nature, animal hybrids, including interracial humans, defy nature's boundaries. In Agassiz's scientific view, having briefly stepped outside the stasis of nature, mixed and mutated examples disturb the equilibrium of nature by corrupting God's perfect design. In the order of nature, these aberrant forms will periodically bubble up and then die out without changing the overall design. Despite the ceaseless activity of its component parts, nature, as Agassiz saw it, is designed to sustain a changeless equilibrium.[28]

To Emerson, there was much to appreciate in Agassiz's life and career. He made important discoveries in natural history and had the talent to invent his own brand of popular science. His lifelong effort to see divinity in nature, the manifold fields of new research he advocated, and the lifetimes of devoted work his teaching career opened for his students represent a most admirable achievement. The spirit in which Agassiz approached nature influenced Emerson's own desire to see human power acting in service of a higher law or a higher good.

The crucial place, though, where Emerson's thought thoroughly rejects Agassiz's is on the implications of change and combination. Agassiz saw nature as self-correcting back to a perfect equilibrium. The "great organic conception" of nature, in Agassiz's vision, takes the form of a static harmony between species and habitat. Nature is a spectacular puzzle in which each piece has a designed place that it fits snugly as a unit in a larger design. The dynamism of it all is God's, not nature's, and for nature to deviate from the original plan is, veritably, the Fall.

Emerson utterly dismisses this static conception of nature. Emerson saw nature as intrinsically progressive. To uncover the activity of Spirit in nature was not to place a thing in a predetermined spot but to reveal the energy that allows its transformation into something better. In "Fate" he refers to this power as "electricity"; in "Self-Reliance" he defines it as "the shooting of the gulf" that occurs "in the moment of transition from a past to a new state." "The soul *becomes* . . . [and] inasmuch as the soul is present there will be power not confident but agent" (*CW* 2:40). In human terms this commitment to transformation is what allows people to transform material things and progress toward a better world. It is of a piece with his view of friendship as a constantly transforming experience that encompasses change in the most basic categories of identity. Emerson's worldview is similar to Agassiz's in the sense that it is grounded in the belief that a universal spirit, as Agassiz states their shared conviction, "unites all organized beings into one great organic conception"; but for Emerson, that organic conception is constantly in motion, constantly morphing, constantly finding ways not just to change but to improve. Improvement, for human civilization, meant transformation toward equality.

By the 1840s, the concept that various subtle types of biological mutation allowed species to adapt to their environments had been around for a long time. Beginning at least with Jean-Baptiste Lamarck's theory that animals adapted in form, transformational theories similar to Darwin's had been an important part of the dialogue about the history of the natural world. Lamarck hypothesized, for example, that giraffes developed long necks as successive generations had to reach higher and higher into trees to graze. He also argued that animals had, over time, developed from simple to complex anatomical forms. That structural change, even progressive adaptations, could occur in animal biology as well as in human civilization had long had believers in the scientific community.[29] In important respects, the difference between the tradition of intelligent design that Agassiz worked in and the transformational tradition that Darwin advanced was not so much the difference between a static and a dynamic "nature" as that between one that followed an overarching plan and one that had unpredictable random change built into its very structure. Given the range of transformational theories available in the nineteenth century, the issue separating Agassiz and Darwin was not so much stasis versus change as design versus chance. Laura Dassow Walls puts the novelty of Darwin's intervention this way: "Darwin's task was not to invent evolution, but to reinvent it so as to demolish design and to enthrone chance."[30]

The implications of moving away from a world that was designed by an external divine intelligence to one that follows its own internal mechanisms were very far-reaching. Scientific debate over the mutability of species, especially the status of hybrids, is important to the antebellum debate over equality because it shaped the assumptions people brought to the debate over the meaning of race. In this respect, Darwinian theory challenged a longstanding construction of human dignity. If all of nature reflects a grand design as Agassiz believed, then it would seem that different races of humans were created to play different roles in the fulfillment of that design. In this model, science serves not as a self-reinforcing epistemological system but as a support to theology. The task of science is to discern God's design and to help social institutions follow it as part of their service to God. In a kind of sideways argument that was crucial to the assault on equality, advocates of divine design argued that design, though static, dignifies each person, no matter how lowly, by situating them in a context of supernatural order and purpose.[31] It connects every person of every race, master and slave, to an act of God. The mutation theory, by contrast, opens the possibility that no human condition is immutable, or even more than the result of good or ill luck.

Until Darwin's theory redefined the debate, the polygenesists' argument provided a powerful weapon in the assault on equality. But even at the height of its influence, polygenism was weakened by an inability to stabilize its own terms. As the polygenesists sought to establish hard boundaries between the races, they found it more and more difficult to define race with any precision. If race itself was an ambiguous phenomenon, how could purity of race ever be factually established? There was consensus neither on the number of human races nor even on the criteria that should distinguish between genus and type. For example, one of the standard criteria for determining animals of the same species had long been their ability to produce fertile offspring. Human beings of different races produce fertile offspring, which would seem to demonstrate the unity of the species. But in the mid-1850s, polygenesists popularized the false idea that different human races could be fertile for up to four generations, at which point mixed-birth unions would produce infertile offspring. Similar fissures in the rhetoric of zoological and demographic categories pervade the discourse of mid-nineteenth-century polygenesis, and these ambiguities undermined the ability of polygenetic scientists to control the discourse that defined the human species. The ambiguity of race as a category made ethnology fluid in its basic terms. It not only left practitioners unable to count the number of races that inhabited the globe but also left wide gaps in the distinctions they sought to establish between biological and cultural traits.

THE "FORMIDABLE DOCTRINE OF RACE"

This resulting ambiguity in the concept of race pervades Emerson's writing. Although he often adopts the rhetoric of the debate over race in passing, his only sustained analysis of "race" occurs in *English Traits* and takes the form of a cultural history of Great Britain. Here, the whole story that he tells is one of ethnic hybridization, and it is a thoroughgoing argument against the idea of biological permanence. It is also emphatically white supremacist. Yet even at his most racist, Emerson emphasizes that the combination of diverse elements was the foundation of British preeminence and is significant in human progress more generally. Mimicking the descriptive rhetoric of the ethnographer, he offers this portrait of the modern Englishman:

> On the English face are combined decision and nerve, with the fair complexion, blue eyes, and open and florid aspect. Hence the love of truth, hence the sensibility, the fine perception, and poetic construction. The fair Saxon man with open front and honest meaning, domestic, affectionate, is not the wood out of which cannibal, or inquisitor, or assassin is made, but he is moulded for law, lawful trade, civility,

marriage, the nurture of children, for colleges, churches, charities, and colonies. (*CW* 5:36)

But rather than being pure, "English" manliness is highly composite. In terms of gender, "the two sexes are co-present in the English mind" (*CW* 5:37). "The English delight," he remarks "in the antagonism which combines in one person the extremes of courage and tenderness." Comically, he even ends the chapter titled "Race" with a literal merger of Englishmen and their horses. While for a couple of centuries the English seemed "to have declined," in "two hundred years a change has taken place.... The gentleman is always on horseback [and] ... a score or two of mounted gentlemen may frequently be seen running like centaurs down a hill nearly as steep as the roof of a house" (*CW* 5:40).

Referring to Robert Knox's study *The Races of Men: A Fragment*, published in London in 1850, Emerson begins his chapter on race by remarking that "an ingeneous anatomist has written a book to prove that races are imperishable." Knox, Emerson notes, distinguishes between race and nation. Whereas race is "imperishable," according to Knox's theory, "nations are pliant political constructions, easily changed or destroyed." Emerson flatly rejects this distinction, arguing that "this writer did not found his assumed races on any necessary law, disclosing their ideal and metaphysical necessity." At the very beginning of "Race" he contests the category by noting that "each variety" of person "shades down imperceptibly into the next, and you cannot draw the line where one race begins or ends" (*CW* 5:24). Contradictorily, he notes that "race works immortally to keep its own," and infamously that "race in the negro is of appalling importance." In addition, "It is race, is it not, that puts the hundred millions of Indians under the domination of a remote island in the north of Europe" (*CW* 5:26). But he unmistakably rejects the idea of racial permanence. The permanence of race "is resisted by other forces. Civilization is a re-agent and eats away the old traits." Indeed, "the formidable doctrine of race suggests others which threaten to undermine it, as not sufficiently based.... [T]hough we flatter the self-love of men and nations by the legend of pure races, all our experience is of the gradation and resolution of races" (*CW* 5:27). The word "resolution" here seems to mean something like "re-solution," as if a race were a liquid solution and the recipe for the solution—the combination of earlier races—is continually changing in its details to make gradation, and gradation, and gradation.

Emerson assumes a connection between race and Britain's economic and military preeminence. The questions he poses, however, do not emphasize the importance of an elusive racial purity but rather ask how have gradation and combination called the English into being. How had they "led to the present stature of the British?" Borrowing from Lamarck's theory that nature evolved from simple to complex organisms, Emerson draws an analogy between the fossil record and the English: "The lowest organizations are simplest; a mere mouth, a jelly, or a straight worm. As the scale mounts, the organizations become complex. We are piqued with pure descent, but nature loves inoculation. A child blends in his face the faces of both parents, and some feature from every ancestor whose face hangs on the wall. The best nations are those most widely related; and navigation, as effecting a world-wide mixture, is the most potent advancer of nations" (*CW* 5:27). He sets the first moment of the ascent of the English at the raids of the Norsemen and follows it through successive invasions and colonization of the British Isles. Over and over, he asserts the importance of combination: "The English composite character betrays a mixed origin. Everything English is a fusion of distant and antagonistic elements. Neither do this people appear to be of one stem; but collectively a better race than any from which they are derived" (*CW* 5:28).

In their myriad combinations the British may be the best race, but they are far from perfect. The brutality of British history proves they are not fully domesticated. "The mildness of the ages that followed Norse, Norman, Danish and Saxon conquest has not quite effaced these traits of Odin; as the rudiment of a structure matured in the tiger is said to be still found unabsorbed in the Caucasian man. The nation has a tough, acrid, animal nature, which centuries of churching and civilizing have not been able to sweeten" (*CW* 5:34). Nonetheless, it is the best that racial promiscuity has been able to produce: "It is not a final race, once a crab always a crab—but a race with a future" (*CW* 5:36). In effect, Emerson situates all animal life in a great, but mutable, chain of being. The chain is linked not by a static divine design but by an infinite number of random mutations. The Englishman stands at the top by virtue of two circumstances: first, a long chain of combinations distributed along a very blurry line between culture and biology; and second, the cultivation of values that are ultimately embodied in the face of "the fair Saxon man." But as advanced as the English are, in some sense they are still as primitive as crabs.

In a journal entry written a few years before his trip to England in 1847 and 1848, Emerson comments on the anemic blood of Americans in comparison to that of the "English race." He reads race here as an effect of culture and sees British culture as pure and strong, while American culture is derivative and weak:

> In America I grieve to miss the strong black blood of the English race: ours is a pale diluted stream. What a company of brilliant young persons I have seen with so much expectation! the sort is very good, but none is good enough of his sort. Every one (an) imperfect specimen, respectable not valid. Irving thin & Channing thin, & Bryant & Dana[,] Prescott & Bancroft. There is Webster, but he cannot do what he would; he cannot do Webster. Then the youth, as I said, are all promising failures. No writing is here[,] no redundant strength, but declamation, straining, correctness, & all other systems of debility. (*JMN* 9:83)

This passage echoes his angst during the Cherokee removal crisis as well as the cultural concerns he shared with John O'Sullivan. Though Emerson is reciting a typical lament on the failure of American culture to shine as brightly as its European counterpart, his use of blood as a metaphor and his identification of cultural leaders as specimens of flexible racial identities underscore the vagueness of the very terms in which he was thinking. The difference between "strong black" and "pale diluted" blood is a difference not so much in the purity of Americans' Anglo-Saxon ancestry but in their failure to combine the raw materials of biology and culture into something higher. Author Washington Irving, religious leader William Ellery Channing, poet and newspaper editor William Cullen Bryant, author and adventurer Richard Henry Dana, historians William Hickling Prescott, and George Bancroft should be able to embody *something* new. They should be able to project a new race in the re-solution of Anglo-Saxon blood with American democratic principles, Indigenous people, and immigrants to produce something more cosmopolitan. Daniel Webster—the Massachusetts senator who had held the Union staunch in the 1832 Nullification Crisis with his famous formulation "Liberty *and* Union, now and forever, one and inseparable"—comes closest to being a perfect specimen, but even he cannot conjure the pseudo-Englishman into the new American "race" that Emerson awaited "with so much expectation!"

In terms of Emerson's assumptions about racial equality here, it is especially important to note that he simply assumes that race is a by-product of culture. If Webster can manage to speak as an authentic American, rather than as some kind of American-British hybrid, he will call a new race into being. The fact that "even Webster can not do Webster" underscores both the muddiness of the idea and the mutability that Emerson attributes to race. Importantly, the path to a new "strong black[ness]" is through more dilution, more hybridization, not through a narrowing of sources back toward British or Anglo-Saxon purity. In his eulogy for Abraham Lincoln, for example, delivered at a funerary ceremony in Concord (which happened to fall on the ninetieth anniversary of the Battle of Lexington and Concord), he closes in a way that exemplifies his understanding of "race" as a mutable phenomenon that integrates biology and culture. In the wake of the assassination, Lincoln's life and death mark the convergence of a ruthless natural history with anthropological change and providential design. He even implies that Lincoln's achievement had opened the door to a new race in post–Civil War America: "There is a serene Providence that rules the fate of nations, which makes little account of time, little of one generation or race, makes no account of disasters, conquers alike by what is called defeat or by what is called victory, thrusts aside enemy and obstruction, crushes everything immoral as inhuman, and obtains the ultimate triumph of the best race by the sacrifice of everything which resists the moral laws of the world" (*W* 11:314–15). He then turns specifically to talk about Lincoln as a vehicle of Providence. In Emerson's idiom of transformation, Lincoln's task is racial rather than political. It is not to sustain government of the people, by the people, for the people, but to create an American race. Providence "makes its own instruments, creates the man for his time, trains him in poverty, inspires his genius, and arms him for his task. It has given every race its own talent, and ordains that only that race which combines perfectly with the virtues of all shall endure" (*W* 11:315). Emerson is placing the martyred president in the role that Webster had failed to perform. Where Webster was a humiliated failure, a man of the past, the defender of property and of a status quo who "resists the moral laws of the world," Lincoln was a man of the future, a person who elides differences, combines the virtues of all existing races, and thus projects the emergence of a new "race."

The "serene Providence," like the "terrible communist" (*CW* 1:231) of "The Young American," represents the process of a progressive history that ruthlessly strikes down heroes. Even Lincoln's gory end is providential. Providence took Lincoln off the stage at the perfect moment in order "to show the world a completed benefactor" (*W* 11:314). Emerson eulogizes Lincoln as a composite character rather than as an embodiment of purity or of

Anglo-Saxon virtue; he is a magazine of frontier clay, gravitas, genius, all rising above his provincial education as "a flatboatman." Of course, this eulogy is hagiographic; most of it marks Lincoln's virtues—a tireless worker, a broad good nature, enormous patience and resolve, eloquence—but Emerson's farewell to Lincoln exemplifies the way he sees cosmopolitan anthropology driving toward universal equality.

As many of his contemporaries did, Emerson tended to use terms for race and ethnicity loosely and even interchangeably. Descriptors such as "race," "nation," "Caucasian," "Anglo-Saxon," "Ethiopian," "Negro," "British," and "American"—which polygenesists in the 1840s and 1850s were trying to distinguish and codify as Linnaean-style categories—never gained consensual definition.[32] The rise of Darwin's theory of random mutation then permanently clouded boundaries between the categories and pushed polygenism into a demimonde. There, it sustained itself as a racist pseudoscience on the margins of nationalism until it reemerged as fascist master race theory in the next century.[33]

Despite the brevity of its ascendence, polygenism gave the idea of racial purity a scientific foundation that would serve the interests of generations of white supremacists. Though Emerson was influenced by polygenetic theories, he never accepts a model of nature in which combination is degrading rather than progressive. His idea of nature relies not on a zoological orderliness that ties organisms to places or identities but on the constant permutation of physical matter to reflect the energy of spiritual law. To seek stasis runs contrary to Emerson's most deeply held convictions about how Spirit works.[34] Material forms are always subordinate to Spirit, and the forms that matter takes are infinitely subject to change. Working his way toward stronger and stronger antislavery statements while polygenetic theory was at its height, Emerson brings from his religious background and Enlightenment convictions a set of assumptions that ruled out a world in which everything had a place and the duty of the public intellectual was to see that everything stayed in it.

If an individual has talents that permit them to eclipse the influence of culture, race, or history, then practical ethics should validate these talents as expressions of universal human potential rather than attribute them to specific races or dismiss them as arrant deviations from type. This deep commitment to an egalitarian ideal of universal possibility combined with the exemplary achievements of heroes enabled Emerson to resist and rebut his own intellectual elitism and racist chauvinism.

EMERSON'S TRANSCENDENTALISM AND COSMOPOLITAN EQUALITY

At the very core of Emerson's Transcendentalism, an elusive but all-powerful benevolent Spirit pervades and unifies everything in the universe. The agonizingly slow movement of civilization and nature toward the visible articulation of this millennial end defines Emerson's conception of history. The dominant tradition of Emerson criticism has tended to treat Spirit as an expression of an almost Christian liberalism that emphasizes individual freedom and potential self-empowerment through acts of reflection that result in self-liberation. But even though Emerson's Spirit acts through the individual, its effect doesn't end there. Emerson's version of the evolution of societies and institutions also underscores the importance of equality to his understanding of Spirit and of how it works in the world. In his 1837 "Politics" lecture, he lists some of the ways granular connections change larger institutions. In the "new age" of global commerce, "the old bonds of language, country, and king give way to the new connexions of trade. It destroys patriotism and substitutes cosmopolitanism" (*EL* 2:80–81).

Though Emerson is often treated as a quintessentially nationalist writer, there is a strong cosmopolitan strain in his writing. In their analyses of Emerson's cosmopolitanism, Branka Arsić and Lawrence Buell both emphasize Emerson's resistance to nationalistic thought. Emerson's politics, Buell argues, represents a type of post-national cosmopolitanism, the stance of "latter-day Puritans standing for the higher law." In Buell's reading, Emerson's writing is "antinationalist" even to the point of trying to redefine his New England identity in universalized cosmopolitan terms.[35] Arsić adds leverage to Buell's effort to pry Emerson away from his narrow reputation as a literary nationalist by arguing that he "consistently advocated a cosmopolitics" that treats nationalism "as a form of personal and cultural immaturity."[36] Arsić cites an 1864 lecture in which Emerson turns from a discussion of the globalization of communication technologies to an imagined future in which people can converse without the veil of national affiliation: "In the great movements on foot for social intercourse, the railroad, and telegraph and the new action for submarine telegraph, it looks as if we should presently . . . forget our savage spites at another province, or another nation, or men of other color, and conquer this till now invincible nationality. Nationality is babyish" (*LL* 2:372–73).

Writing as the Civil War was grinding into its third year of mass slaughter, Emerson here bluntly asserts a position on the universality of human equality that he had been articulating in other ways since the very beginning of his career. National identities always lag behind the transformational impulses of his Transcendentalist idealism. He frequently treats race and nationality as objective realities, but often he does so to mark an obstacle or boundary that needs to be negotiated to achieve authentic civility. The reality of racial domination may represent the work of fate, what he calls an "irresistible dictation" of nature, but to accomplish the domestication of culture, this circumstance also represents an unjust human condition that needs to be overcome.

In his book on race and law in the American nineteenth century, Gregg Crane addresses this ambiguity by integrating Emerson's thought on politics and science into a forward-looking theory of "cosmopolitan constitutionalism." Crane takes advantage of the flexibility in Emerson's terminology to emphasize the way the two words "constitution" and "blood" signify in simultaneously material and symbolic terms. In Emerson's hands, blood becomes a metaphor for the constitution-making moral commitments that can permit the Americans to fashion a "blood" that itself expresses the ideal of progressive combination. This redefinition away from a context in which ancestry determines identity and toward a population built around combination and synthesis negates the backward-looking idea of racial purity and even anticipates the emergence of new races out of existing ones.

Crane writes that by redefining the political process of constitution making as "a trope for a diverse moral consensus, Emerson suggests that it is the justice we enact and not our heritage that defines us."[37] He explains that as ethnographic theories were developing, the meanings of basic terms of racial identity were also especially fluid and subject to redefinition. Rather than marking scientific boundaries, the multiple meanings of "blood" defined variables that also offered opportunities for progressive redefinition. Crane concludes that Emerson mediates the problems posed by racist science through an act of translation in which the principles of egalitarian racial recognition become the constitutional "blood" of a pluralistic, democratic society. Taking blood out of the material realm and treating it as a metaphor enabled Emerson to incorporate the whole body of racist science into a narrative that culminates in an egalitarian process of racial combination. Races and cultures, literally reconstituted and recombined in individuals, come to embody a progressive, pluralistic, and *advancing* national identity.

On the one hand, as an interpretation of Emerson's thought about race, Crane's argument allows consensus to be as tolerant of racial diversity as it is of religious diversity.[38] On the other hand, as a practical analogy, Crane's idea of validating a "diverse moral consensus" in antebellum America does not explain much because the intensifying assault on equality in the 1850s eroded broadly recognized values that could sustain a national identity rooted in "moral consensus." Rather than promoting consensus, Emerson had to choose: purity or combination.

Where Crane emphasizes "constitutional cosmopolitanism" to describe Emerson's effort to separate race from predetermined capabilities, Ian Finseth identifies a form of "blood cosmopolitanism" that stands as an alternative to politics altogether. Finseth gives material forces greater weight than Crane but nonetheless emphasizes Emerson's interest in imagining a world in which spiritual forces dominate material facts. In Finseth's reading, by studying the long tradition of evolutionary theory that led up to Darwin, "Emerson came to believe that the volatile energy of racial conflict, like that of individual dissent, would serve not to disrupt the Union, but to provide the dialectic of change and progress necessary to its well-being."[39] The idea of a synthesis, and the integration of races that was represented by combining the blood of diverse peoples, acted powerfully on Emerson's imagination and is completely consistent with his overall bias toward processes of disintegration and recombination.[40] For Finseth, blood cosmopolitanism describes a process of racial integration that Emerson saw as necessary to the progress of civilization. Emerson's "recognition of widespread intermixture advises us," Finseth concludes, "to see Emerson as both advocating a deracialized moral and political consensus and as seeking to create a usable, proactive narrative of the undeniable fact of human miscegenation."[41] Purity of blood points backwards; blood cosmopolitanism points forward toward the next "resolution." Miscegenation, Emerson implies, will be necessary to produce the "American race." By 1844, anyway, Emerson seems open to this idea. The moral and political consensus to which Finseth alludes represents the egalitarian multiculturalism that would necessarily underpin relationships among such diverse identities. As he puts it, "The sine qua non of this cosmopolitanism was Emerson's irreducibly humanist belief that the biological and spiritual bonds linking humanity into one whole were more important and more fundamental than national allegiance, cultural background, or environmental circumstance."[42]

In their use of the metaphor of blood as a mystified material essence similar to the way people use DNA metaphorically today, Crane and Finseth both underscore the polar antagonisms of stasis and combination in Emerson's defense of equality. In their readings, cosmopolitanism refers to social structures that unify diverse sources, whether ideological, religious, cultural, or racial. Both the virtues and challenges of cosmopolitanism reside in its emphasis on universal human similarity and equality. Crane's "constitutional cosmopolitanism" and Finseth's "blood cosmopolitanism" build on this foundation by highlighting the intellectual gymnastics through which Emerson struggled to mediate between his desire to see things converge and the static categories of racist science that were so central to the antebellum assault on equality.

Emerson hems and haws over the antagonism of cultures, races, and nations, but as the assault on equality was strengthening the ideology that underpinned slavery, he took sides with the forces of egalitarian pluralism over the forces of gradation, caste, and hierarchy. His faith in the universal accessibility of Spirit acted as a counterforce against the rising emphasis on immutable inequalities. Crane and Finseth thread the needle between universalizers and multiculturalists by constructing Emersonian cosmopolitanisms that welcome all races and cultures but that also imply their eventual unifying synthesis generation on generation. Yet both cosmopolitanisms are necessarily egalitarian. In the context of slaveholding, white supremacist, and increasingly xenophobic America, both versions of Emersonian cosmopolitanism reflect a far more radical cultural intervention than his argument that popular culture is more important than classical learning or that Americans should try to project a national voice onto the world literary stage.

The bedrock assertion of cosmopolitan equality is that every human person is irreducibly similar and should have rights that must be universally respected if the idea of personhood is to be meaningful.[43] Notwithstanding his universalizing of an ethnocentric emphasis on individuality, no assumption is more basic to Emerson's thought than the claim that every individual should have an equal scope in which to pursue their natural talents. In Emerson's view, "there are no common men. All men are at last of a size, and true art is only possible on the conviction that every talent has its apotheosis somewhere. Fair play and open field! And freshest laurels to all who have won them!" (*CW* 4:18).

Two moments of resistance to identities that chafed his sense of personal independence reflect Emerson's impulse to reach toward an ideal that rejects exclusionary identities in order to embrace cosmopolitan universality. Very early in his career, he considers the sectarian struggles that would define his generation of ministers. He looks at the sectarian divisions within Protestantism and tries to find a position that puts all people on an equal spiritual footing. He notes in his journal:

> I suppose it is not wise, not being natural, to belong to any religious party. In the Bible, you are not directed to be a Unitarian or a Calvinist or an Episcopalian. Now, if a man is wise, . . . he will say to himself I am not a member of that or any party. I am God's child. . . . Religion is the relation of the Soul to God, & therefore the progress of Sectarianism marks the decline of religion. (*JMN* 3:259–60)

The identities offered by Presbyterian, Congregationalist, or even Unitarian doctrine strike Emerson as unnatural because they "save a man from the vexation of thinking" (*JMN* 3:260) and thus prevent the spirituality that will move identity away from the "babyish" distinctions of identity politics and bring it closer to a self-conscious universality.

Years later, and addressing a crisis with higher stakes, he also writes in frustration at the inability of his contemporaries to rise above identity politics. Rebutting the argument that enslaving some people is the only way to support advanced societies, Emerson acknowledges the power of the argument but rejects the legitimacy of the position. This time his topic is racial domination rather than religious affiliation. In his essay "Fate," he treats the anaconda's merciless suffocation of its victim as an analogy to the enslavement of Africans by Europeans. This brutality is a serious aspect of the human condition and must be either accepted as necessary or rejected with a strong rationale. "Our America," he writes, "has a bad name for superficialness. Great men, great nations, have not been boasters and buffoons, but perceivers of the terror of life, and have manned themselves to face it" (*CW* 6:2). In society as in nature, progress seems to inch along, steeped in blood, through a merciless predation: "The crackle of the bones of his prey in the coil of the anaconda,—these are in the system, and our habits are like theirs. You have just dined, and, however scrupulously the slaughterhouse is concealed in the graceful distance of miles, there is complicity,—expensive races,—race living at the expense of race" (*CW* 6:4).[44] In this analogy, Emerson closes the gap between the world of the anaconda and a human civil society in which race preys on race. But against this similarity between predator and prey in the Amazon jungle and the perverse boasting about inherent superiority that would validate similar relations among humans, he exempts human beings from the necessity of living by such standards. Persons are neither snakes nor mice, and race need not prey on race because "man is not order of nature. . . . But the lightning which explodes and fashions planets, maker of planets and suns, is in him" (CW 6:12). This exemption from the predatory order of nature allows each individual, as he puts it later in the essay, to "take sides with the deity" rather than accepting any practice or institution as binding in the future (CW 6:8). Slavery is not a fact of nature but a cruel and predatory institution that can be reversed by humane people acting in harmony with the universal Spirit.[45] As deeply as the essay "Fate" recognizes history as a circumstance, Emerson does not accept circumstance as definitive. Facing the terror of life means recognizing that acting like an anaconda is a personal and civil choice and not a fated demand of God or Nature.

In recent criticism "Fate" has supplanted "Experience" as the essay in which Emerson most directly addresses the powers that resist progress, unity, and Spirit, but it is also important to recognize that in "Fate," Emerson offsets his fatalism with the affirmation that "a part of fate is the freedom of man" (CW 6:18). In spite of all he had learned about the limitations of the power of the individual in the years between *Nature* in 1836 and *Conduct of Life* in 1860, in "Fate" he reaffirms his faith in the possibility of progressive evolutionary change. The watershed this essay marks in his thought is not a turn toward either skepticism or fatalism but a recognition that progress may *not* be inevitable, that a positive moral arc may *not* be built into the order of nature, that the "arc of the moral universe" does not "bend toward justice," but that it is much harder for benevolent genius to gain an upper hand over greed, egotism, and demagoguery than he had ever before recognized.[46] Affirming this posture, he closes his 1854 essay on the Fugitive Slave Law with the words "I hope we have come to an end of our unbelief, have come to a belief that there is a Divine Providence in the world which will not save us but through our own co-operation" (AW 89).

The topics of these two examples define a pattern that characterizes Emerson's response to identity politics. When faced with a choice between two competing identities, rather than choosing one and rejecting the other, he sweeps them both aside and affirms an aspirational identity that envisions a cosmopolitan democracy in which every person is sovereign and equal. This double gesture represents one of Emerson's most consistent intellectual moves: he recognizes fate as the power of circumstance to determine each person's identity, but he also avers the power of co-operation with Providence to verify the necessity of unity and the possibility of equality. This gesture is indispensable to Emerson's egalitarian thought because it permits him to envision people liberating themselves from local prejudices and imagining better selves living in a better world. In Emerson's reasoning, continually defaulting to an anticipated cosmopolitan universalism is the necessary first step in any larger process of social change because self-reliance is not just about self-empowerment; it is also about transformation toward higher standards of communication, recognition, and equality.

THE "SIMULAR MAN" AND THE "ARRESTED UNDERTYPE"

Given the facts that the United States was a slave nation, that respected scientists such as his friend Louis Agassiz were advocating racial hierarchy as part of a divine plan, and that Emerson had long been drawn to elitist ideas about genius that lifted a select few above the crowd, how is it that he came to stand with the egalitarians rather than the racists? Theodore Parker and Thomas Carlyle went in the other direction. Emerson could easily have refined his belief in the special genius of inspired poets and scholars into a theory that linked Spirit and genius to Anglo-Saxon racial superiority. Why did Emerson move toward the perfectionist spirituality of William Lloyd Garrison and the integrationist egalitarianism of Frederick Douglass instead? Despite his long engagement with them, the spiritual and scientific claims of the assault on equality failed to change Emerson's conviction that combination is essential in both Spirit and nature, and that progress is defined by movement toward universal equality rather than white male supremacist hierarchy.

In a journal passage written in 1844, relatively early in the ramping up of an emboldened slave power, Emerson argues against the nativists who sought to define a national identity based on ethnic origins. Rather than linking American identity to Anglo-Saxon racial purity, Emerson proposes indiscriminate ethnic and racial combination as a means of transforming the "pale diluted stream" of American "blood" that could make a Daniel Webster but not a Thomas Carlyle:

> I hate the narrowness of the Native American party. It is the dog in the manger. It is precisely opposite to all the dictates of love & magnanimity: & therefore, of course, the opposite of wisdom. It is the result of science that the highest simplicity of structure is produced, not by few elements, but by the highest complexity. Man is the most composite of all creatures, the wheel-insect, *volvox globator*, is at the beginning. Well, as in the old burning of the Temple at Corinth, by the melting & intermixture of silver & gold & other metals, a new compound more precious than any, called the Corinthian brass, was formed so in this Continent,—asylum of all nations, the energy of Irish, Germans, Swedes, Poles, & Cossacks, & all the European tribes,—of the Africans, & of the Polynesians, will construct a new race, a new religion, a new State, a new literature, which will be as vigorous as the new Europe which came out of the smelting pot of the Dark Ages, or that which earlier emerged from Pelasgic & Etruscan barbarism. (*JMN* 9:299–300)

Writing here vigorously and in pique, almost certainly in response to something he had read in the popular press, Emerson responds to the nativists with the same reflexive scorn he had directed at Democratic operative Cyrus Stowe, who "respected only numbers" as the legitimate use of democratic equality (*JMN* 7:99). The idea of linking the rights of citizenship to heritage incites Emerson to interweave historical allusion, scientific description, and demographic argumentation, all of which culminates in the emergence of a new race and culture. He momentarily hesitates in his inclusiveness, listing European ethnicities that all fall within the polygenesists' category of European or Caucasian: Germans, Swedes, et cetera, even the Irish, restocking the old English and Scottish bloodlines. But then, with his hesitation at the promiscuity of incorporating other races set off by a comma and a dash, he decides even to include Africans and Pacific Islanders in the "composite" that will "construct a new race." This brief rant is of a piece with his assimilationist stance in the Indian removal crisis.

In his view, the narrowness of the nativist party, a narrowness that seeks to establish an American race by insulating "American" bloodlines, works against the order of nature. Rather than seeking purity, nature progresses by "melting & intermixture," reaching toward continually new combinations.

To parallel this evolutionary process, Emerson slides race toward culture as ethnic and racial combinations create new worship, politics, and literature. This direction follows modern natural history as well as the demands of "love & magnanimity." The new people who emerge from this process will be analogous to the alloy that emerged from the burning of the temple at Corinth.

Ironically, even as he spouts manifest destiny/melting pot nationalism, he is unambiguous in his assumption that the combination and intermixture of diverse elements trump racial purity as both a natural fact and a value. It may be, Emerson argues, that Anglo-Saxons dominate the world. But if the history of civilization proves anything, it is that racial preeminence is a temporary state and is always on the defensive. It is a question much truer to history, as Emerson understood it, to ask: What will come next? What is over the horizon? Just as he remarks in the 1844 "Politics" essay that civil laws are mere political "memoranda" always subject to revision, so race is a cultural memorandum and subject to revision, and even to improvement.[47] All races represent raw materials that are waiting to be transformed (CW 6:26). In the context of his assumption about continual transformation, Emerson's anthropological categories of race and nationality retain a highly provisional quality. As he had put it in "The Young American": "Remark the unceasing effort throughout nature at somewhat better than the actual creatures: *amelioration in nature*, which alone permits and authorizes amelioration in mankind. The population of the world is a conditional population; These are not the best, but the best that could live in the existing state of soils, gasses, animals, and morals; the best that could *yet* live; there shall be a better, please God" (*CW* 1:230–31). Or, reiterating his argument in "Fate," using the same terms he had in "The Young American," he brings the contradictions between his own white supremacism and his aspirational egalitarianism directly into the essay:

> The face of the planet cools and dries, the races meliorate, and man is born. But when a race has lived its term, it comes no more again.
> The population of the world is a conditional population; not the best, but the best that could live now. (*CW* 6:21)

Emerson never wavers in his antislavery. But his attitude toward racial equality is more complex. Following the standards of contemporary natural history and ethnography, he slides back and forth between what are today more clearly distinguished sociological, political, and cultural referents. The only frame that fully contains his thought about "melting & intermixture" or of hierarchy in the diverse "population of the world" is stasis versus mutability. Within this frame, his deepest reflex is to project continual transformation as a principle and a necessity. His thought is also defined by an aspirational utopianism which usually implies that transformation results in growth or improvement. The possibility of equality is there, and in his view, it must be the aspirational goal of humankind.

To prepare his 1844 address on emancipation in the British West Indies, Emerson studied the history of slavery, and this research brought about an important change in his sensibility because it motivated him to add his voice to the ranks of antislavery activists. This new public commitment shows not only an antislavery "conversion" but also a desire to rethink the obstacles to the progressive changes that could make his society more decent and humane.[48] As this strain of thinking develops, the question that underpins his thought shifts from a spiritual question—How can one live in harmony with Spirit?—to a contextual question: What are the forces that thwart Spirit's influence in the world? Beginning with his emancipation address, the long history of shameless racial exploitation and bald-faced hypocrisy in religious and political discourse amplified Emerson's interest in the historical forces that shaped the trajectory of equality. His attention moved beyond the Transcendentalist's focus on the powers of the self and even the moral suasionist's effort to change the world one soul at a time. His study of the history of slavery made him attentive to modes of exploitation that are intentionally reproduced generation after generation. By turning from a focus on science and ethnology to a focus on history and politics, Emerson begins to see the place of slavery in the assault on equality in a very different light.

The hypocrisy and insincerity of proslavery rhetoric provoked some of his most emphatic egalitarian statements. In the period of alternating anger, despondence, and combative hopefulness that followed the 1850 passage of the Fugitive Slave Law, Emerson confides in his journal:

> These thirty nations [the US states] are equal to any work. They are to become 50 millions presently & should achieve something just & generous. For the future of slavery is not inviting. But the destinies of nations are too great for our spanning & what are the instruments no policy can show[,] whether Liberia, whether flax[,] cotton, whether the working them out by Irish & Germans none can tell . . . by what scourges God has guarded his law. But one thing is imperative[:] not to do unjustly, not to steal a man, or help steal him, or to call stealing honest. (*JMN* 11:407)

In this passage he by and large reiterates the substance of his ruminations in the 1830s, when he first addresses race in his journals—except that the tone is much more fierce. The end of this entry is especially revealing because Emerson's assertion of personal ethics was added at a later date as a means of asserting an imperative that conflicted with the responsibilities that the Fugitive Slave Law imposed on him. In its determination to enforce an individual discipline, this emendation echoes comments Emerson was making as early as 1835: "I pray God that not even in my dream or in madness may I ever incur the disgrace of articulating one word of apology for the slave trader or slave-holder" (*JMN* 5:15). But these steely private vows do not mean that he would refuse to echo the most degrading assumptions of the polygenesists. A comment from 1840 reveals his reflexive white supremacy and shows how deeply the terms of natural history influenced his thought and his own sense of place in an evolutionary history. Extending the analysis of a topic he had raised before, Emerson makes vivid this conflict within his egalitarianism. He writes: "The negro must be very old & belongs, one would say, to the fossil formations. What right has he to be intruding into the late & civil daylight of this dynasty of Caucasians & Saxons? It is plain that so inferior a race must perish shortly like the poor Indians." And he goes on to say as part of the same entry: "Yet pity for these was needed, it seems, for the education of this generation in ethics. Our good world cannot learn the beauty of love in narrow circles & at home in the immense Heart, but it must be stimulated by somewhat foreign & monstrous, by the simular man of Ethiopia" (*JMN* 7:393).

In characterizing the African as a "simular man," Emerson cites the principle that allowed his cosmopolitan egalitarianism to stand alongside his Anglo-Saxonist supremacism. Although the "Ethiopian" in this entry is trapped in a condition of simulation, Emerson assumes that the same is true of all people and all races. In 1845 he notes: "Well & it seems there is room for a better species of the genus homo. The Caucasian is an arrested undertype" (*JMN* 9:212). The best example he offers of this condition is Daniel Webster. In his 1851 speech on the Fugitive Slave Act, he argues that in defending the law, Webster "crossed the line, and became the head of the slavery party in this country." He gestures at an explanation, speculating that "Mr. Webster perhaps is only following the laws of his blood and constitution" (*AW* 66). He uses the same language a few years later when he asserts that even though "Mr. Webster had a natural ascendancy of aspect and carriage," his failure to defend the right to liberty proved a general point: "You cannot rely on any man for the defense of truth who is not constitutionally, or by blood and temperament, on that side" (*AW* 75).

Emerson's emphasis on progressive combination and transformation ascending from simulation to an authenticity that has not "*yet*" been achieved defines an important context for Emerson's racism. He feels a racial hierarchy and believes in it, but he nonetheless also believes that persons, African or British or American, black or white, all embody simular man.

Despite their assumption of racial malleability, in their white supremacist dehumanization of Africans, these are the most damning lines in all of Emerson's journals and lectures. They not only embrace the degradation of Africans but also position Africa's people as the literal antithesis of love and home. In the onward progress of combination, in this particular moment, Emerson does not restrain the racist impulse to see Africans as "foreign & monstrous." Their enslavement is a lesson in ethics for "Caucasians & Saxons." Antislavery, rather than the progress of justice, becomes an education in pity for himself and those he considers his racial equals. It is almost as if he is projecting into the future a time after "this generation" when a more cosmopolitan identity better understands "the beauty of love" by recognizing equality outside the narrow circle of the familiar.

The necessity of racial transformation that permits Emerson to see an evolutionary narrative of moral progress embedded in natural history is similar to the cosmopolitan transformation he anticipates in the "Address on Emancipation in the British West Indies." This address represents Emerson's most sustained analysis of the relationship between racism and history. His narrative of natural history, which distinguishes between "very old" races and the present "dynasty" of Caucasians, defines his reading of racial progress. It presents both his white supremacist assumptions and his validation of universal liberty as a step toward universal cosmopolitan egalitarianism.

Writing a few years earlier, in "Self-Reliance," he had dismissed the "angry bigot" who came to update him on "the latest news" from the West Indies with some tart advice: "Go love thy infant: love thy woodchopper; be good-natured and modest; have that grace; and never varnish your hard uncharitable ambition with this incredible tenderness for black folks a thousand miles off" (*CW* 2:30). His visceral disgust with the cosmopolitan philanthropist who loves the idea of humanity but cannot see suffering in his immediate surroundings mirrors Charles Dickens's attitude toward his character Mrs. Jellyby in *Bleak House*, whose eyes could focus on nothing closer than Africa.

But in preparation for the 1844 address on emancipation, Emerson put himself through a program of reading that compelled him to recognize that West Indian slaves were indeed his own woodchoppers and that the veils of distance between Concord and Ethiopia did not change the intimacy of the connection between New England's wealth and Caribbean slavery. Emerson details his own recent education on the topic, sketching the global network of slave transportation and exploitation that linked Europe, Africa, the Caribbean, and the United States. He underscores the historical evolution of slavery and the slave trade, highlighting the distances between sites of exploitation in Africa and the West Indies and the sites in which slave produce is consumed. He also underscores the way those distances obscure the brutality of a global society reliant on slavery.[49]

As he summarizes the British antislavery campaign that culminated in the illegalization of slavery in Britain's West Indian colonies, Emerson returns to the ground of the Cherokee removals and describes a cultural dialogue about the boundaries of human rights. Whereas the context of his letter to Martin Van Buren was the removals crisis, which he saw as a disgrace to his identity as a citizen of the United States, the emancipation address faces slavery explicitly and self-consciously in the context of a global movement to advance a universalized standard of human rights. It shows a cosmopolitan perspective emerging from a national one. Emancipation in the British West Indies is not just an expression of British virtue but a turning point in world civilization. It marks the possibility of a new and higher standard of civility for the world as a whole.

As a newly defined norm articulated by the world's most powerful nation, Great Britain, the liberation of slaves in the West Indies had important implications for the relative moral stature of the United States. Emerson juxtaposes his sense of national shame against the achievement of the British by confessing, "Whilst I have read of England, I have thought of New England." As he "walked in the pastures and along the edge of the woods," he was trying to keep mental company with the British activists and politicians, the "patriots and senators who have adopted the slave's cause." Given the company he must keep as an American, he feels that the British antislavery heroes reject him. In his thoughts, "—they turned their backs on me," he says (*AW* 23).[50] As he was quick to recognize, the British Empire had adopted a standard of human rights that shamed the United States as a barbaric society resisting progress toward a new standard of cosmopolitan equality. Using the word "Africa" as a metaphor for the African diaspora, Emerson laments that regardless of what his countrymen tell themselves, the implication for progress is both clear and global: "America is not civil whilst Africa is barbarous" (*AW* 31).[51]

In the context of the global antislavery movement, Emerson's shaming the United States has a clear egalitarian function. To open the address, Emerson situates West Indian emancipation in a progressive narrative of expanding civility: "We are met to exchange congratulations on the anniversary of an event singular in the history of civilization; a day of reason; of the clear light; of that which makes us better than a flock of birds and beasts: a day, which gives the immense fortification of a fact,—of gross history,—to ethical abstractions" (*AW* 7). For the British to have achieved a peaceful end to slavery in their West Indian colonies rewards not just the decades of labor by antislavery activists, and not just the ability of deliberative government to achieve major reforms; most importantly, it validates a cosmopolitan idea of humanity. It is a "singular" event, a clear break with tradition in the name of the most humane standard of reason. Speaking at an American commemoration, Emerson underscores his sense that this acknowledgment of the right to liberty is not just a decision made by one government but an event that makes the idea that "all men are created equal" something more than just "glittering and sounding generalities." His first point is that emancipation is like the structure of a fort. It is solid and defensible. The possibility of universal emancipation now has a new rampart, a fact, a "gross history" that can be weighed and measured. It makes the possibility he speaks for easier to defend and harder to attack. The ability of the British to give up slavery and of the emancipated slaves not to claim their right to blood vengeance embodied equality winning out against a human condition where raw domination had been the norm since prehistory.

Later in the essay, Emerson refers to his opening observation that emancipation was a "singular" event in "the history of civilization": "I said, this event is signal in the history of civilization" (*AW* 19). In the shift from "singular" to "signal," Emerson reorients global antislavery to emphasize the direction it sets for the future. Despite its idealism, what makes the event a signal directing future change emerges out of Emerson's own racist construction of culture and civility. It underscores the limitation of his own ability to recognize the equality of liberated Afro-Caribbeans. What strikes him as a portent of the future is not just that the Africans' right to liberty was recognized by the empire; Emancipation was a signal event because it "came mainly from the concession of the whites" (*AW* 30). The British Empire, surely, was powerful enough to maintain slavery by force. But in Emerson's analysis, emancipation embodied a kind of moral learning *by the British*. For their part, the terms of emancipation were disappointing to many British abolitionists. West Indian freed persons were required to work as "apprentices" for six years, for nominal pay; refusal to work was punishable by whipping. Slaveholders also received compensation under the terms of the Emancipation Act.[52]

In the narrative of civil, or even constitutional, progress that he anticipates, "one feels very sensibly in all this history that a great heart and soul are behind there, superior to any man, and making use of each in turn, and infinitely attractive to every person according to the degree of reason in his own mind" (*AW* 26–27). This is the direct action of Spirit, the "opening of human doors," as he puts it in "The Divinity School Address." Emerson does not attribute emancipation to the inherent qualities of the English "race"; neither does he attribute it to the insight of a specific hero or poet. Even in noting that it represents the work of a "great heart and soul," he adapts the terms of the "immense Heart" evolved by the doomed and miserable simular man he had remarked four years earlier. The evolution of humankind toward cosmopolitan racial equality here takes the form of a universal ethical ideal working its way into the consciousness of the British people until at last it takes hold and expresses itself as positive law. That kind of change was possible. Yet, as he wrote, the direction of the future hung in the balance, and his own countrymen were well into the process of doing the opposite by mocking equality and expanding slavery.

Equally important to what he sees as the "concession" of the British, Emerson stands amazed at the restraint of the freedmen. The "civility" with which they celebrated their liberation underscores Emerson's sense that this emancipation marks the dawn of a new era. He quotes the report of the governor of Jamaica: "It is impossible for me to do justice to the good order, decorum, and gratitude which the whole laboring population manifested on that happy occasion. Though joy beamed on every countenance, it was throughout tempered with solemn thankfulness to God" (*AW* 18). The pious humility of this response strikes Emerson as important because it was counterintuitive and thus embodied an "idea" that might herald a peaceful, just, multiracial society. A vengeful race war would have represented a completely understandable expression of hatred. But the impossible peacefulness with which the wronged people greeted their independence spoke, to Emerson, of something transcendent. He awkwardly welcomes this new idea as a great event in the domestication of culture: "The first of August marks the entrance of a new element into modern politics, namely, the civilization of the negro. A man is added to the human family. Not the least affecting part of this history of abolition, is the annihilation of the old indecent nonsense about the nature of the negro" (*AW* 29). The awkwardness of these lines, and Emerson's own inescapable racism, gets more palpable as he describes a historical anthem as his version of adding a new voice to the choir of civilized peoples:

> I esteem the occasion of this jubilee to be the proud discovery, that the black race can contend with the white; that in the great anthem which we call history, a piece of many parts and vast compass, after playing a long time a very low and subdued accompaniment, they perceive the time arrived when they can strike in with effect, and take a master's part in the music. The civility of the world has reached that pitch, that their more moral genius is becoming indispensable, and the quality of this race is to be honored for itself. (*AW* 31)

Emerson's intention here is praiseworthy. He wants to mark the instantiation of a new identity for former slaves as an event that defines a new era in the civility of the world. In doing so he constructs a metaphor that recognizes difference while also attaching honor, even mastery, to "the black race." From his point of view, the generosity with which the West Indies' slaves greeted liberation is Africa's first solo performance in the progress of civilization.

But aside from his dismissal of "the old indecent nonsense about the nature of the negro," who would quote this passage to demonstrate Emerson's commitment to equality? Doesn't it assume that as reason slowly enlightened the British slave owners, the "more moral genius" of the West Indian slaves was learning piety, humility, and forgiveness? Describing the murderous history of slavery on sugar plantations as a "low and subdued accompaniment" in the anthem of history trivializes the very degradation that he was describing a moment earlier. Emerson's voice here is also so awkward because he is speaking in the idiom of natural history rather than his own idiom of individuality-centered egalitarianism. History is a "great anthem" in which different races have had more and less prestigious parts to perform. After centuries in the back rows, Africans can now stand downstage in the glow of the footlights and sing alongside the "master" singers?

In contrast to this clumsy effort to capture the importance of a successful antislavery campaign, Emerson speaks with conviction when he describes a universalized model of humanity represented not by groups but by individuals. As he puts it: "The arrival in the world of such men as Toussaint [Louverture] and the Haytian heroes, or of the leaders of their race in Barbadoes and Jamaica, outweighs in good omen all the English and American humanity. The anti-slavery of the whole world, is dust in the balance before this,—is a poor squeamishness and nervousness: the might and right are here: here is the antislave: here is man: and if you have man, black or white is an insignificance" (*AW* 31). Far from being simular, this is the idea of cosmopolitan humanity realized in actual, distinct individuals. In the broadest sense these "heroes" and "leaders" represent an aspirational equality toward which all could aim.[53]

Where the cosmopolitan strain of Emerson's thought underscores the universalizing dimension of his egalitarianism, what is most important for the relationship between Emerson's attentiveness to antebellum ethnography and his defense of equality is the way racist science boomeranged to strengthen both his belief in equality and his conviction that sincere communication was at its foundation. As he was in the process of rejecting racial purity as a standard for assessing human potential, let alone as a guiding principle for civil justice, he came to see the hypocrisy and political intimidation that linked racist ethnography to the debate over slavery through a lens of contempt that caused him to grow every bit as appalled and frustrated as Abraham Lincoln became in the late 1850s. He began to see proslavery science and proslavery rhetoric less as sincere voices in a dialogue aimed at advancing knowledge and more as a cynical political alliance of pseudoscientists and bankrupt politicians intent on advancing the interests of slavery no matter what; and the protection of slavery meant refuting the idea that equality was either good or possible.

THE ASSAULT ON EQUALITY AND PUBLIC SINCERITY

Race had entered Emerson's thought as a consistent thread in the mid-1830s. It occurs just as William Lloyd Garrison's *Liberator* was raising the profile of immediate abolitionism and the defenders of slavery were changing their voice in the aftermath of the Nat Turner rebellion. At the same time, the defenders of slavery were beginning to push hard against equality as a value. The post–Nat Turner defense of slavery came as a surprise, even to many defenders of the institution. The slave rebellion led by Turner, a charismatic lay preacher, killed up to sixty-five whites in Southampton, Virginia, in August 1831. In its immediate aftermath, many assumed the rebellion finally confirmed that slavery was too volatile to sustain, and that Virginia would follow neighboring states and adopt a plan for gradual manumission. But the Virginians went in the opposite direction. Beginning with discussion of the rebellion in the Virginia legislature's 1831–32 session, the slave states began to pivot away from an apologetic stance and toward an intensive defense of slavery as a "positive good." The legislators of Virginia decided to strengthen the power of slaveholders and amplified the state's control over the manumission of slaves.

Following the debate in the legislature, Thomas R. Dew, president of the College of William & Mary in Williamsburg, Virginia, published his "Essay in Favor of Slavery," in which he defended the institution in positive terms. It is a crucial document in the assault on equality. Dew's essay was published in the Philadelphia-based *American Quarterly Review* and then widely circulated as a pamphlet. He argues that the very inequality of the slave system promotes virtue among its members and exemplifies a humane community. He describes a system that fosters love through a hierarchy of duties and obligations. In his telling, the master–slave relationship becomes a counterpart of familial affection: "There is nothing but the mere relations of husband and wife, parent and child, brother and sister, which produces a closer tie, than the relation of master and servant." Each of these, Dew emphasizes, represents a relationship in which one partner is subordinate and obliged to obey, and the other has an equal moral duty to be benevolent and generous. Far from being subjected to a "degrading submission," as Thomas Jefferson claimed, the slave is accustomed to look at his or her master as a "supporter, director, and defender."[54]

This duty of submission is grounded in inherent differences analogous to humans' inferiority to God. White people, Dew argues, "might rather die than be the obscure slave that waits at our back." Yet happy in his station, the slave has a different motivation: "His ambition is to excel all his fellow slaves in the performance of his servile duties." Should the *"wily philanthropist"* whisper "into the ears of such a slave" that he is equal and should be free, he would be reenacting the crime of the "serpent that entered the garden of Eden" and destroyed Paradise. In regard to the fulfillment offered by slave society to all its members, Dew holds, "We have no doubt but that [the slaves] form the happiest portion of our society. A merrier being does not exist on the face of the globe than the negro slave of the United States."[55]

Dew's analysis is important because it introduced a new agenda that became the most important front in the assault on equality. In quick order, Dew's "Essay in Favor of Slavery" became a handbook of arguments in defense of slave society. Desire for such a defense was strong enough that shortly after its publication, the Calhounite *United States Telegraph* argued that it was time for slaveholders to abandon all the "cant" about the evils of slavery and begin to defend rather than apologize for the institution.[56] In 1837, in response to a speech by John Quincy Adams against the gag rule that tabled antislavery petitions in Congress, John C. Calhoun, then a representative from South Carolina, gave a speech defending the gag rule and framing slavery as beneficial. "I hold," Calhoun maintained, "that in the present state of civilization, where two races of different origin, and distinguished by color, and other physical differences, as well as intellectual, are brought together, the relation now existing in the slaveholding States between the two, is, instead of an evil, a good—a positive good."[57]

An entry in Emerson's journal from about a year before Calhoun's speech makes vivid just how difficult it was for Emerson and many of his white contemporaries to separate ideas about race from the fact of slavery. His notes also demonstrate how little the millennia-long history of legal slavery had done to legitimize the institution in his eyes. As he writes, respect for an idealistic assumption about equality of capabilities and, therefore, for the justice of equality of opportunity competes with equally reflexive assumptions about the racial superiority of whites. Writing, probably in early 1836, in one of the notebooks he used to organize thoughts for lectures, he jots down some scattered notes on race and slavery that engage racial equality, political equality, regional identity, equality of access to public speech, and even equality of respect. He makes a series of rough notes in outline form as if he is trying to orient himself to a question he had not yet thought about with any seriousness:

Duty to us
Duty to Negro
Practicability
Slavery
    Wholly iniquitous
    Self destructive
    A dreadful reagent

The Abolitionist; his plan
> To awaken the conscience

Its aspect to us
> A question for discussion
> A question for action
>> For New England
> Importance of discussion
> The vote & the assertion of his right
> Beyond this I do not feel a call to act
> Nearer duties (*JMN* 12:151–52)

In these notes Emerson moves away from a focus on race and slavery to address his sense of the abolitionist's effort to awaken the conscience in favor of abolition. He talks of duty self-reflexively, in terms of his obligations to himself. He also talks about it in terms of duty not to support the enslaved but to defend the rights of the abolitionists who had been active in New England. He asserts a personal responsibility to defend the activist's right of public speech and commits to vote only for antislavery candidates. Then, however, he tries to draw a line that limits his personal obligation to speak alongside the abolitionists by noting that while total devotion to antislavery may be the calling of full-time abolitionists like Garrison, he had "nearer duties." In other words, he faces slavery only to compartmentalize it and then move on to things he cares more about. But as the entry goes on, he is unable to put slavery out of mind. He immediately begins to enumerate "the present aspects of the Slavery Question," in which he defines two responsibilities: first, a civic obligation "to open our halls to the discussion" of "the new value of the private man"; and second, he condescendingly defines a personal obligation to serve as an ally of his "fellow man the Slave":

> We are to assert his right in all companies
> An amiable joyous race who for ages have not been permitted to unfold their natural powers we are to befriend. (*JMN* 12:152)

He briefly looks back at the ancient history of enslavement and sees it in terms of stolen opportunity. The rhetoric of this passage is subtle. Emerson recognizes equality at a foundational level by linking personal duty to assert the slave's natural right to liberty "in all companies." Implicitly equal, at least in that one sense, the enslaved have had their natural powers suppressed by violence in ways that free people had not. When he makes this connection, he is speaking the cosmopolitan language of universal human rights. The path that leads him to this conclusion opens with a general defense of free speech and a claim that the rise of individual rights, of "the new value of the private man" embodied by the expansion of democracy, functions as a form of antislavery activism because it asserts the equal right of all persons to act as free agents in the world. This leads him to recognize a personal responsibility to assert the slaves' equal right to the opportunity to "unfold their natural powers."

But this recognition of civil standards, of his own criteria for casting his vote, of the abolitionists' right to free speech, and of the fact that African Americans have had their "natural powers" suppressed is as far as he goes in asserting the equality of enslaved black persons. The whole passage, written probably within a year of Frederick Douglass's escape from slavery, is abstract and hypothetical. At the time of writing, Emerson feels no imminent presence of degradation. He amplifies the fact of his distance from personal friendship or more than transactional acquaintance with any Africans or African Americans by finally putting the issue to rest.[58] He may have a duty to defend the rights of abolitionists and slaves when slavery comes up in conversation, but it is more or less a passive ethical responsibility. In the 1830s he seems to feel there is a firewall of culture between Concord, where he lives, and the slave states.

In the last section of this entry, his thinking takes one more turn. Rather than following the line of thought that begins with the cosmopolitan assertion of equality, Emerson ends this reflection on race and enslavement with a remark that echoes the ethnographic mapping of the polygenesists: "I think it cannot be maintained by any candid person that the African race have ever occupied or do promise ever to occupy any very high place in the human family. Their present condition is the strongest proof that they cannot. The Irish cannot; the American Indian cannot; the Chinese cannot. Before the energy of the Caucasian race all the other races have quailed and done obeisance" (*JMN* 12:152). The twists and turns of this journal entry are representative of many patterns in Emerson's thought and in antebellum American thought more generally. When Emerson is thinking about slavery and racial domination in philosophical terms, imagining individuals as generic but singular human beings, he invariably argues for equality. But when he addresses the world as a polyglot set of races and cultures, he adopts the tropes of white supremacy.[59] When he shifts away from the individual person to look at race through the lens of ethnography, he sees natural history more like an inevitably genocidal force rather than a force that gives momentum to Spirit's cosmopolitan egalitarianism. When he is thinking in terms of race rather than persons, he assumes that history is a brutal competition among races in a winner-take-all evolutionary process. This line of thought even allows Emerson to envision racial succession as a progressive structure similar to that which enabled civil society to progress from tribe to kingdom, empire, republic, and finally to democracy. He describes this progression in his essay "History." Even in his 1844 antislavery speech commemorating emancipation in the British West Indies, he articulates a race-against-race competition for survival: "If the black man is feeble and not important to the existing races, not on a parity with the best race, he must serve, and be exterminated. But if the black man carries in his bosom an indispensable element of a new and coming civilization, for the sake of that element, he will survive and play his part" (*AW* 31). These lines are especially striking because they divest the perpetrators of responsibility for the conditions under which "the black man" has lived. Emerson implies that the "black race" must stand the test of natural history, while members of other races passively observe the success or failure of Africans' struggles. The quick moves from perspective to perspective in this journal entry reveal the competing civil and scientific discourses that structured the antebellum debate over racial equality. Emerson asserts his personal conviction that a standard of universal equality is both good and inevitable, but he then scoffs at the idea that non-Caucasians could ever take advantage of the very equality he had just recognized. This tension between egalitarian principles and racist impulses was not unusual among white antislavery activists. Frederick Douglass moved to Rochester, New York, to start his career as an editor largely to get away from the racist condescension of the Garrisonians.[60] Louis Agassiz was both intensely racist and emphatically antislavery; so was Abraham Lincoln.[61]

Theodore Parker is a good example of the tension between a principled commitment to equality and a tendency to accept the claims of an anthropology that assumes racial hierarchy. Despite his idealistic optimism, his abolitionism, and his advocacy of workers' rights, Parker believed that profound differences in natural ability distinguished the races. He expresses his sense of the differences among races as he opposes the Mexican-American War.

In one of his sermons on the war, Parker predicts that "before many years, all of this Northern Continent will be in the hands of the Anglo-Saxon race. That of itself is not a thing to mourn at. Could we have extended our empire there by trade, by the Christian arts of peace, it would be a blessing to us and to Mexico; a blessing to the world."[62] The industriousness of Anglo-Saxon immigrants to North America, Parker holds, represents a boon that will inevitably subjugate the Indigenous-African-Iberian peoples of Central America. This "energy," as Emerson had characterized the same racial difference, will compel the Mexicans to "quail and do obeisance." Parker's objection to the war has nothing to do with Mexicans' rights to self-determination. It is a purely technical question of process. Racial domination by Anglo-Saxons is inevitable, but racial domination should be achieved by trade relations that culminate in the peaceful transfer of property and power from Mexican to Yankee. Parker's only complaint is that the United States was forcing the transfer at the point of a gun. It is especially striking that Parker uses the word "hands" to express domination here, because one of his most powerful essays on workers' rights revolves around the degradation of working people to the mere "hands" of industry.[63] In his pioneering work *Race and Manifest Destiny*, Reginald Horsman treats Parker as a kind of test case for the shift from eighteenth-century universalist cosmopolitanism toward the scientific racism promoted by the polygenesists. Comparing Emerson and Parker, Horsman concludes that "far more than Emerson, Parker was willing to think in broad terms of superior and inferior races with specific characteristics."[64] When this ethnographic point of view enters his thinking, it leads him to question the possibility of equality.

Despite the hold that white supremacism had on his generation of educated whites, Emerson consistently moves toward the belief that greed and sadism, not nature, are at the root of racial inequality in America. Still, the chauvinistic bigotry of his comments on the Africans, Irish, Indigenous Americans, and Chinese stand in sharp contrast to the racial egalitarianism he expresses four pages farther on in the same notebook. Thinking not of scientific categories but of social relationships, Emerson reverses the implications of recent claims by natural historians for the validity of scientific racism: "Is it thought that there is a race of beings in this earth[,] an exception to all which we have yet found in nature, one, namely, whose existence cannot be maintained except by another's usurping its independence: except by crime?" (*JMN* 12:151–53). The idea that Africans *need* slavery, or that it is natural and good—a bedrock claim in the post–Nat Turner defense of the institution—strikes Emerson as absurd, even insulting in its cynicism.

Despite his participation in the language of Anglo-Saxonist racial superiority, his sense that slavery was a crime never wavers, nor does his advocacy of change toward greater racial and social equality. What does change, though, is his attitude toward the broad range of voices that were promoting inequality. Rather than accepting that, especially in politics, anti-egalitarian and proslavery voices were sincere in their claims, Emerson increasingly came to see scientific racism and proslavery politics as cynical and intentional hypocrisies meant to manufacture legitimacy for something everyone knew to be degradation, exploitation, torture, and theft.

Emerson was in his late twenties at the time of the Nat Turner rebellion. It is possible that the early denunciations of slavery in his journals were reactions to the new and more assertive defenses of slavery derived from Dew and Calhoun. Along with many others, by the time of the Kansas-Nebraska Act twenty-four years later, it came to be his sense that the rhetorical defense of slavery had become a nearly perfect example of hypocritical cynicism. It exemplified what German social theorist Jürgen Habermas defined as "strategically distorted communication"—a systematic effort to recode key terms so that they suppress understanding of a speaker's true intentions. It reflects the rhetorical strategy of a secret or hidden agenda.[65] By the time Emerson delivered his addresses on the Fugitive Slave Law in 1851 and 1854, he had felt the defense of slavery ratchet up in strength and confidence through the secession crisis of 1832, the Fugitive Slave Law and the rendition of Anthony Burns, and the Kansas-Nebraska debate. A few years into the future, the *Dred Scott* decision by the Supreme Court would give the coup de grâce and effectively nationalize slavery. All these were supported by the scientific-political campaign to redefine slavery as a positive good.

In his second essay on the Fugitive Slave Law (1854), delivered in the wake of Kansas-Nebraska, Emerson characterizes the change in aspect of proslavery public discourse. He and Lidian traveled to New York, where he delivered the address on the fourth anniversary of Webster's March 7, 1850, speech supporting the bill that included the Fugitive Slave Law. Much of Emerson's address is about the rhetoric of Webster's speech. Looking back to that speech as an inflection point in American public discourse, Emerson remarks that in 1850, "Mr. Webster decided for slavery. And *that* when the aspect of the institution was no longer doubtful, no longer feeble and apologetic, and proposing soon to end itself, but when it was strong and aggressive and threatening an illimitable increase" (*AW* 78). To Emerson, the event of Webster's betrayal marked the fall of a potential rhetorical bulwark against the expansion of slavery. Webster's sophistry had not only given an aura of patriotism to northern acceptance of an emboldened slave power but also offered a model for the intentional and cynical corruption of public speech.

By 1854, the rhetorical distortions Webster sanctioned had become entrenched. They threatened to redefine the meaning of ideas such as "Union" and "patriotism." In the damage it could do, it sent chills down the spines of those working to preserve integrity in public dialogue, which was the lifeblood of an egalitarian public sphere. On the timeline Emerson describes, beginning with Webster's speech, the possibility of developing a more sincere public dialogue, a more dignified model of democratic citizenship, and a more equal society was diverted toward the suppression of antislavery public speech. Webster's speech undermined the very ground on which Emerson's own defense of equality was built. Without sincerity, there could be no aspirational vision or leveling upwards toward equality. If the meanings of words were all inverted, universalization meant universally accepting hierarchies of domination and submission rather than the universalization of aspiration to broader and more inclusive recognition of equality. By 1856, the redefined meaning of patriotism would allow a senator from Massachusetts, a man who was also a renowned constitutional scholar, Rufus Choate, to advise responsible voters to treat the human rights universalism of the Declaration of Independence as something trite and ephemeral.

Instead of speaking the plain truth about slavery, even if it was moderated for the Senate and less incendiary than that of Theodore Weld or Frederick Douglass, Webster could still have explained the price so much of the country—and so much of Massachusetts—felt it was paying for slavery. Instead, Webster gave a speech that made biting one's tongue and consciously lying an act of patriotism. Sincerity was even coded as sedition. "Opposition" to the new law, Emerson reminds us, "was sharply called *treason* by Webster and prosecuted so. He told the people at Boston that 'they must conquer their prejudices,' that 'agitation on the subject of slavery must be suppressed'" (*AW* 79). By 1854, for Emerson, everything had changed, and he felt no "nearer duties" than lending his voice to the project of ending slavery. To steer back toward that goal, the strategic distortion of basic terms would have to be called out and identified as the weapons they had been turned into as part of the assault on equality.

In his rhetorical analysis of Webster's March 7, 1850, speech, Emerson focuses on the waves of hypocrisy that were dictating the nation's priorities. Webster, "the most American man in America," had told his countrymen "that slavery was now at that strength that they must beat down their conscience and become kidnappers for it" (*AW* 78). It would have been one thing if Webster had made his speech, and it had effervesced and then been forgotten. But that's not what happened. The consequence that Emerson brings into focus is its impact on the integrity of public bodies of all sorts and on their potential influence over the citizenry. Webster's defense of the Fugitive Slave Act was allowing other deliberative bodies to cultivate rhetorical illusions that defined crime as a high virtue:

> The end for which man was made is not stealing, nor crime in any form. And a man cannot steal, without incurring all the penalties of the thief; no, though all the legislatures vote that it is virtuous, and though there be a conspiracy among scholars and official persons to hold him up, and to say, *Nothing is good but stealing.* A man who commits a crime defeats the end of his existence. He was created for benefit, and he exists for harm. (*AW* 84)

He is specifically talking here about the logic of "patriotic" speech that follows Webster's example of inversion: The Fugitive Slave Law will help to preserve the Union; the Union is good; therefore you are virtuous when you defend the Fugitive Slave Law. The "him" in Emerson's phrase "hold him up" here refers to the thief or criminal. Emerson buries Webster by arguing that the effect of his defense of slavery was to "hold . . . up" the lying, thieving criminal as a new George Washington, worthy of being put on a pedestal, worthy of statues, because affirmation of his actions by legislatures, scholars, and government officials had made the criminal into the savior of the Union.

In his first speech on the Fugitive Slave Law, the "Address to the Citizens of Concord," delivered in May 1851, Emerson had gloated prematurely over the government's inability to shut down criticism of the law: "Mr. Webster's measure was, he told us, final. It was a pacification, it was a suppression, a measure of conciliation and adjustment. These were his words at different times: 'there was to be no parleying more'; it was 'irrepealable.' Does it look final now?"

(*AW* 63–64). On the contrary, when it was passed, Emerson believed that the passage of the law had "dislocated the foundations" of northern trust in government and would lead to an organic reassertion of faith in equality. The demands the law placed on northerners would surely be rejected. The Fugitive Slave Law was so egregious that "it has been like a university to the entire people," Emerson continues. "It has turned every dinner-table into a debating club." At this point, he trusts the people to turn the law into a dead letter because the "sentiments" of the people will make its enforcement impossible. No fancy rhetoric, Emerson had believed, could "draw a sponge over" the "crime" that it mandates. The popular press and public opinion will rescue the country: "unless you can suppress the newspaper, pass a law against bookshops, gag the English tongue, all short of this is futile" in the effort to justify the law in the mind of the people (*AW* 61). Already he finds the distortion of language to be a risk. Looking back over the long span of history, he considers it remarkable that "tyrants" had relatively rarely been able to enact blatantly "immoral" laws; "some color, some indirection, was always used." But here was a statute that openly "enacts the crime of kidnapping" (*AW* 57). Its open criminality will prove its Achilles' heel, dooming it because people's inherent moral sentiments will make it impossible to obey a law that legislates "wrong pure from any mixture of right" (*AW* 57).

But the organic connection between statute law and "higher" law, morality, or natural law proved less potent than Emerson anticipated. As part of the assault on equality, slavery's defenders simply worked to redefine the meaning of key words. In the 1851 address, Emerson is already concerned that intentional insincerity was casting a shadow over the language. He fears that "the names of conscience and religion" will "become bitter ironies, and liberty the ghastly mockery which Mr. Webster means by that word" (*AW* 68).

Toward the end of the 1851 address, as he faces the "question, What shall we do?" he refers to the change that had already taken place in the debate over slavery since the 1830s. He asks: "Since it is agreed by all sane men of all parties (or was yesterday) that slavery is mischievous, why does the South itself not offer the smallest counsel of her own? I have never heard in twenty years any project except" strengthening fugitive slave laws, which perpetuates slavery and implicates the North more deeply in its practice. He can find few reasons to be hopeful. He ticks off meager options that he hardly seems to believe in: compensated emancipation, appeals to religion, economic arguments that slavery is obsolete, Liberia; he even mentions something that seems like Indian Territory in Oklahoma—alluding to the size of "the national domain"—but these pass quickly, and he ends up circling back to the issue of sincerity in public speech as the hill on which opponents must make their stand. He recalls the citizens of Concord to their regional identity and implores them to act with "rectitude," even repeating the term for emphasis. He sums up his proposition for action this way: "Here," in the "fastness" of Concord and Massachusetts, "let us not lie, nor steal, nor help to steal; and let us not call stealing by any fine names, such as 'union' or 'patriotism'" (*AW* 71).

The 1851 speech is preoccupied with criticizing the Fugitive Slave Law and detailing the healthy result a backlash to it might produce. By contrast, the 1854 reprise in New York concentrates on defining the corrosive legacy of Webster's speech and the importance of insulating discussion among "scholars and students" from the trend toward the strategic distortion of basic terms in democratic self-government (*AW* 73–74). Emerson pauses to emphasize that although he is speaking of an elite, he also means "when I say the class of scholars and students,—that is a class which comprises in some sort all mankind,—comprises every man in the best hours of his life" (*AW* 74). He offers a tepid defense of the value of the newspapers, but in contrast to the intensity of his faith in 1851 that open discussion would suffocate the law because "this dreadful English tongue is saturated with songs, proverbs, and speeches that flatly contradict and defy every line of" the fugitive slave "statute." By 1854, his priority is different. He wants to protect the possibility of sincere dialogue against the threat that *everyone* will begin to "call stealing by ... fine names" that undermine the aspirational force that might eventually allow all people to meet and talk as equals. In the later essay he seems to have lost confidence that rough debate in the press will squelch enforcement of the law. He imagines a scene of commuters quietly consuming a "second breakfast" as each silently reads his paper on the ride to work (*AW* 61).

The rapid progress of the assault on equality in the years since Webster chose to stand with the slaveholders "has given a disastrous importance to the defects of this great man's mind" (*AW* 77). Emerson details Webster's rise and the development of his unique standing. He singles out his presence at the dedication of the monument on Bunker Hill in 1843. Webster's mere presence was awesome to Emerson. People "looked at him as the representative of the American continent. He was there in his Adamitic capacity. . . . There was the monument, and here was Webster" (*AW* 76). Emerson explains Webster's talent as an orator, describing him as "so thoroughly simple and wise in his rhetoric—he saw through his matter,—hugged his fact so close,—went to the principal or essential, and never indulged in a weak flourish" (*AW* 76). But oratorical skill and moral judgment are two different things, and even though he had been given a clear choice, when his moment came, Webster quailed before the slave power:

> Here was the question: Are you for man, and for the good of man; or are you for the hurt and harm of man? It was a question, whether man shall be treated as leather? Whether the negroes shall be, as the Indians were in Spanish America, a species of money? Whether this institution which is a kind of mill or factory for converting men into monkeys, shall be upheld and enlarged? And Mr. Webster and the country went for quadruped law. Immense mischief was done. People were all expecting a totally different course from Mr. Webster. If any man had in that hour possessed the weight with the whole country which he had acquired, he would have brought the whole country to its senses. (*AW* 79)

Webster's defense of permanent inequality disunited his constituents by reinforcing an unspoken law that slavery was "always to be varnished over" with falsehoods, even though every "sane man" knew that the studied dishonesty of rhetoric about the Union referred to "one crime" and turned "free-statesmen" into "accomplices to the guilt." The practice had inverted the words most vital to democracy and undermined the foundations of sincere public dialogue. At an 1856 Kansas relief meeting, Emerson makes his most explicit statement on the state of political discourse: "Language has lost its meaning in universal cant. *Representative Government* is really misrepresentative; *Union* is a conspiracy against the Northern States which the Northern States are to have the privilege of paying for; the *adding of Cuba and Central America* to the slave marts is *enlarging the area of Freedom. Manifest Destiny, Democracy,* fine names for an ugly thing" (*AW* 113–14). The loss of sincerity in public discourse was more than just a frustration. Emerson often used the metaphor of transparency, as in the "transparent eyeball" of *Nature*, to denote authenticity or sincerity. It is a pretty apt metaphor, since insincerity is clouded with hidden motives and cynical agendas. To take a word like "democracy," which in his lifetime had taken on a new and more expansive meaning that he judged a giant step toward equality, and then to cloud it under the new connotation that democracy meant ignoring slavery was to ask people to repress the possibility of aspirational dignity, to embrace cowardice in their hearts, and passively to accept that equality was no longer among the United States' canonical values. Rufus Choate had sent his letter to the Maine Whigs mocking the universal human rights values expressed in the Declaration of Independence on August ninth, a month and a day before Emerson spoke at the Kansas Relief Meeting in Cambridge on September tenth.

Compared to the challenge he anticipates after passage of the Kansas-Nebraska law, Emerson finds the Revolution to have been a relatively small accomplishment. By compromising on slavery back then, the Founders had given his generation an even harder task: "The hour is coming when the strongest will not be strong enough. A harder task will the new revolution of the nineteenth century be, than was the revolution of the eighteenth century. I think the American Revolution bought its glory cheap" (*AW* 115). Emerson's son Edward was twelve years old at the time. When hostilities began five years later, Edward tried to join the army but was rejected for health reasons.

The effort to define physical bodies, especially distinguishing races and sexes, in terms of inherent hierarchy rather than equality is in many ways the most tenacious line of argument developed in the assault on equality. As late as the 1960s, ethnological claims that reach back to *Crania Americana* were still being cited by American courts to justify anti-miscegenation laws and sustain the idea of purity of race as a meaningful concept.[66] In the 1830s the polygenesists' theory became the connector in efforts to combine religion, history, ethnology, and biology into a canon of authoritative knowledge that would reserve human rights for a narrow sliver of Anglo-European white males. The rhetoric of scientific inferiority and superiority that this voice in the assault on equality proposed struck deep roots in American culture and long outlived the influence of polygenism as a scientific theory explaining the origin of race.

Emerson was thinking, writing, and speaking at the antebellum high point of this debate. At no time did he ever speak in support or defense of slavery. He was deep in the fray, and he found some elements of the polygenesists' theory to be plausible. Theories of racial hierarchy were consistent with emerging models of natural history. When generalized from the individual to the group, they were also consistent with Emerson's own belief in the transformative power of genius. He was never able fully to discard a visceral sense of superiority to blacks and Irish. These are truths that shaped but do not define the role he played in the defense of equality. His own struggle against "the old indecent nonsense about the nature of the negro" is more a window into the influence of scientific racism than it is into Emerson's thought.

On the issue of transformation, Emerson's universalizing model of equality would either have to include or exclude race within its boundaries. As a universalizer, he chose inclusion and equality. Whereas his brief involvement in the Cherokee removals crisis was expressed in terms of lost identity—the loss of a certain idea of American citizenship—his path through anthropological thought expressed his most basic commitment to equality. In this debate, Emerson rejected arguments that precluded transformation because these same arguments also precluded the possibility of progress toward an equal society. Finally, even in its convolutions, Emerson's thought about racial equality goes deeper than commitment to procedural democratic egalitarianism or social egalitarianism. Emerson articulated the necessity of racial egalitarianism as part of the rigor of self-reliant individuality. His never quite expressed conclusion is that to rule out a person, any person, as an equal misses the whole point of the domestication of the idea of culture. Spirit functions through connections that make people more equal. In his thought, that conviction applies to the right of persons of every race or no race to be known as equals as much as it does to the right of every person to participate in government or to stand as equals in marriage and friendship.

4

LIBERTY, PROPERTY, AND SOCIALISM

The year Emerson published *Nature*, class issues dominated presidential politics. By the time the 1836 campaign began, the Whigs had coalesced as a political organization and were effectively countering the Democrats' claim to be the voice of the people. Rather than campaigning in the republican tradition, which emphasized ideals of virtuous citizenship and civic-minded representation of the common good, Whigs were trying to play what they considered the Democrats' game. They accused their opponents of anti-democratic conspiracies and tried to make candidate Martin Van Buren personally unacceptable to the electorate. Even the dignified William Henry Seward, a New York antislavery Whig who would move Emerson deeply with his "Higher Law" speech and would go on to serve in Lincoln's cabinet, condemned Van Buren as a "crawling reptile" who had tricked Andrew Jackson into a corrupt alliance.[1]

Though slavery was an issue in the presidential campaign of 1836—especially in relation to the possibility of war between Mexico and Texas—the election turned on economic issues related to the Bank of the United States and the contrast between hard and paper currency.[2] The hard money debate even finds its way into Emerson's *Nature*. As Emerson explains his belief that language loses force as it gets more abstract, he compares the predictable insincerity of partisan rhetoric to the abstract value of banknotes. They just do not inspire confidence the way solid gold does. As a new breed of popular politician was learning to bob and weave for the more expansive electorate, "old words are perverted to stand for things which are not; a paper currency is employed when there is no bullion in the vaults" (*CW* 1:20). Just as partisan elections seemed to be turning democracy into a rhetorical confidence game, paper money was threatening to undermine real value with all manner of fraud. By analogy, words disconnected from referents were degrading the value of language. Who could tell if banknotes represented tangible assets, bullion in the vaults? Who could tell if a politician's words were sincere or just the noise of a demagogue's cynicism?

The Democrats won the presidency in 1836, but it was a brief ascendance, and it set the stage for a period of economic turmoil. Financial panic in 1837 catalyzed underlying anxieties to provoke serious thought about the role of wealth and property in American society. Though it didn't develop the way Emerson had hoped, it was probably a good thing that the electoral system had stabilized, because shortly after Van Buren's election, the economic downturn combined with the improving organization of the Whigs made the election of 1836 the last time that the Democracy would have clear dominance in national politics. Van Buren's presidency became a casualty of changing politics much as John Adams's had a generation earlier. He served only one term as president before a Whig won office. The party structure defined by Jackson and the Democrats in the early 1830s held up pretty well as power shifted back and forth from Democrat to Whig and back again. Between Van Buren's loss in 1840 and Lincoln's victory in 1864, no president would achieve reelection to a second term. Three presidents, including Lincoln, would die in office between 1841 and 1865. The Liberty Party, Free Soil Party, and American Party would briefly claim factions from both the Whigs and Democrats before the Republican Party found a way to construct a coalition that could unite Free Soil Democrats and antislavery Whigs across the northern states.

When Emerson published *Nature* in late summer 1836, though, financial panic seemed unlikely, and to all appearances the Democrats were at least as strong as they had been in 1834, when he witnessed the congressional election in New York.[3] During this phase of his career, and even after the 1837 collapse, Emerson was buoyed by the economic vitality of the times. He admired trade and commerce as a model of independent creativity, will, and energy. He shared the common view that individual enterprise in the market embodies a form of inventive reason that liberates people and weakens the power of hereditary wealth. Capitalism opened the door for equality because it became a visible antithesis of the arbitrary power of theocracy and despotism. But even very early in his career, Emerson's affirmation of capitalism coexists uneasily with reservations about the effects of capitalism on human dignity and equality. The development of his thought on capitalism is not unlike that of his thought about democracy. Both marked progressive transformations that held the potential to expand and dignify every person, but they were both being hijacked by unscrupulous actors. Too many of his countrymen were undermining themselves by investing heart and soul in politics and business. Those priorities could lead people to see themselves as commodities or even as extensions of their political party.

While the danger of partisan or factional strife is deeply rooted in thought about democracy, it is usually explained as a type of risk, one of the ever-present weaknesses of democracy as a majoritarian form of government. At the other pole, in the identity of the individual, which was what Emerson hoped to influence, there is an additional danger. Thinking of oneself as a form of property and of grounding individual rights on property law or on the principle of self-ownership is one of the most important ways of understanding the right to liberty and even equality: all people are equal in the sense that each has an inalienable right to self-ownership. But linking liberty and equality so tightly to the same principle that gives one the right to sell a plot of land would also become one of the most important subjects of debate in the defense of equality.

At the same time that liberal democratic principles were advancing movements for democracy, modern socialism was taking shape in European thought and quickly found adherents in the United States. The same liberation of creative energy and invention that capitalism encouraged had the negative effect of creating factory towns with populations of immiserated workers. The conditions that Emerson could see taking hold in New England as the textile industry mechanized were resulting in dead-end lives that, for workers, canceled out the liberating equality that commerce offered to enterprising individuals who had access to capital.[4] Textile mills with spreading company slums a half-day's ride from Concord showed Emerson what the future might look like for some of his countrymen.[5]

Nonetheless, just as Emerson believed that democracy was a necessary context for equality, he believed that the freedom to create, bargain, and trade was a human right and essential to equality. Commerce had utopian qualities. In theory, the nature-like workings of the market could replace the arbitrary power of tradition with genuine meritocracy. For individuals, the free market could assess innovative creativity, assign it a value, and reward that creativity and invention with wealth and prestige.

Yet commerce also had flaws that, for Emerson, eventually outweighed the value of capitalism. His thought about economics is unique in that it does not involve a critique grounded in class tension or even dwell on the emergence of large-scale industrial capitalism. The problem, as he saw it, lay not in trade or commerce but in the idea of private property itself. Private property encouraged materialism over idealism and egotism over humanitarianism.[6] Emerson's economic thought contrasts with that of people such as Orestes Brownson, who, in "The Laboring Classes," opposes hereditary wealth; or Theodore Parker, whose "Thoughts on Labor" distinguishes between the oppressed "hands" who do productive work and the "mouths" whose wealth allows them to live in idleness; or Seth Luther, whose "Address to the Workingmen of New England" denounces child labor and attacks the claim that ten-year-old children who work sixty hours a week have an equal chance alongside peers who can afford to attend school.[7] Instead, Emerson's thought is grounded in an effort to rebut the assumption that capitalist economic relationships are in any way natural or necessary. As he puts it in 1844:

> I think the best argument of the conservative is this bad one; that he is convinced that the angry democrat who wishes him to divide his park & chateau with him, will, on entering into the possession, instantly become conservative, & hold the property & spend it as selfishly as himself. For a better man, I might dare to renounce my estate; for a worse man, or as bad a man as I, why should I? All the history of man with unbroken sequence of examples establishes this influence. Yet it is very low & degrading ground to stand upon. We must never reason from history, but plant ourselves on the ideal. (*JMN* 9:113)

Despite the "best argument of the conservative" against a more equal distribution of wealth, Emerson finds he has to reject history and seek an ideal that relates trade and commerce to the general welfare rather than to the claim that greed and self-interest are universal and dominant. Progress toward this "ideal" probably doesn't lie with the "angry democrat," but he is sure that it doesn't lie with the propertied conservative either.

As he moved away from capitalism and toward socialist egalitarianism between 1836 and 1844, Emerson was trying to imagine a society in which some principle or force could ensure that the enterprise and inventiveness of capitalism could not become a source of exploitation or degradation. Despite all its virtues, the problem with commerce, Emerson concludes, is that it threatens people's sovereignty by inviting them to see themselves as commodities with high or low value as the market dictates.[8] Just as his response to Jacksonian politics addressed the question, What is the point of democracy if it leads to mesmerized mobs cheering the harangue of a demagogue?, his response to the economics of early industrial capitalism addresses the question, What is the point of commerce if it turns the whole world into a market where people are bought and sold?

NATURE AND COMMERCE FOR THE PUBLIC GOOD

Nature builds toward idealism and Spirit, but it is grounded in the nitty-gritty of commerce. Emerson's 1836 essay *Nature* intervenes in the political economy of Jacksonian democracy in two ways. First, it emphasizes the public nature of labor by treating the manipulation of "commodity" as a social good rather than as a form of individualized appropriation. Second, it defines the highest value of commerce not as a testimony to the superiority of the inventor or entrepreneur, but as a source of universal progress that dignifies all humanity. As much as *Nature* is about the unrealized spiritual potential of individuals, it is also about doing things with matter, or "commodity," as Emerson calls it, that makes the world a better place for everyone. When *Nature* is read as a text about the creative manipulation of commodity, raw materials, or capital, its core idea is that doing useful things in the world adds to the common weal.

In *Nature*, Emerson assumes that individuals live in communities. Even the alienation from original sources of power that motivates *Nature* is explicitly grounded in social metaphors. He details a project of levering his community out of an egotistic and materialistic mode of relating to nature and lifting it toward a spiritual and philanthropic understanding of economic value. The progression from matter to spirit is explicit in the structure of the essay. As it proceeds from chapter to chapter, Emerson works from material to spiritual issues. He begins with the manipulation of physical objects in chapters titled "Commodity," "Beauty," and "Language." Then, in "Discipline," which serves as the transitional fulcrum of *Nature*, he explores how the manipulation of physical objects structures the mind. He concludes with "Idealism" and "Spirit," chapters that examine the relation between the mind and the universal laws that govern nature.⁹ The goal of structuring the text so that it proceeds from matter to spirit is to offer what Emerson calls a "progressive" (*CW* 1:31) theory that will point the whole community toward ideals that explicitly rebut the possessive individualism of Jacksonian America.

In the long history of civilization, science, commerce, the Reformation, and the American Revolution, among other phenomena, had proven the creative liberty of the individual and enabled the rise of liberal humanist values. But this movement of the individual to the center of philosophy will have little real value if most people live in the shadow of a few geniuses. As he puts it in 1836 in the introduction to his "Philosophy of History" lecture series, "Progress belongs to the individual and consists in becoming universal" (*EL* 2:13–14). By structuring *Nature* so that it progresses from commodity to Spirit, Emerson defines Jacksonian materialism as a groping effort to meet a standard of dignity that recognizes the liberty of the individual but also insists that *all people* are entitled by nature to the highest standard of human recognition. Progress may begin with the insight of an individual, but it counts as progress *only* when the value of spiritual insight is transformed into something practical, which then becomes public property.

Toward this end, Emerson subordinates material to spiritual methods of interacting with nature. On the material level, animal instinct is analogous to human understanding, which enables the manipulation of physical nature. But on the higher, spiritual level, creative "reflection" is analogous to reason, which allows one to articulate the universalizing value of spirit—the way inventiveness can enhance many people's lives.¹⁰ For civilization to progress, and for all human beings to attain the dignity each deserves, even property must aspire toward that higher level. Distinguishing between the material as "active" and the spiritual as "reflective," Emerson describes the difference: "So long as the active powers predominate over the reflective, we resist with indignation any hint that nature is more short-lived or mutable than spirit.... To the senses and the unrenewed understanding, belongs a sort of instinctive belief in the absolute existence of nature." But "Reason mars this faith... If the Reason be stimulated to more earnest vision, outlines and surfaces become transparent, and are no longer seen; causes and spirits are seen through them" (*CW* 1:30). These causal forces are by definition universally accessible and thereby also necessarily public. To approach the "causes" of commodity relations with a possessive or property rights perspective is to disregard the public utility of creative labor and to live with a purely egotistical relation to the world. From that viewpoint, things with "outlines and surfaces" are either yours or not yours, and that's it.

Yet manipulating the material world with a "renewed understanding," or an "educated will," as Emerson calls it at the very end of the essay, allows the civic value of invention to leapfrog over the private wealth that it offers. For example, in the chapter "Commodity," Emerson addresses the role that the rudimentary manipulation of natural resources has played in the progress of civilization. In untouched nature, "all the parts incessantly work into each other's hands for the profit of man. The wind sows the seed; the sun evaporates the sea; the wind blows vapor to the field." Agriculture and irrigation simply capture and organize the effects of wind and sun. With civilization, people who understand the laws behind physical phenomena harness natural occurrences for the benefit of all: "The useful arts are reproductions or new combinations . . . of the same natural benefactors," which become the public property of all humankind. "The private poor man hath cities, ships, canals, bridges, built for him," and thus the achievements of individual genius are shared by everyone (*CW* 1:11–12).[11]

This point, that utilitarian invention always becomes a form of common property, Emerson holds, is so obvious that he does not have to go into depth about it: "There is no need of specifying particulars in this class of uses. The catalog is endless, and are the examples so obvious, that I shall leave them to the reader's reflection." But before he moves on from "Commodity" to "Beauty," he pauses to underscore the point that the value of manipulating material to create new uses lies in the way it contributes to the public good. He concludes the chapter with a "general remark": "that this mercenary benefit [the social use-value of commodity], is one which has respect to all farther good. A man is fed, not that he may be fed, but that he may work" (*CW* 1:12). Invention may bring wealth, power, and fame to the creative genius; but if he works as an egotist, acting only to satisfy his personal appetite, then he has failed to appreciate the value of his creativity. The act of working dignifies the human being, but it dignifies him or her only because it produces a benefit that the genius cannot himself own or consume. The personal benefits genius produces—wealth, fame, prestige—are relevant only as means of accounting for its contribution to the common good.

In the chapter "Beauty" Emerson underscores the civic quality of acting in the material world by describing the public benefits of creativity. Deploying a figure who would become one of his signal representatives of genius,

Emerson juxtaposes Christopher Columbus against the New World as a fitting image of heroic individuality. Columbus is important to Emerson for his combination of idealism and egotism. For Emerson, Columbus's self-reliance symbolically and literally called a new world into being. But Columbus's role as a representative of transformative thinking is more important than his geographic discoveries. "Columbus's purpose," in Emerson's thought, as Kris Fresonke observes, "was not to discover America . . . but to overcome intellectual routine." Fresonke explains this remark by referring to a passage from Emerson's journals of 1830: "Five or six facts independently of almost no value, made the discovery of America in Columbus's mind & secures it[;] which is to him altogether frivolous but inestimable to the race when seen in connexion with another fact not known for 100 years after" (*JMN* 3:176).[12] The beauty of Columbus's discovery was his willingness to put together disparate facts and "seek their intentions" as natural phenomena. As Emerson carries this idea forward in the "Idealism" chapter of *Nature*, when the right facts get combined to capture "centuries of observation in a single formula," then "the solid seeming block of matter has been pervaded and dissolved" (*CW* 1:34). Disparate, apparently unrelated facts led Columbus to a magnificent contrarian idea, and he actually had the courage and the luck to see it through to a conclusion. Then, in his moment of sublime vindication, a moment that for Emerson exemplifies beauty because it collapses spirit into phenomena, Columbus stands on the shore of Hispaniola, and the New World clothes him as "fit drapery" for his daring enterprise.

But posed brutal and heroic against a backdrop of "purple mountains" (*CW* 1:15), Columbus is not alone as an exemplar of beauty.[13] In the chapter "Beauty" he is a member of a group that begins with "Leonidas and his three hundred martyrs," who sacrificed themselves to save Sparta from Xerxes's army. There is also Arnold von Winkelried, a medieval knight who altruistically defended Swiss independence.[14] After Emerson describes Columbus's victory over intellectual inertia, he reverses the image of beauty so that virtue's heroes appear as martyrs rather than conquerors. He thus situates beauty in an explicitly political context that emphasizes how loyalty to an idea can enhance human dignity even as its representative man is sacrificed:

> When Sir Henry Vane was dragged up the Tower-hill, sitting on a sled, to suffer death as the champion of the English laws, one of the multitude cried out to him, "you never sate on so glorious a seat!" Charles II, to

intimidate the citizens of London, caused the patriot Lord Russell to be drawn in an open coach through the principal streets of the city on his way to the scaffold. "But," his biographer says, "the multitude imagined they saw liberty and virtue sitting by his side." (*CW* 1:15)

Columbus, Leonidas, Winkelried, Henry Vane, and Lord Russell are all linked together as examples of beauty.[15] But whereas Columbus represents the beauty of self-reliance overcoming the stagnation of intellectual routine and opening doors to new worlds of wealth and culture, the others stand alongside him because they embody an idea that dignifies everyone against the arbitrary and degrading power of tyranny. Each of their individual acts is beautiful because it embodies an aspirational ideal that, if universally shared, would dignify everyone. The crowds who gathered at the executions of Henry Vane and Lord Russell shout out their recognition that the martyrs stand for principles that will liberate and ennoble each witness to the event. The condemned are not just brave and principled; they embody the progress of idealism and signal its movement toward a new standard of equality. They represent movement toward a world in which each individual can claim equality of respect.

The examples Emerson uses here to describe the public benefits of idealism are similar to the relation Margaret Fuller describes between men and women in her 1844 *Woman in the Nineteenth Century*. Fuller describes boys and girls quarreling on a playground as a metaphor for the immaturity of humankind. "Man has gone but little way" toward realizing his full potential, Fuller writes, and "now he is waiting to see whether woman can keep step with him, but instead of calling out, like a good brother, 'you can do it, if you only think so' . . . he often discourages with school-boy brag: 'Girls can't do that, girls can't play ball.'" But every now and then, for a brief moment, something different happens on the playground. When one of the girls decides to "defy their taunts, break through and be brave and secure," the children "rend the air with shouts" because everybody—the boys included—recognizes that their schoolmate has overcome childish convention and lifted up all of humanity.[16] At that moment, the brave girl is transcendent; she embodies an unattained and aspirational equality, and all the others children instinctively recognize the real meaning of her defiance and find themselves cheering that ideal of human possibility.

Emerson's defiant crowds and Fuller's cheering schoolmates are applauding the same concept. What Emerson frames in the "Beauty" chapter of *Nature* in relation to equality of access to resources is the same thing that Fuller imagines in relation to gender equality. Both reflect efforts to envision progress toward equality of respect. These moments embody a deferred beauty because they arrange the materiality of the world in ways that gesture toward a civility in which the perfection of individual character and a broad standard of civil equality flow from one to the other as cause and effect. When the ideal becomes visible in the act of an individual, however briefly, everybody has had the opportunity to claim that standard as their birthright.

While the chapters "Commodity," "Beauty," and "Language" all address the materiality of things in the world, "Discipline" bridges external and internal worlds. This transitional chapter explains how acting on commodity forces new structures on the mind. It is important to the egalitarian strain of Emerson's thought because it describes the logic by which private insight attains universal value by adding to the common stock of knowledge and power.[17]

In the chapter "Discipline," Emerson contrasts private and public values of nature. Through the "creative antagonism" of human will working on stubborn fact, the tiniest and most mundane acts, the "disputing of prices" with vendors, calculating the "interest" of various choices in daily life all teach the "necessary lessons of difference, of likeness, or order." All these little battles between individual will and economic law shape the "hand of the mind" (*CW* 1:27). Ultimately, if the lessons of discipline are well learned, this antagonism makes the mind powerful enough to lift itself up from instinct, understanding, and commodity, and into the realm of reflection, Reason, and Spirit. Discipline allows circumstances that seem immutable to be transformed by epoch-changing insight: "The first steps in Agriculture, Astronomy, Zoology . . . teach that Nature's dice are always loaded; that in her heaps and rubbish are concealed sure and useful results." Concave shapes displace water and float. Stars map the sea at night. Serving all humankind, discipline turns "the powers of nature to the domestic service of man, so that the ocean is but a waterwheel and the solar system but a clock" (*CW* 1:25). As an expression of the public good, Emerson's larger point is that each new law discovered, each increment of instrumental leverage gained over nature, represents an advance for humankind as a whole. By Emerson's reasoning, it would be a fool's mistake to organize society so that invention privatizes value or commoditizes scientific truth. On the contrary, discipline teaches that trying to own, or patent, or copyright processes of transformation is both impossible and wrong. In *Nature*, intellectual property is a contradiction in terms.

With the public value of invention in mind, Emerson posits that the highest discipline is the recognition that "nothing in nature is exhausted in its first use. When a thing has served its end to the uttermost, it is wholly new for an ulterior service." The endless mutability of objects in nature symbolizes the fruitlessness of private appropriation. According to this "doctrine of use" for the common good, the recycling of commodity from one socially useful form to another represents an "ethical character" inherent to all valid creative acts.[18] Michael Lopez uses a line from Emerson's 1862 essay "American Civilization" as the epigraph for his chapter on the doctrine of use: "Use, labor of each for all, is the health and virtue of all beings" (*CW* 10:403). The ethical requirement of discipline, that the individual seek to be useful, underscores the final impossibility of appropriating nature for private purposes. Beyond the fact that nature resists privatization, as an ethical standard for behavior, the doctrine of use inculcates a recognition that even *seeking* to appropriate nature degrades the material object of use and alienates its owner from the community.

At the end of the discussion, Emerson reemphasizes this "ethical character" as an indispensable quality of "Discipline": "Whatever private purpose is answered by any member or part, this is its public and universal function, and is never omitted" (*CW* 1:26). If one is to claim the power that discipline allows, one must embrace the knowledge that, as he will put it in "The Young American," this "Genius or Destiny is of the Sternest Administration, though rumors exist of its secret tenderness. It may be styled a cruel kindness, serving the whole even unto the ruin of the member; a terrible communist, reserving all profits to the community, without dividend to individuals. Its law is, you shall have everything as a member, nothing to yourself" (*CW* 1:231).

The "Discipline" chapter of *Nature* defines interactions with the material world in order to recognize the historical boundaries of human power *and* to put pressure on those boundaries. It enables individuals to adopt an egotistical relationship toward nature even as they seek to harmonize the current of their efforts with nature's unrevealed causes and spirits. But the purpose of this paradoxical antagonism is less to achieve the personal transcendence of the transparent eyeball than it is to produce goods that can be shared equally by all as nature, the "terrible communist," moves slowly forward.

Emerson concludes *Nature* by imagining utopian circumstances that transform both civil society and the individual. As self-culture moves people away from the commodification of nature and toward harmony with its causes, and as knowledge accrues and the domestication of the idea of culture proceeds, Emerson imagines an "influx of the spirit" that will reshape the world. "As when summer comes from the south," he projects, and "the snow-banks melt and the face of the earth becomes green before it, so shall the advancing spirit create its ornaments along its path." A new spring will transform society. In its wake, "spiders, snakes, pests, madhouses, prisons," even "enemies, vanish" because "they are temporary" and not part of the destined condition of humankind. As human beings learn to draw out their own ideal character, the universal mind that all people share will act like a magnet that attracts good and repels evil: "It shall draw beautiful faces, warm hearts, wise discourse, and heroic acts, around its way," improving life "until evil is no more seen." In the end, when spirit extirpates evil, humankind will reclaim its original Edenic estate: "The kingdom of man over nature, which cometh not with observation—A dominion such as now is beyond his dream of God—he shall enter without more wonder than the blind man feels who is gradually restored to sight" (*CW* 1:45). This utopia will emerge through acts that interpret nature and allow Spirit to spread from individual to individual until the benefits are widely shared.

This vision of a society transformed by the universalization of Spirit is interwoven with an alternative conclusion in which Emerson atomizes the society into separate individual universes. He even parses the opposition between a universalized and an individualized vision down to the level of specific tradesmen:

> Every Spirit builds itself a house, and beyond its house a world, and beyond its world a heaven. Know then that this world exists for you.... All that Adam had, all that Caesar could, you have and can do. Adam called his house, heaven and earth; Caesar called his house, Rome; You perhaps call yours, a cobbler's trade; a hundred acres of ploughed land; or a scholar's garret. Yet line for line and point for point your dominion is as great as theirs, though without fine names. Build therefore your own world. (*CW* 1:44–45)

So which is it? Is Emerson's vision of the realized end state of history a condition in which Spirit will produce a society so wonderful that the state can close its prisons and psychiatric hospitals? Or is it that the "influx of the spirit" will teach the cobbler that he is Caesar's equal and that his little shop is as great as Rome? The answer, of course, is both; and this is the core tension so often deferred in the aspiration of Emerson's egalitarianism. He vacillates back and forth between a point of view that is explicitly social, even communitarian, that explicitly imagines self-reliance as a continual but loosely connected *mutual* self-reliance; and an alternative point of view that treats the individual as an autonomous universe who perceives community obligations as a threat to autonomy. This tension between a libertarian point of view and a broader and more communitarian view of social connection runs throughout Emerson's thought. In its internal logic as well as its development in his thought, though, its resolution leans toward the communitarian pole. Even when he wavers in his perspective, the paradox of social reliance and individual isolation underscores the instability of the radically liberal position. It implies layer after layer of isolation—culture, community, family, even language as a medium for building one's own world. Each of these layers is constantly interrupted by everything from giggling kids in the next room to congressional bombshells. A communitarian vision comes to dominate the liberal autonomy of self-reliance because the individual, even the individual of *Nature*, is too engaged, too encumbered by history and community to stand aloof. This bias toward self-reliance as a public and egalitarian force is rooted in the way Emerson defines Spirit. Spirit may be unique to each person, but it is singular only in the Romantic sense of being embedded in each individual soul. In its agency and the values its agency would embody, it is a universal sentiment, exclusive to no one and shared by all.

In the progression from "Commodity" to the utopia where humankind fulfills the highest ideals it can imagine for itself, *Nature* asserts a new economy of civil value. It aims to turn the individual away from the shop counter and the politician's soapbox and toward recognition that unless his or her labor adds to the common good, it is empty egotism. In the most literal sense, by Emerson's logic, the "doctrine of use" makes things *good*; and this goodness is defined by the communal value that the labor of individual genius produces.[19]

"POLITICS" IN 1837: FREE TRADE AND UTOPIA

As his vision of organic utopia in *Nature* implies, Emerson's foundational political assumptions are not rooted in the choices of social contract theory. Rather, they are akin to religious ideals of prelapsarian unity between the individual and God.[20] Unlike Hobbes, Locke, or their contemporary James

Harrington, Emerson's state of nature refers to a spiritual rather than a civil condition. The inventors of philosophical liberalism sought to imagine the individual outside of all social forms in order to frame the most basic requirements of civil society. For these earlier theorists, society begins when an imaginary human encounters another imaginary human in the state of nature. But Emerson's thought about the foundations of society begins in a different place; it begins with a Platonic contrast between ideal and actual conditions. This reasoning from the ideal has pervasive implications for Emerson's thought about equality. As he puts it in his 1837 lecture on politics, the assertion of a universally shared human condition has immediate consequences for civil society: "Government, society is possible, only because all men have but one mind, and in consequence really but one interest. The consciousness of this fact is the root and prolific cause of all revolutions in favor of freedom. [']God is our father and all we are brethren,['] instinct whispers in the ear of every man. Down topple before this absolute spiritual right, all the tyrannies, all the hierarchies, all the artificial ranks of the earth" (*EL* 2:70). Civility is rooted not in a contract that regulates the natural war of each against all but in an instinctive recognition of the same universalizing cosmopolitanism that obviates racial hierarchy. This cosmopolitanism allows Emerson to bridge the gap between the universality of Spirit and the private whisperings of "instinct." Harmony between the two legitimizes "revolutions in favor of freedom" because the "absolute spiritual right" of each person to live as a sovereign state articulates "the one great interest" that each human person shares with every other. Artificial ranks and castes—relations crucial to the alternative posed by those seeking to undermine equality by defending slavery as a positive good—simply violate the natural fact of universal similarity. The mere existence of ranks and castes justifies revolution in favor of freedom.

Emerson clarifies his own utopian assumptions in the same lecture. Just "as it is only on the supposition of a common nature, of an identical mind that any government is possible, so always the bases of politics must be explored and all corrections of political errors derived out of the ideal commonwealth" (*EL* 2:70). The practical goal of political thought, Emerson assumes, is similar to Plato's in *The Republic* or Augustine's in *The City of God*, not in their formal details but as efforts to reason from the ideal, to reason in ways that direct civil society toward the highest aspirational ends.[21] His own version of politics, far from being the art of the possible, begins as a process of reverse incrementalism. It represents the work of drawing an alienated "ideal commonwealth," or "mind's Republic," as he also calls it, from the realm of repressed memory into a place of publicity and political authority.²²

Emerson delivered his 1837 "Politics" lecture as part of his "Philosophy of History" lecture series. As the series develops, the elements of the repressed "mind's republic" incrementally become social as they find outlets in science, culture, politics, and so on. Inching progressively forward, history leads to philosophy as new forms of knowledge add to the common stock of inherited skills. This process frees individuals from mental enthrallment and erodes tyrannies and artificial hierarchies into dust.

In its recognition of political equality, the Democracy of Jacksonian America makes every citizen an independent public power, a sovereign state—and this achievement is as important as any other in human history. But despite its empowerment of the individual, in Emerson's "ideal commonwealth," citizenship has a strong civic republican strain: "The education of every man is bringing him ever to postpone his private to the universal good, to comport himself, that is, in his proper person, as a State, and of course whilst a whole community around him are doing the like, the persons who hold public offices become mere clerks of business and in no sense sovereigns of the people" (*EL* 2:78). As an expression of economic freedom that complemented the rise of political democracy, Emerson's vision of individuals eclipsing government by acting as sovereign commercial entities reflects a widely shared sense that commerce equalized and empowered individuals by creating new opportunities to achieve economic independence.²³ With equal voting rights established, at least for white men, he goes on to consider a question of economics: If matter, or commodity, is best understood as a substance that people use to create objects of public value, what principles should guide distribution and compensation of that value? He approaches this question not under the heading of economics, business, or even political economy but as an integral question of politics. This approach is not surprising, because just as Emerson was defending equality at the same time as he was weighing the merits of evolutionary theory against the claims of the polygenesists, he was speaking to audiences of young men entering business just as the mercantilist policies of the eighteenth century were giving way to theories of "free trade" which called for minimal government regulation of economic relationships.

The rising arguments for free trade, understood along the idealistic model that grew out of eighteenth-century liberalism, claimed that unrestricted trade will empower individuals and create global interdependencies that are mutually profitable and mutually beneficial. It would help diverse people interact with one another as equals. Free trade underscores common interests rather than antagonisms. A broadly liberal market in goods of all kinds appealed to Emerson in its imagery of free individuals engaged in constant creative enterprises that turned inert commodity into value. Rather than representing greed, the rise of trade signaled a progressive liberation of human potential from a static mercantilist system governed by autocrats to an exuberant capitalist democracy of inventors and adventurers. As a vehicle for legitimizing property, this new model of economics enhanced the sovereignty of the individual by equating the ownership of private property—especially land—with the autonomy that offered the freeholder a realm of state-like sovereignty.

As Emerson saw it, advocating trade was not merely vital to the defense of liberal autonomy; trade also had a crucial egalitarian dimension. Like others, he associated free trade with political equality because it gave people new opportunities to acquire wealth and, eventually, to claim political power. In trumpeting pacifistic and utopian theories of capitalism, Emerson imagines the role trade can play in promoting intercultural friendship, cosmopolitan egalitarianism, and the global dissemination of useful goods and ideas. Trade, he argues, allows previously impoverished people to gain property and thus both provides economic, political, and cultural empowerment and advances equality.

The belief that trade supports human rights was especially strong in the early and mid-nineteenth century. Richard Cobden, leader of the Anti–Corn Law League, whom Emerson met in Manchester, England, in 1848, for example, saw his own advocacy of global free trade as part of the pacifist movement for world peace. In the spring of 1842 he wrote a colleague: "It has struck me that it would be well to try to engraft our free trade agitation upon the Peace Movement. They are one and the same cause. It has often been to me a matter of the greatest surprise, that the friends [Quakers] have not taken up the question of free trade as the means—and I believe the only human means—of effecting universal and permanent peace."[24] Connecting commerce, individual autonomy, and world peace was not uncommon among the Enlightenment thinkers whose economics shaped Emerson's early thought about property. Adam Smith collected the threads of the free trade argument in *The Wealth of Nations* to make a strong case for free trade as an instrument that would advance liberty, promote economic equality, and make war obsolete. Writing twenty years after Smith, Immanuel Kant published "On Perpetual Peace" partly to underscore disconnection between the welfare of a monarch's people and the wars for which European dynasties conscripted tens of thousands of subjects. Kant grounds his cosmopolitanism partly in the role that international trade had come to play in undermining the arbitrary power of monarchs. But equally he recognized that the brutality of the slave trade and the imperial rivalries fueling it meant that before international commerce could be an instrument of peace, it had to be grounded in a universalized standard of human dignity. The peace movement that coalesced after the Napoleonic Wars ended in 1815 acted on this idea by proposing a Congress of Nations and other instruments of global governance to subordinate trade to a worldwide legal regime of human rights.[25]

Economic theorists early on claimed the rhetoric of natural rights to define the marketplace as a place for community as well as hard-nosed bargaining. In a 1696 essay advocating the liberalization of trade, Charles Davenant, an English Tory politician, made the case that import-export tariffs were "unnatural" for societies with long traditions of international commerce: "Laws to compel the consumption of some commodities, and prohibit the use of others, may do well enough, where trade is forced, and only artificial. . . . But in countries inclined by genius, and adapted to it by situation, such laws are needless, unnatural, and can have no effect conducive to the public good." In a 1701 essay titled "Considerations Upon the East India Trade," Henry Martyn argued that God created the seas to fulfill the natural desire to trade. The oceans are there so "that our wants at home might be supplied by our navigation into other countries. . . . By this we take the spices of Arabia, yet [we] never feel the scorching sun which brings them forth, we shine in silks which our hands never wrought, . . . we only plough the deep and reap the harvest of every country in the world." Martyn argues that God designed the world to have economic specialization according to geography and climate, and that this diversity was intended to foster a natural equality among trading peoples because it facilitates the movement of one society's surplus goods to distant places where they have greater value. Jacob Vanderlint would extend this claim a generation later, making the argument that "all nations of the world, therefore, should be regarded as one body of tradesmen, exercising their various occupations for the mutual benefit and advantage of each other." Advocating from a complementary liberal perspective, Francis Hutcheson, who taught Adam Smith moral philosophy at the University of Glasgow, presents the industriousness of the trader explicitly in the language of natural rights: "As nature has implanted in each man a desire of his own happiness, and many tender affections toward other(s) in some nearer relations of life . . . tis plain each one has a natural right to exert his powers, according to his own judgment and inclination, for these purposes, in all such industry, labour, or amusements, as are not hurtful to others."[26] Trade fulfills the natural desires of the individual, even as it promotes equality between trading partners.

The integration of trade into the rhetoric of natural rights is important in connecting the emergence of liberal autonomy with ideas about private property because it naturalizes global economics, nudging it away from a preoccupation with dynastic rivalry and treating it as an expression of inherent human desire: not power but enterprise. *The Wealth of Nations*, especially, Kathryn Sutherland remarks, worked to drive "the economic impulse deeper into the recesses of human personality as the natural basis of our psychological and social existence."[27] Accepting Smith's naturalization of the capitalist's motive by nurturing the impulse to trade would foster the individual's natural desire to produce social goods. Rather than promoting egotism or selfishness, Montesquieu's "doux commerce" or Adam Smith's "invisible hand" translates individual ambition into goods that benefit all people. Emerson's initial assumptions about commerce follow this line of thinking.

Even John Stuart Mill, as suspicious as he was of forces that invite individuals to give up independent thought, also understood free trade as a vital engine in the advancement of human rights. Writing on the eve of the 1848 revolutions, Mill remarks: "It is commerce which is rapidly rendering war obsolete, by strengthening and multiplying the personal interests which are in natural opposition to it. And it may be said without exaggeration that the great extent and rapid increase of international trade, in being the principle guarantee of the peace of the world, is the great permanent security for the uninterrupted progress of the ideas, the institutions, and the character of the human race."[28] A few years earlier, in a gesture that attracted Emerson's attention, Richard Cobden popularized anti-tariff politics by reframing the issue as one of individual rights rather than philosophical principle. Cobden presents free trade in unabashedly utopian terms, describing it not as geopolitics but as interpersonal communication. In his representations, commerce is purely a communicative act, disconnected from profit-driven exchanges of privately owned goods and services. Free trade promotes equality because it is "drawing men together, thrusting aside the antagonism of race, and creed, and language, and uniting us in the bonds of eternal peace." It will "change the face of the world, so as to introduce a system of government entirely distinct from that which now prevails." Making war obsolete, imperialism and aggressive nationalism will "die away" as "man becomes one family, and freely exchanges the fruits of his labor with his brother man."[29]

This vision of unrestrained global commerce blossoming into cosmopolitan utopia appealed to Emerson in its imagery of free individuals engaged in constant creative enterprises that turned inert commodity into value. In his 1837 "Politics" lecture, and in the lecture titled "War" which he delivered to the American Peace Society in the summer of 1838, Emerson emphasizes the utopian, cosmopolitan, and pacifistic implications of commerce. Above all, trade requires discipline. Trade inches along on a delicately advancing threshold of social benefit and self-interest. Demanding exhaustive energy to extract a narrow margin of gain, it forces all of an individual's faculties into active engagement: "It calls out all force of a certain kind that slumbered in the former dynasties" and puts it into motion. Even though trade is materialistic, it treats commodity as a means rather than an end. Trade, he puts it in "The Young American," "is a very intellectual force. This displaces physical strength, and installs computation, combination, information, science in its room" (*CW* 1:233). Activity, creativity, disregard of borders, and self-reliance all work in trade, not just to undermine arbitrary power but also constructively to embody equality, communal investment, and a life devoted to improving the world.

In Emerson's view, the expansion of commerce was discrediting the regimes of forced labor that characterized feudalism and monarchy. To ground civil society in a just distinction between persons and property would reintegrate the whole because it establishes a natural relationship between reason and commodity. It would "destroy the whole magazine of dissimulation for so many ages reckoned the capital art of government; it would purge that rottenness which has defamed the whole science until politics has come to mean cunning" (*EL* 2:79). The science of government, like religion and philosophy, functioned to dominate rather than liberate the individual. Specifically, through cunning and dissimulation it worked to justify feudal and monarchical power relationships that violated human rights.

Like Mill, Emerson anticipates an egalitarian cosmopolitan utopia emerging from the expansion of global trade. The growth of independence movements and of liberal politics throughout Europe and South America, Emerson holds, is inextricably connected to the role of commerce in redefining people's sense of equality. But unlike Cobden, Emerson emphasizes the importance of private property both to liberal autonomy and to citizenship. "The last ages," he argues, "have been characterized in history by the immense creation of property... and that by millions, not by a few, involves necessarily so much education of the minds of the proprietors." It "has been the creation of lovers of order, knowledge, and peace" (*EL* 2:80, 81). By his reasoning, gaining a bit of property domesticates people and makes them good citizens. But it does so not because people want to protect their newfound wealth. Rather, the idea that each individual has a natural right of ownership in the value of his or her labor was replacing the idea that the private individual was a social inferior who owed service to a king or a state. The freeholder or self-employed tradesman loves order and peace, in Emerson's eyes, because their labor is justly compensated with accumulating capital, and the esteem that goes with useful work. As he presents it in the 1837 "Politics" lecture, the global expansion of trade and property rights provoked revolutions in Europe and South America that seemed on the verge of sweeping away Europe's dynasties and replacing them with a world order grounded in cosmopolitan liberalism.

Emerson had good reason for taking such an optimistic view. Between 1811 and 1830, thirteen nations in Central and South America had gained independence from the Spanish and Portuguese Empires. In Europe, beginning with the Greek Revolution in 1821, movements for economic and political reform gained voice from Portugal to Russia. Lord Byron, of course, died while fighting in Greece. Emerson himself introduced Lajos Kossuth, the hero of the short-lived Hungarian Revolution, while the European rebel was on a lecture tour in America. As part of the conclusion to the 1837 "Politics" lecture, Emerson imagines free trade leading to a cosmopolitan utopia: "The projects with which the minds of philanthropists teem, are themselves a sure mark of progress. The black colony of Liberia, the proposition of the Congress of Nations to arbitrate controversies between two states... these are projects the bare starting of which in any practicable shape, proves civilization and Christianity" (*EL* 2:82). In opposition to dynastic rivalries and global war, commerce promotes international peace. In the Peace Society address he writes that as commerce had expanded, "war has been steadily on the decline." He continues:

> Nothing is plainer than the sympathy with war is a juvenile and temporary state. Not only the moral sentiment, but trade, learning, and

whatever makes intercourse, conspire to put it down. Trade, as all men know, is the antagonist of war. Wherever there is no property the people will put on the knapsack for bread; but trade is instantly endangered and destroyed. And, moreover, trade brings men to look each other in the face, and gives the parties the knowledge that these enemies over sea or over the mountain are such men as we; who laugh and grieve, who love and fear, as we do. And learning and art, and especially religion, weave ties that make war look like fratricide, as it is. (*CW* 10:185)

Imagining free trade in intimate, personal terms rather than through global institutions or international treaties, Emerson presents it as a communicative act that "weave[s] ties" by bringing diverse individuals face-to-face. In trust and mutual engagement as well as in its anticipation of future meetings, trade was analogous to friendship. Emerson does not talk about trade promoting racial equality through mutually beneficial enterprises, but his personalization of trade as a practice that "brings men to look each other in the face," and his recognition that "these enemies . . . laugh and grieve . . . as we do," is a far cry from the rhetoric of contemporaries who were promoting Anglo-Saxon superiority and asserting a natural right to subordinate and exploit the people of the global South.

Referring to the rise of Peace Societies like the one he was addressing, Emerson optimistically claims that the prospect of world peace grounded on global commercial ties "has now become so distinct as to be a social thought: societies can be formed on it" (*CW* 10:188). The rapid growth of the peace movement even allows him to treat war as an obsolete by-product of barbarism and feudalism. As culture is domesticated through a fabric of global person-to-person ties, war will seem increasingly infantile: "It is not a great matter how long men refuse to believe the advent of peace: war is on its last legs; and the universal peace is as sure as is the prevalence of civilization over barbarism, of Liberal governments over feudal forms. The question for us is only *How soon?*" (*CW* 10:189). In the Peace Society address, as in the "Politics" lecture, Emerson cites proposals for a Congress of Nations as a sign of cosmopolitan progress: "The proposition of the Congress of Nations is undoubtedly that at which the present fabric of our society and the present course of events do point" (*CW* 10:201).

As the world moves away from dynastic tyranny and toward democracy and free trade, everything begins to change. The recognition of universal human equality discredits hereditary power and legitimizes political democracy. By envisioning each individual as a sovereign state, Emerson places the capitalist entrepreneur at the vanguard of a global revolution in which commercial activity expands wealth through the creative acts of citizen-sovereigns. On the assumptions of classical liberalism that Emerson echoes here, the free market embodies an economic tabula rasa by which all have equal access to resources and opportunities. Free trade will promote cosmopolitan equality as private citizens accumulate wealth. Bourgeois property will facilitate the expansion of political democracy. The disciplined creativity of individuals all over the world will immeasurably increase everyone's opportunities and access to culture. This strain of optimism about the way commerce releases creativity, brings diverse people face-to-face, and generally works to domesticate culture runs in Emerson's thought at least through "Wealth" and "Culture," published as part of *The Conduct of Life* in 1860.

But it also coexists with a parallel suspicion of capitalism that starts out early in his career, focused on the way commerce infects selfhood by promoting greed and expands toward a general critique of private property. In mid-career, this suspicion shifts from psychological concerns about the integrity of the self to material, social concerns. In addition to the risks capitalism poses to character, wealth inequality troubles Emerson more and more. After 1837 Emerson begins to reverse course, emphasizing how property rights—not so much the activity of trading but the power of ownership—undermine autonomy and corrupt democratic politics at least as much as they liberate creativity. His advocacy of trade and his subsequent rejection of private property create a thoroughly conflicted economic theory. The conflict is focused on the way commerce and private property either aid or harm the expansion of equality. Whereas he is strongly inclined to advocate trade and private enterprise, his attitude toward private property is highly critical. The terms on which he attempts to reconcile the right to property with the cosmopolitan assumptions about empowerment that he saw in commerce mark the beginning of a critique that will conclude with a sharp move to the ideological left in the 1844 version of the "Politics" essay.

SELF-OWNERSHIP AND THE RIGHTS OF PROPERTY

Second to the idea that persons are free and morally responsible actors in the world, the belief in an individual right to private property has been the strongest canon of liberal ideology. John Locke even flips these, holding the individual's right to property in oneself as the foundational principle that legitimizes the right to liberty. The conflict between these types of rights—liberty and property—is that property rights are not only about property. The rules that govern property rights have also long defined social relationships and thus overlap with the right to liberty. As legal scholar Jeremy Waldron puts it, "The concept of property is the concept of a system of rules governing access to and control of material resources."[30] Rights of access and use of resources underpin norms that govern many of the postures we adopt as we move through the physical world: trespass, theft, usufruct; the behavior of visitors, guests, travelers, hosts; the rights of owners, employees, customers, and so on, all of which are determined by recognition that certain objects or spaces are the private property of particular persons. From the very origin of liberalism, the ownership of property has been almost inseparable from the ideas of selfhood and of society.

Emerson's rhetoric of liberal autonomy draws deeply on the reservoir of metaphors that equate selfhood with self-ownership. Neal Dolan details how Emerson used economic metaphors to define the process of self-liberation: "Throughout Emerson's early writing . . . property was a name not only for beautiful estates or profits from interest but for an inward achievement of human freedom—for a fluid, ever-ongoing, and intimately personal interchange of consciousness and world." Dolan's reading explains the subtle symbolic meanings of property that operated powerfully in eighteenth-century liberal political thought, especially in the juxtaposition of abstract "properties" that the individual cultivates within the self and the ownership claims that individuals can make in the world. As Dolan notes about Emerson's 1837 "Politics" lecture, it would be "hard to imagine a clearer repudiation of the egalitarian spirit of Jacksonianism, which was itself rather safely liberal by comparison to emerging European socialism. Emerson is indeed engaged in class politics" in this lecture, "but only of a conservative-liberal American Whig variety."[31]

Dolan treats property as a pun linking will and matter in much the same way that Stanley Cavell tends to treat Emerson's use of the word "constitution" as a pun that links politics and character.[32] By this reading, Emerson's commitment to freedom is largely unconnected to his investment in equality, such that his politics exemplifies the ideals of republican self-discipline and bourgeois entrepreneurship. In Dolan's analysis, Emersonian selfhood is realized in the autonomy that comes from creative labor. Expressing one's inherent properties, self-ownership builds toward something similar to

George Kateb's ideal of "mental self-reliance," or the ability to address issues in the world through one's own intellectual resources rather than through conventional tropes or ready-made opinions. Self-reliance, Kateb holds, is a kind of self-possession; it consists of "thinking one's thoughts and thinking them through."[33] In the long tradition of liberal self-ownership that Dolan reconstructs, the Emersonian subject achieves property in themselves only when they are able to think beyond internalized discourses of church, party, or state. These properties of self-ownership animate key terms Emerson uses for autonomy. "Man Thinking," "know thyself," and "Self-trust" (*CW* 1:53, 55, 63) in "The American Scholar" and "obey thyself" (*CW* 1:82) in "The Divinity School Address" all ask the individual to claim the autonomy that liberal thinkers connect to self-ownership.

Between 1837, when he wrote "Politics" as a lecture, and 1844, when he published a heavily revised version of it in the second series of *Essays*, Emerson came to see private property less as a support to self-reliance and more as an obstacle to equality and thereby to the progress of civilization.

In his 1837 "Politics" lecture, Emerson argues that the empowerment of individuals requires the state to protect private property. He explains: "It is plain that there are two objects for whose protection government exists, 1. Persons, 2. Property. . . . Whilst thus of persons the rights of all as persons are equal in virtue of the access of all to Reason, their rights in Property are very unequal" (*EL* 2:70–71). As a starting point, he understands inequality in the distribution of wealth to be a measure of individual industry, explaining that variations in property depend "primarily upon the skill or virtue of the parties, of which there is every degree" (*EL* 2:71). His assessment of the relationship between talent, work, and property at the beginning of this lecture echoes the coldheartedness of his comments in the "Discipline" chapter of *Nature*. Just as the intellectual discipline it takes to manipulate ideas is learned by trial and error,

> the same good office is performed by Property and its filial systems of debt and credit. Debt, grinding debt, whose iron face the widow, the orphan, and the sons of genius fear and hate;—debt, which consumes so much time, which so cripples and disheartens a great spirit with cares that seem so base, is a preceptor whose lessons cannot be forgone, and is needed most by those who suffer from it most. Moreover, property, which has been well compared to snow,—"if it fall level to-day, it will be blown into drifts to-morrow,"—is the surface action of internal machinery. (*CW* 1:24)[34]

Reiterating labor as the standard for ownership in the "Politics" lecture, he stipulates: "It will be admitted that in the earliest society they who have the wealth have a right to it. It is the product of their labor and virtue" (*EL* 1:71). Even though he sees labor in terms of civic contribution, he unambiguously accepts the Lockean model of defining private property as the result of the transforming of commodity, or raw material, through creative labor. The transformed material may add value accessible to everyone, but as an object, it has become the property of the inventor.

Yet even in the 1837 lecture, this is as far as Emerson is willing to go in accepting property as a legitimate institution. As long as property "visibly comes to the owners in this direct way, no other opinion would arise in any virtuous society than that property should make the law for property and persons the law for persons" (*EL* 2:72). But what if property comes to a person from some source other than "their labor and virtue"? Strictly speaking, Emerson recognizes a right to private property only when an object is the direct "product of . . . labor." As he acknowledges, this standard applies most obviously to "the earliest society," which places almost all legally recognized property in 1837 outside the pale of legitimacy. For example, the wealth he inherited from his first wife's family, which he claimed through a lawsuit, did not come from his own "labor and virtue," and thus would not be authentically his.

In the 1837 lecture he dodges the exploitative nature of property in his own day by treating tension between property rights and human rights as a technical problem rather than as an inherent flaw in the idea of private property. He concludes that economic theory is just incomplete. In order to legitimize property rights fully, political philosophers simply have to find the principles that will distinguish property rights from human rights. "No distinction," he writes, "seems to be so fundamental in politics as this of persons and property. . . . [A]nd throughout history the errors of political societies have arisen from confounding these two classes of rights" (*EL* 2:73). With liberal capitalism and democracy on the verge of displacing feudalism, the next great advance in civilization will be to develop a "philosophy of property" that legitimizes wealth but prevents it from transgressing the rights of persons. Discovering an authentic means of keeping these two types of rights from hobbling each other, Emerson anticipates, will "open new mines of practical wisdom which would in the event change the face of the world" (*EL* 2:79).

The path to this end, however, is unclear. Norms governing persons and property continually trip each other: Crimes against property are often punished with the loss of personal liberty. Persons are protected against injury and exploitation by paying taxes rather than by personal service. The rich tend to overestimate the legitimate authority of property. The poor do the same with individual rights. As Emerson puts it: "On the one hand, the obvious inequality of rights of property has led the rich and strong to assume a like difference in personal rights, which assumption legalized is tyranny; on the other, the manifest equality of personal rights has led the many to assume a like equality of rights over property, which is Agrarianism" (*EL* 2:73). In the former case, economic exploitation unrestrained by respect for human equality leads to chattel and wage slavery. In the latter case, equalizing the distribution of wealth distorts appropriate remuneration for invention. This second path was articulated during the 1840s in the free land policies of George Evans and the National Reform Association, and by the bans on inherited property proposed by Thomas Skidmore and Orestes Brownson.[35]

The problem Emerson approaches here is that from its very origin, the construction of liberal autonomy has been contingent on the ability of persons to claim sovereign spheres of power, but this objective is subverted by the fact that autonomy within these spheres often includes arbitrary power over other persons. In the 1837 lecture, Emerson tries to look beyond this overlap by imagining a philosophical innovation that will resolve the problem. He recognizes the way property rights impinge on persons, but then balks at criticizing the right to property.

There were potent overlaps between the assault on equality and the debate over wealth inequality and private property. Though Virginia lawyer and essayist George Fitzhugh has a notoriety that exceeds his actual influence, his 1854 pamphlet "Sociology for the South, or, The Failure of Free Society" and its expanded 1857 version, *Cannibals All! Or, Slaves without Masters*, illustrate how the terms of these debates could be contorted to argue that equality promoted the brutal heartlessness of wage slavery, while the slave and caste society of southern plantations was a form of benevolent socialism. In fact, Fitzhugh explicitly defines equality as a reversion to a pre-civil savage state and slave society as a forward-looking socialist utopia.[36]

In Fitzhugh's thinking, to combine economic freedom and equality before the law simply facilitates unrestrained exploitation: "Free trade, when the American gives a bottle of whiskey to the Indian for valuable furs, or the Englishman exchanges with the African blue-beads for diamonds, gold, and slaves, is a fair specimen of all free trade when unequals meet." What the ideal of liberal equality fails to recognize, Fitzhugh argues, is that the inherent inequality of peoples such as "Indians" and the "African" made them vulnerable to exploitation. When inherent inequality is factored into the liberal equation, free society becomes a form of cannibalism. It reproduces the savage state by leaving inferior people defenseless: "They who act each for himself, who are hostile, antagonistic and competitive, are not social and do not constitute a society. We use the term free society for want of a better; but, like the term free government, it is an absurdity: those who are governed are not free—those who are free are not social." In effect, for Fitzhugh, the very idea of equality implies a Hobbesian state of nature. "We have heard a distinguished" political economist, Fitzhugh observes,

> object to negro slavery because the protection it afforded to an inferior race would perpetuate that race, which, if left free to compete with the whites, must be starved out in a few generations. Members of Congress, of the Young American party, boast that the Anglo-Saxon race is manifestly destined to eat out all other races, as the wire-grass destroys and takes the place of other grasses. Nay, they allege this competitive process is going on throughout all nature; the strong are everywhere devouring the weak; the hardier plants and animals destroying the weaker, and the superior races of man exterminating the inferior.

To defend against the chaos of equality, the weak are forced to band together in order to restore the very security that equality had destroyed. Fitzhugh cites the Chartists, Odd-Fellows, Temperance societies, trade unions, and utopian associations as examples of the chaos that ensues when equality is forced on people who need protection rather than equality. Paradoxically, on Fitzhugh's reasoning, slave society represents an advanced form of communism. As he puts it, "A well-conducted farm in the South is a model of associated labor that Fourier might envy." Indeed, slavery is symbiotic and mutually protective, he argues:

> Every southern slave has an estate in tail, indefeasible by fine and recovery, in the lands of the South. If his present master cannot support him, he must sell him to one who can. Slaves too have a valuable property in their masters. Abolitionists overlook this—overlook the protective influence of slavery, its distinguishing feature and no doubt the cause of its origin and continuance.... What a glorious thing to man is slavery, when want, misfortune, old age, debility and sickness overtake him. Free

society, in its various forms of insurance, in its odd-fellow and temperance societies, in its social and communistic establishments, and in ten thousand other ways, is vainly attempting to attain this never-failing protective, care-taking and supporting feature of slavery.[37]

Fitzhugh's assault on equality interweaves scientific, economic, and cultural critique. *Cannibals All!* exemplifies how comprehensively the opponents of equality sought to discredit egalitarian assumptions. In contrast to Kant's shuddering recognition that imperial rivalries invented the seventeenth-century slave trade and thus required a global regime of human rights law that would protect *everyone*, Fitzhugh holds that since God made Africans inferior to Europeans, "the protective influence of slavery" is "no doubt the cause of its [slavery's] origin and continuance." The possession of persons is not a problem for Fitzhugh because he assumes that all social relationships can ultimately be traced back to the idea of property. In his view, both ownership and being owned were part of God's benevolent plan.

C. B. Macpherson, in his reconsideration of the theory of possessive individualism, defines a contradiction in the belief that natural law requires that persons and property have equal representation under the law. While Fitzhugh's reasoning shows ways in which property rights were combined with religious and historical thinking to advance the assault on equality, Macpherson's analysis makes vivid the problem that Emerson tried to resolve by fantasizing an organic principle that could separate human rights from property rights. As the theory of self-possession took hold in the seventeenth century, connecting the ownership of property to enfranchisement, Macpherson argues, gave meaning to individual rights. Within the limits of his property, every man really could be imagined as a sovereign with an independent state. In that environment, treating property as a sacrosanct realm of autonomy advanced liberal equality because it placed a limit on the intrusive power of the national government.

The contradiction is that the assumptions about independence that had legitimized equal legal protection for persons and property in the seventeenth century were no longer valid in the nineteenth century. But assumptions about personhood and opportunity that supported the self-ownership model of liberal identity (or, more accurately, masculinity) had not been amended to reflect the advent of industrial production. Living within this contradiction, when the belief that hard work and self-control marked the path to autonomy, comfort, and respect remained strong despite overwhelming evidence that capitalism, self-ownership, and the legal protection of property were *also* vehicles of mass degradation, Emerson, Mill, Cobden, and their generation were caught in a kind of time warp: possessive individualism still served as an ideal, but the prerequisites that had once offered enfranchised men a rough equality of opportunity obtained less and less. In effect, Americans of Emerson's generation were watching self-ownership turn on itself as capital and labor markets mocked the idea that one's possession of spirit, ingenuity, ambition, and the capacity to labor embodied autonomy in any meaningful way. Although possessive individualism has no room for chattel slavery because the individual's right of self-ownership is inalienable, it also has no mechanism to prevent the slave-like immiseration that a "free" labor market was making a reality for so many people.

In summary, when seen as a form of intercultural dialogue, commerce projected the highest ideals of cosmopolitan equality and individual freedom. It underscored belief in a universally shared humanity and validated industry as a praiseworthy endeavor. But this vision of cosmopolitan community supported by egalitarian assumptions about self-ownership suppressed the fact that commerce is not just a communicative act. As Emerson revised the 1837 "Politics" lecture for publication in 1844, the coercive power of private property came to represent for him a critical obstacle to the achievement of liberal autonomy.

While many people in Emerson's America could claim the formal qualities of liberty, few had the economic opportunities that made possessive individualism an appealing model of identity. On the contrary, possessive individualism became a source of alienation. Stephen Simpson, a Baltimore newspaper editor, specifically contrasts political equality with the economic inequality he saw around him. The political equality that had recently been gained by workingmen, Simpson argues, was mocked by a "funding system" that favored capital over labor. "Did the Constitution intend," Simpson writes, "to provide for nothing beyond *mere political right*? Does not the political embrace, necessarily, the *moral equality*? Does it not declare that equality is the basis of the whole social compact, and that all laws and regulations, customs and usages, shall bear equally upon all the members of the community?" As Simpson saw it, the root of the increase in economic inequality was that a corrupt banking system was degrading the power of labor to claim ownership of the value it had produced. "From the earliest epochs of civilized society,"

Simpson declares, "the *producers* of wealth have . . . been degraded to the condition of slaves, serfs, vassals, or servants, and this degradation has even extended to the present day."[38] Until the laborer can claim just compensation, the republic is little more than a conspiracy.

Making the exact same assumptions about the right to property that Emerson makes in *Nature*, Simpson argues that the pro-monopoly legal and banking system was corrupting a natural distribution of wealth:

> It was never designed by the people who framed this government to grant the power that *Law* should regulate the distribution of wealth instead of industry. I use the term Law as a generic word, embracing all the details that affect the distribution of wealth, such that moneyed corporations, chartered monopolies, and that endless chain of levers which move industry to empty her gains into the lap of *capital*, and which effectually frustrate and defeat the grand object of rational self-government on the basis of individual freedom and personal merit.[39]

The legal corruption of the labor market undercuts the dignity of workers by reducing their power to claim just compensation for labor. This not only insults natural equality but also threatens to create a revolutionary situation. If productive labor ceases to be respected as a form of self-reliance, which partly means being compensated in a way commensurate to its contribution to the public good, a core ligament in the civil body snaps, and war between capital and labor becomes inevitable. The whole situation is as much about equality, or "the family tie of the race," as it is about wages:

> When the children of toil are as much shunned in society as if they were leprous convicts just emerging from loathsome cells, the most powerful obstacle is erected between them and all that can make them estimable and happy. The family tie of the race is snapped asunder; and man thus degraded and oppressed would be less than man, if he did not feel enmity towards his oppressor and view with resentment an order of things so contrary to the dictates of justice and humanity, so broadly in contradiction to his political rights, and so basely in violation of his equal attributes as a man. Here is the fountain, the sacred fountain of all revolutions.[40]

Even as Jacksonians promoted an ideal of political equality combined with economic opportunity designed to empower the common man, the emergence of factory production and capital-intensive industry marked an increasingly important arena in the assault on equality. By the mid-1820s, the deteriorating power of individual laborers in the market was motivating a union organizing movement. By the early 1830s, laborers had emerged as a new though relatively weak voice in public discussion of equality.[41] In a report published by a Pennsylvania workingman's organization, laborers both publicize their working conditions and call on others to begin speaking out: "We are obliged by our employers to labor . . . from 5 O'clock in the morning until sunset, being fourteen hours and a half, with an intermission of half an hour for breakfast, and an hour for dinner, leaving thirteen hours of hard labor." The factory floor had "an atmosphere thick with dust and small particles of cotton, which we were constantly inhaling to the destruction of our health, our appetite, and strength." Their wages, of course, were paltry, and their savings nil: "We return to our labor in the morning, as weary as when we left it; but nevertheless work we must, worn down and debilitated as we are, or our families would soon be in a starving condition, for our wages are barely sufficient to supply us the necessaries of life. We cannot provide against sickness or difficulties of any kind, by laying by a single dollar, for our present wants consume the little we receive."[42]

The early labor movement's efforts at consciousness-raising, mutual assistance, inter-trade cooperation, unionization, and work stoppage were all driven by the desire of propertyless workers to claim some measure of economic equity, respect, and opportunity. It emerged to provoke a dialogue with a class of masters and capitalists who seemed intent on cutting off all possible avenues through which workingmen could accumulate property and thereby achieve the economic independence that made self-ownership a viable model for liberal equality. The alternative was to accept the status of a lower caste. The conditions described by Simpson and the workingmen of Pennsylvania evoke both the practical and the psychological effects of trends in property rights and economic development that would undermine equality by establishing a caste society characterized by impassable barriers between people with access to property and those without. By the mid-1840s, the economic makeup of local mill towns such as Lowell, agricultural villages such as Concord, and metropoles such as Boston were achieving unmistakable differentiations that were drawing Emerson's thought toward questions about self-ownership, property rights, and the distribution of wealth.

"THE YOUNG AMERICAN"

In 1844 Emerson revised and published his 1837 "Politics" lecture along with "The Poet" and "Experience" in the second series of *Essays*. The year began with an address to a group of aspiring young office workers. The "Young American" address and the "Politics" revision that he would work on later in the year show Emerson very consciously rethinking his understanding of the impact private property has on equality in civil society. The position he takes in these essays contrasts sharply with the free trade libertarianism of the 1837 "Politics" lecture. In the revision of this lecture, Emerson reconsiders the theory of possessive individualism and explicitly rejects the argument he had presented in 1837.

The 1844 essays show Emerson's political thought changing in two important ways, both of which juxtapose cosmopolitan egalitarianism against the growing wealth inequality that had become more obvious in the intervening years. First, he rethinks his attitude toward the right of property to legal status equivalent to human rights. Second, he tries to draw into focus the long-term implications of the experimental socialist communities that were challenging relationships between labor and capital. In combination, these two changes of opinion define a transition in which the threats to equality that he was beginning to associate with property come to outweigh the connections between creativity and liberty that in the 1830s he had associated with commerce. What results is a transition in which Emerson rejects a liberalism rooted in self-ownership and property rights in favor of a cosmopolitan liberalism that subordinates property rights to human rights. In these two essays Emerson refutes the conservative argument that strong legal protections for private property are the best way to incorporate natural law into statute law.

The shift is important to the defense of equality for several reasons. It marks an effort to connect liberal freedom to communitarian expectations about the distribution of wealth. It also severs the connection between property and autonomy as a foundation for liberal identity. But most importantly, it clarifies a hierarchy of values. All the creative science that had remade the world since Copernicus and the scientific revolution should serve the public good rather than the vanity of a few magnates and their heirs. But as events seemed to be shaking out, millions of people were being immiserated because property laws gave people with capital the power to control other people's lives. In this situation, property rights were promoting barbarism rather than culture and should give way to something better.

Though Emerson criticizes the power of property directly in the 1844 essay, since the 1830s he had been arguing against the internalized identities that commerce promoted. In the introductory lecture of the "Present Age" series, delivered in early December 1839, he develops an extended critique of commerce, dealing with it as a form of seduction that puts the body where the spirit should be. The materialist dimension of commercial invention has an almost mystical power, Emerson argues, because it "removes from nature that mystery and dread which in the infancy of society defend man from profanation before yet his prudence and conscience are enlightened" (*EL* 3:19). Thus, he says bluntly, "there is nothing more important in the culture of man than to resist the dangers of commerce" (*EL* 3:190). His interest in the "Present Age" series is not in the structural implications—both good and bad—created by the rise of trade but in the way that materialism infects the motivations and perspectives of individuals. In Jacksonian America, trade "encroaches on all sides" and threatens to transform the individual into a purely sensual agent who "has no reverence" for anything above material gain. "The end, *to be rich*, infects the whole world" so that "education is degraded" and becomes simply a training ground for the skillful accumulation of wealth. Even religion becomes "a mere lever out of the spiritual world" by equating wealth with virtue (*EL* 3:190–91).

The danger commerce poses in the "Present Age" lectures is similar to the danger materialism posed in *Nature* or sensualism posed in "Love." Like the ability of genius to transform commodity into spectacular expressions of beauty and usefulness, "commerce, dazzling us with the perpetual discovery of new facts, of new particulars of power, has availed so far to transfer the devotion of men from the soul to that material in which it works" (*EL* 3:191). Materialism, commerce, and possessive individualism impel people toward idolatry: "It seems to realize to the senses the sovereignty which the soul claims" (*EL* 3:190). This temptation to treat the material object as the end of creativity rather than the symbol or articulation of a life in harmony with Spirit is the long-running antagonist in Emerson's ambivalence about the economic qualities of democratic society. Just as he supported democracy but opposed partisanship as an identity, he supported trade and commerce but opposed accumulating property as its goal or as a criterion of self-esteem. There is also, however, an important difference: whereas the trend toward partisanship is a tragedy because it squanders so much human potential, the rise of commerce is both a tragedy and a crime: It is a tragedy because it encourages people to value the wrong things. It is a crime because it legalizes all manner of theft.

In 1844, when he published "The Young American" and "Politics," the dangers posed by commerce were no less pressing than they had been when he delivered the "Present Age" lectures, but in the 1844 essays Emerson's perspective is both more focused and more critical. In "The Young American," he situates trade in a very long-term, epochal historical context. Commerce is "in the midst of its career," and despite the many forces in motion around his countrymen, trade is "the political fact of most significance to the American at this hour." He then shifts to the political left, arguing that capitalist commodification had become corrosive to communities and thus to the liberty of individuals. He had long been criticizing capitalism for encouraging people to see themselves in base material terms, but in this essay he moves toward the values of the socialists. He presents the capitalist marketplace as a site that sucks everything into itself and reduces all value to exchange value. He captures the complex relationship between creative opportunity and commodification that he sees in liberal capitalism by emphasizing the simultaneity with which it facilitates individual liberty and promotes human degradation:

> Trade goes to make the governments insignificant, and to bring every kind of faculty of every individual that can in any manner serve any person, *on sale*. Instead of a huge Army and Navy and Executive Departments, it tends to convert Government into a bureau of intelligence, an Intelligence-Office, where every man may find what he wishes to buy, and expose what he has to sell; not only produce and manufactures, but art, skill, and intellectual and moral values. This is the good and this is the evil of trade, that it would put everything *into the market*; talent, beauty, virtue, and man himself. (*CW* 1:233–34)

Capitalism may reward invention and industry, but it also makes human skill or labor indistinguishable from non-human commodities. Like vegetables and precious metals, human talents may trade low or high, but they are all for sale in the marketplace. At exactly the same time, Karl Marx, an obscure German economist working in England, was arguing that the only truly non-commodified labor was the unique creative work of the artist, Emerson was reaching almost the exact same conclusion. By Emerson's logic, since the progress of humankind lies not just in advancing instrumental power over nature but also in constructing a society that offers each individual the maximum standard of liberty, dignity, and opportunity, capitalism, and the materialism that drives it, must play its role in the domestication of culture and then accept a subordinate status.

At its very origins, civilization began with "the patriarchal form of government" and proceeded through feudalism to "commerce." As he writes, civilization seems to be reaching toward the future with "association" as the next foreseeable stage of social evolution. "Trade," Emerson reiterates, has served as a great liberating force. When "feudalism grew to be a bandit and a brigand . . . trade was the strong man that broke it down and raised a new and unknown power in its place." As he explains it, trade "is a new agent in the world, and one of great function; it is a very intellectual force. This displaces physical strength and installs computation, combination, information, science in its room." As "the historian will see, . . . [trade] was the principle of Liberty; that trade planted America and destroyed feudalism; that it makes peace and keeps peace, and it will abolish slavery" by demonstrating that talent is distributed regardless of rank or race (*CW* 1:234). One of the ways in which Harriet Beecher Stowe communicates degradation in *Uncle Tom's Cabin*, for example, is in having the slave George Harris clearly express bitterness that his own mechanical innovation for processing hemp has been stolen by the factory owner he is forced to serve.[43]

What is crucial to Emerson's developing thought about economic equality is that even in his metaphors of meteoric speed, he positions commercial society as a transitional social form. Although it is the dominant force in his society, and it has many virtues, its real purpose lies in its capacity to destroy ancient forms of arbitrary power and to prepare the ground for a world in which persons can transcend commodity status to stand individual, equal, and sovereign. In introducing this revolutionary change, he asserts that "the uprise and culmination" of the age of commerce is the vital fact of the moment. But he also situates the commercial age as a dark night trending toward a new Renaissance. Like Marx, Emerson simply takes it for granted that socialism will break the back of capitalism in the same way that capitalism broke the back of feudalism. "Trade was one instrument" of liberating persons and advancing human rights, but as a portent of the coming era, Emerson notes, "the time is full of good signs. . . . Witness the new movements in the civilized world, the Communism of France, Germany, and Switzerland; the Trades' Unions, the English League against the Corn Laws; and the whole *Industrial Statistics*, so called" (*CW* 1:235). Each of these movements anticipates a step forward for civil society because it asserts the priority of people over property. With the exception of Cobden's Anti–Corn Law League, every one of the movements he cites advocated for the rights of industrial workers.

As he looks around and surveys his country's most important resources, Emerson searches for a way to imagine a politics that can maintain the virtues of trade while avoiding the harms of private property. Listing the issues he sees as most important for the future, he highlights three conditions for the young American to consider: first, the vast geography of the continent; second, the bustling commerce and energetic optimism of its youth. Then, for the third condition, he turns toward that future:

> Government has been a fossil; it should be a plant. I conceive that the office of statute law should be to express, and not to impede the mind of mankind. New thoughts, new things. Trade was one instrument, but Trade is also but for a time, and must give way to somewhat broader and better, whose signs are already dawning in the sky.
>
> 3. I pass to speak of the signs of that which is the sequel of trade.
>
> In consequence of the revolution in the state of society wrought by trade, Government in our times is beginning to wear a clumsy and cumbrous appearance. We have already seen our way to shorter methods. The time is full of good signs. Some of them shall ripen to fruit. All this beneficent socialism is a friendly omen. (*CW* 1:234)

Emerson's ambivalence about the Association movement is well documented, but in "The Young American" he unhesitatingly presents socialism as the path to a better society.[44] The Associationists' efforts to reconstruct labor, politics, and property were just in their infancy. As he puts it, "This is the value of the Communities; not what they have done, but the revolution which they indicate as on the way" (*CW* 1:237). The "revolution" he anticipates will preserve the economic and creative powers through which liberalism undermines tyranny, but it will also redefine civil and legal practices so that they refuse to allow the owners of property to violate the rights of individuals.

Though the communities are clumsy prototypes, he understands them as efforts to universalize equality by reimagining civil society outside of a capitalist framework. In theory, free trade should go hand in hand with political democracy, but in the world he saw around him, government was far more protective of property than it was of people. Reform oriented toward "beneficent socialism" was required to advance equality because government had been drawn into the marketplace, where it served the interests of property rather than those of people. Socialist movements in the United States and abroad, he wrote, emerged

> from a feeling that the true offices of the State, the State had let fall to the ground; that in the scramble of parties for the public purse, the main duties of government were omitted,—the duty to instruct the ignorant, to supply the poor with work and with good guidance. These communists . . . proposed, as you know, that all men should take a part in the manual toil, and proposed to amend the condition of men by substituting harmonious for hostile industry. (*CW* 1:235–36)

The motives of "these communists" contrast with the motives of laissez-faire liberalism in that they seek to redefine the relationship between labor and capital. Those interested in mitigating coercive labor relations must incubate new forms of government, because even small government liberals like Emerson had lost Adam Smith's confidence that the market could be relied on to protect human dignity. In fact, commercial society seems actually to undermine the ability of people to behave decently. Commercial life, Emerson complains, "reveal[s] a public mind so preoccupied with the love of gain, that the common sentiment of indignation at fraud does not act with its natural force" (*CW* 1:240). Reclaiming a more republican civility, though, would have to come out of something like the Association movement rather than the free market, because efforts to amplify the power of property over people had utterly corrupted politics. In order to advance humane measures, he tells his audience of young businessmen, we cannot "rely on our money, and on the state because it is the guard of money" (*CW* 1:241).

His concern has another side to it, though. The momentum of his thought toward communitarian politics made him uneasy, and immediately after denouncing a politics corrupted by money, he tries to adapt the goals of the socialists to the freedom he associates with commerce. Imagining a system that "would put everything *into the market*," but that can also serve human dignity, he argues:

> It would be but an easy extension of our commercial system, to pay a private emperor a fee for services, as we pay an architect, an engineer, or a lawyer. If any man has a talent for righting wrong, for administering

difficult affairs, for counseling the poor farmers how to turn their estates to good husbandry, for combining a hundred private enterprises to a general benefit, let him in the country-town, or in Court Street, put up his sign-board, Mr. Smith, *Governor*, Mr. Johnson, *Working king*. (*CW* 1:237–38)

Despite the comic hyperbole of an aspiring emperor hanging a shingle to offer his services, Emerson is serious about threading a needle here. The eye of the needle is a vision of society that provides the maximum of individual freedom with an absence of exploitation (or a maximum of equality). The thread he is trying to pass through the needle is a model of liberal selfhood that can sustain such an aspirational idea. Turning to the market allows him to preserve, even if ironically, an ideal of political order without arbitrary power. If a citizen objects to Mr. Smith's government, they needn't buy his wares. Emerson mocks himself as he extends the metaphors of liberal commerce into the realm of government—a place not designed for individual profit, but where the common good is paramount. To project an alternative to the commercial entrepreneur as a model of identity for the Young American, he turns back to the individual, but drawing on his ideal of a domesticated culture, he returns to his core metaphor for individual sovereignty. In a passage strangely adapting the internalized spirit and the aspirational universalizing of "Self-Reliance," Emerson describes the reflexes that the "American nobleman" will show in an authentically egalitarian society:

> The private mind has access to the totality of goodness and truth, that it may be a balance to a corrupt society; and to stand for the private verdict against popular clamor, is the office of the noble. If a humane measure is propounded in behalf of the slave, or of the Irishman, or the Catholic, or for the succor of the poor, that sentiment, that project, will have the homage of the hero. That is his nobility, his oath of knighthood, to succor the helpless and oppressed; always to throw himself on the side of weakness, of youth, of hope, on the liberal, on the expansive side, never on the defensive, the conserving, the timorous, the lock and bolt system. (*CW* 1:240–41)

Exhorting his audience to show these reflexes, Emerson asserts, will turn them into the natural sovereigns of a more humane society. As he puts it: "Let your powers be well directed, directed by love, and they would everywhere be greeted with joy and honor. The chief is the chief all the world over, only not his cap and his plume. It is only their dislike of the pretender, which makes men sometimes unjust" to the accomplished person (*CW* 1:241).

In "The Young American" Emerson argues that commercial society, as much good as it has done to assert the autonomy and power of the individual, has also failed to dignify the human being fully. Capitalism, as he hoped his countrymen were learning, liberates human energies only to make them indistinguishable from non-human commodities. Since the real destiny of humankind is not just the power offered by greater control over nature but rather a society that offers each individual the opportunity to become singular, capitalism must serve its progressive purpose and then wither as it is supplanted by a higher form of culture.

"POLITICS" IN 1844: THE SEQUEL TO TRADE

The revised "Politics" essay that Emerson published a few months after delivering "The Young American" continues to develop his critique of capitalism by homing in on the legal status of private property. Whereas he connects global free trade to the expansion of liberal human rights in the 1837 lecture, in the revised essay he connects the power of property to the corruption of democratic politics. The tone of the 1837 lecture is optimistic and cosmopolitan, addressing the global expansion of trade as a foundation for the expansion of democratic politics; by contrast, the 1844 essay is critical and national, focusing on the inability of American politicians to project models of character that rise above the corrupting influence of money. On one level, the revised essay articulates an explicit and carefully thought-out change of opinion about the role of property in the "mind's republic," as he had put it in the 1837 version. On another level, it expresses a set of inchoate frustrations that the political system defends property so well, but has so little interest in promoting the sincere dialogue that produces the egalitarian individuality that democracy offers.

The opening lines of the revised argument reframe the topic of politics away from the grand theory and images of organic unity that linked the 1837 original to the "one man" metaphor of "The American Scholar." Instead, Emerson emphasizes the provisional nature of government and statute law: "In dealing with the State we ought to remember that its institutions are not aboriginal, though they existed before we were born; that they are not superior to the citizen; that every one of them was once the act of a single man; every law and usage was a man's expedient to meet a particular case; that they are all imitable, all alterable; we may make as good, we may make better." Rather than reasoning from a Platonic ideal of organic social unity, the "mind's republic" begins by situating existing practice in historical context and emphasizing the malleability of law. As he puts it: "The law is only a memorandum. . . . The statute stands there to say, yesterday we agreed so and so, but how feel ye this article today?" (*CW* 3:117–18).

Quickly, he then moves to his reasons for rethinking the role of property in politics. Explicitly referencing his own earlier conclusions, he remarks that reconsideration is necessary because "doubts have arisen whether too much weight had not been allowed in the laws, to property, and such a structure given to our usages, as allowed the rich to encroach on the poor, and to keep them poor." This encroachment represents an important transgression of the right of each person to an equal chance in life. But more than just recognizing that property rights can outflank opportunity and force people into conditions of generational impoverishment, even with all the liberties he associates with self-ownership, he concludes that private property *itself* obstructs the path to authentic human dignity. His objection is not just that concentrated wealth has coercive power; it is that self-ownership as a justification of identity is inconsistent with either liberty or equality. It cannot function as a foundation for the aspirational idealism of Emerson's defense of equality. He is unable to quite put his finger on the source of the problem, but he feels that the legal status of property pulls the definition of human personhood away from an emphasis on Spirit—which takes the name "character" in this essay—and toward an overemphasis on commodity. "Partly," as he puts it, property rights allow economic exploitation. But "mainly," as he also puts it, he objects to the high legal standing of property because "there is an instinctive sense, however obscure and yet inarticulate, that the whole constitution of property, on its present tenures, is injurious, and its influence on persons deteriorating and degrading: that truly the only consideration for the state is persons" (*CW* 3:119–20). The power that concentrated capital gives owners over workers here overlaps fully with an "inarticulate" sense that the legal standing of property is "injurious" to "persons." The state should not divide its moral responsibility by considering the rights both of persons and of property. The law should defend *only* persons. Emerson is somewhat tentative, unwilling to give up on the idea of private property root and branch, but he is surely suggesting that the concept of property may have done all the good it can and has begun to undermine progress toward a more equal society.

The constitution of selfhood within capitalism not only gives those with more private property the power to exploit those with less, but also it asks all people to fetishize commodity and to equate themselves with their property. Worse, it asks people to look at the world through a lens in which property is the end and persons are the means. To look at the issue from a political perspective, for government to represent property and persons on equal terms exacerbates economic exploitation. In fact, in "Politics" Emerson derives the origin of exploitation in exactly the same way as Jean-Jacques Rousseau. In his *Discourse on Inequality* Rousseau writes: "From the moment any one man needed help from another, and as soon as they perceived that it was useful for one man to have provisions for two, equality disappeared, property was introduced, work became necessary, and vast forests were changed into pleasant fields, which had to be watered with human sweat and in which slavery and misery were soon seen to spring up and grow with the crops." For Rousseau, the emergent distinction between capital and labor is the very fall of humankind. This initial distinction in which capital calls wage labor into being then expands to create other forms of inequality: "The strongest did more work; the most skillful turned his to better advantage; the most ingenious found ways to curtail his work. . . . Thus, natural inequality spread along with contrived inequality, and the differences among men, developed by different circumstances, make themselves more obvious, more permanent in their effect, and begin, in the same proportion to influence the fate of individuals."[45] The "fate" that Rousseau refers to here gestures toward the emergence of caste societies.

Emerson's analysis of the same transition away from a strict equality of property is equally subtle. He continues Rousseau's analysis by extending exploitation from power relationships between individuals to the political defense of property:

> Whilst I do what is fit for me, and abstain from what is unfit, my neighbor and I shall often agree on our means, and work together for a time to one end. But whenever I find my dominion over myself not sufficient for me and undertake the direction of him also, I overstep the truth, and come into false relations to him. I may have so much more skill or strength than he, that he cannot express adequately his sense of wrong, but it is a lie, and hurts like a lie both him and me. Love and nature cannot

maintain the assumption: it must be executed by a practical lie, namely by force. This undertaking for another, is the blunder which stands in colossal ugliness in the governments of the world. (*CW* 3:218–19)

Where Rousseau discusses physical strength, technical skill, and inventive cleverness, Emerson talks of the extension of "dominion." Where Rousseau talks of "natural inequality" blurring into "contrived inequality," Emerson turns to ethics. By extending his dominion, he violates another person's sovereignty. Even if the relationship is somehow mutually beneficial, it is asymmetrical and unequal, and even if the master-and-hand status goes unexpressed, the violation of sovereignty creates a "sense of wrong" in those who find themselves somehow maneuvered out of the state of natural equality. They are no longer a "neighbor" but more like a dependent. Even though the difference originates in what Rousseau would call a "natural inequality," for Emerson this difference is irrelevant. The new relationship has distorted the two persons' ability to interact as equals. In some sense the new relationship must originate in strategic communication because Emerson can't imagine anyone voluntarily giving up a standing as precious as equality in one's own eyes. He even links the change to an inability to relate as equals in honest dialogue, framing skill and strength as forms of cunning. The change in status leaves the neighbor knowing he had made a bad bargain, even if "he cannot express adequately his sense of wrong." This inability doesn't change the fact that the new relationship is "deteriorating and degrading" toward a "false relation." Emerson explains it in terms of communication: "It is a lie and hurts like a lie both him and me."

Rousseau talks of these differences of power becoming "more obvious, more permanent in the effect" until they emerge as hereditary classes. Emerson compresses this long process into single moment: "Love and nature cannot maintain the assumption" of such power, "it must be executed by a practical lie, namely, by force." He is talking about the exact moment when one individual acts to "undertake the direction" of another and thereby violates that person's sovereignty.

The specific proposal he makes in the revised "Politics" essay is not to eliminate private property but to eliminate its protection under statute law. He proposes to do away with it as a legal category and leave the defense of property to nature. As commodity, property is a real thing and therefore will force recognition even without protection in statute law. In Rousseau's idiom the law is a contrivance; in Emerson's it is "a man's expedient." But since property will be defended by natural law, Emerson infers, government can be single-minded in its focus on the defense of human rights. He reasons that "things have their laws, as well as men; and things refuse to be trifled with." Whether or not it has political representation or legal standing, "property will be protected" (CW 3:120). But by suggesting that his countrymen remove legal protections for property, Emerson effectively reverses his former argument. Rather than imagining the law as an honest broker separating and protecting the rights of property equally with the rights of persons, he proposes that government now accept the responsibility of protecting the rights of persons without any regard to the rights of property. In many respects, the 1844 "Politics" essay argues that "the whole constitution of property" is part of the assault on equality and needs to be restrained, rethought, and reversed. When he writes that "there is an instinctive sense, however, obscure and yet inarticulate" that "the whole constitution of property" is "injurious" and "degrading," he may be talking only about his own vague sense. But he is more likely trying to capture and express something in the atmosphere of 1844 New England. As this instinctive feeling gains clearer and clearer articulation, he anticipates that politics will become less and less about finding equilibrium between property rights and human rights and more about defending human equality against the degrading powers of economic inequality.

The single most vivid image of the degradation that Emerson attributes to property is in his "Ode, Inscribed to W. H. Channing." Emerson wrote this poem in 1846 to mark the death of Charles Turner Torrey, a minister from Salem, Massachusetts, who was convicted of helping slaves to escape. Torrey died in prison.[46] Emerson attended Torrey's funeral and listened to Channing, who, along with Garrison, had become a strong advocate of disunion. Emerson was impressed with Channing's passionate commitment, but he rejects Channing's disunionism on the grounds that dissolving the Union would not address the fact that property, not Union, was the problem. Even if Massachusetts were to promote separation from the slave states, property—or "things," as he calls it—had turned much of New England into its beast of burden. Things would hold the reins and act as sovereign:

> Boston Bay and Bunker Hill
> Would serve things still:—
> Things are of the snake
> . . . . .

> 'Tis the day of chattel,
> Web to weave, and corn to grind;
> Things are in the saddle,
> And ride mankind.
>
> There are two laws discrete,
> Not reconciled,—
> Law for man, and law for thing;
> The last builds town and fleet,
> But it runs wild,
> And doth the man unking (*CW* 9:147–48)

He reverts here to the idea that there are interconnected sets of law for persons and for property. Emerson validates his belief that commerce had transformed the world for the better, but it had not drawn out Spirit or improved human character. It had done the opposite, causing people to internalize the principles of property rather than seeing themselves and every other person as equal and sovereign.

The integration of property—both in the law and in metaphors of personal identity—has allowed the idea of private property to claim priority over the idea that each person must recognize the liberty and equality of each other person. Not just in chattel slavery but in the ways even fully enfranchised citizens are invited to see themselves and one another, the influence of property was dragging the idea of personhood down toward the level of commodity when personhood as an idea should be reaching upward toward equality. In the stifled liberalism that was emerging as the assault on equality was making the promise of community grounded in universal equality harder to imagine, it had also been knocked a step backwards by allowing a new materialist "government of force" to use property rights as a weapon.

Reaching for a model that would redeem liberalism by prioritizing equality as a value but that would also neutralize the "law for thing[s]" by subordinating property rights to human rights, Emerson combines the broadest standard of egalitarianism in the abstract with ongoing faith in the ability of each individual to call forward a better self. In "Politics," using the term "self-government" as a synonym for individuality, Emerson observes that "the tendencies of the times favor the idea of self-government, and leave the individual, for all code, to the rewards and penalties of his own constitution." The movement toward self-government "separates the individual from all party, and unites him, at the same time, to the race." This quality Emerson presents as the foundation of a radical egalitarianism grounded not in a Hobbesian war of each against all but in a standard of universal recognition and mutual appreciation. The impulse toward self-government "promises a recognition of higher rights than those of personal freedom, or the security of property. A man has a right to be employed, to be trusted, to be loved, to be revered." A politics grounded in these rights, in Emerson's view, represents the contrast between "the government of force" and lies, and "the broad design of renovating the State on the principle of right and love" (*CW* 3:128).

Indeed, he pushes the idealism of his metaphors of domesticity in "Politics" as far as it goes in any of his essays: "The power of love as the basis of a state has never been tried. We must not imagine that all things are lapsing into confusion, if every tender protestant be not compelled to bear his part in certain social conventions; nor doubt that roads can be built, letters carried, and the fruits of labor secured, when the government of force is at an end" (*CW* 1:128). Proposing "the power of love as the basis of a state" in the penultimate paragraph of the essay may be an echo of Emerson's early pastoral training, but it is a voice that holds reciprocity and recognition above other values. In the next two sentences he contrasts "the government of force" with the possibility that a society could be "a nation of friends." To close the essay, he admits that for the time being, such visions are far-fetched, but he presents them as aspirational goals nonetheless. The 1844 "Politics" ends by accepting mockery, much as he had accepted mockery after delivering his "Divinity School Address." Or, in the same volume, at the end of "Experience." Solitude offers a sanity and healing power that speak to each discouraged person: "Never mind the ridicule, never mind the defeat: up again, up again, old heart!—it seems to say,—there is victory yet for all justice; and the true romance which the world exists to realize, will be the transformation of genius into practical power" (*CW* 3:49). In "Politics" he encapsulates his defense of equality by contrasting the government of force with a government grounded in an egalitarian dialogue among friends and lovers. "Such designs" as "renovating the State on the principle of right and love,"

> full of genius and full of fate as they are, are not entertained except avowedly as air-pictures. If the individual who exhibits them, dare to think them practicable, he disgusts scholars and churchmen; and men of talent, and women of superior sentiments, cannot hide their contempt.

> Not the less does nature continue to fill the heart of youth with suggestions of this enthusiasm, and there are now men,—if indeed I can speak in the plural number,—more exactly, I will say, I have just been conversing with one man, to whom no weight of adverse experience will make it for a moment appear impossible, that thousands of human beings might exercise towards each other the grandest and simplest sentiments, as well as a knot of friends, or a pair of lovers. (*CW* 3:129)

The central dynamic of the 1844 "Politics" essay is the pressure of reconciling contrasting utopian visions. On the one hand, Emerson advocates the internalization of the ethical responsibilities of government in the individuality of the "wise man." On the other, he envisions the community acting so that "the private citizen might be reasonable, and a good neighbor, without" being threatened by "the hint of jail or a confiscation" (*CW* 3:128).

The most famous lines from "Politics" articulate this process of transition from politics to self-government: "To educate the wise man the state exists; and with the appearance of the wise man, the state expires. The appearance of character makes the State unnecessary. The wise man is the State" (*CW* 1:126). Emerson also implies that the wise man is both a heuristic and an egalitarian. As a heuristic, he represents the conditions under which formal government could literally dissolve into anarchy because every individual has perfectly domesticated culture and is a model of self-government. This anarchy represents the end state of history. It has the freedom of the individual at its center, but in context, individual freedom is possible only because the citizen will always respect the equality of each person they encounter. The "wise man" recognizes that to "undertake the direction" of another is to institute the government of force. The wise person chooses to abstain from that assumption of power over another.

In this version of an atomized society with equality as its foundational value, Emerson builds a just society around radically free individuals. The wise man is a version of the minister, scholar, or poet; but he is also a version of the communal "one man" to which Emerson refers at the beginning of "The American Scholar." The wise man is a metaphor for a just state in which the individual is unbound by institutions. Rather than being "minutely subdivided and pedaled out," such an individual maintains an organic unity through egalitarian respect for and recognition of every other person's rights. In fact, Emerson interprets the actual forms of representative democracy as efforts to simulate this form of government. As a community looks for leadership, it turns to "the will of the wise man." But since the "wise man, it cannot find in nature . . . it makes awkward but earnest efforts to secure his government by contrivances; as, by causing the entire people to give their voices on every measure; or, by a double choice to get the representation of the whole; or by a selection of the best citizens." He here enumerates the basic procedure of direct democracy, representative democracy, and civic republicanism, respectively. But each of these institutions is only a stand-in for the authentic authority of Spirit, because "all forms of government symbolize an immortal government, common to all dynasties and independent of numbers, perfect where two men exist, perfect where there is only one man" (*CW* 3:125).

In regard to "commodity," from as early as *Nature*, Emerson was thinking about the types of activity that create private property in relation not just to its reflection of unalienated labor but in relation to public value. His early thought about trade and commerce partly parallels his thought about democracy in that he sees things like the "cobbler's shop" as a place where people can achieve a form of dignity that neutralizes the difference between a storefront business and an empire. But for my purpose it is mainly important for the way it reflects his progressive idealism. History, for Emerson, is a voyage toward equality. Commerce, in its subversion of ancient forms of arbitrary power, was a crucial leveler and contributed to the emergence of democracy by allowing new outlets for independent creativity that leads to economic independence and contributions to the public weal. In the combination of creative liberty and political equality, Emerson finds a potential set of conditions that, if understood properly, could offer a higher level of dignity to each and all than had ever been known before.

Conclusion
EMERSON'S CULTURE WAR

The culture wars of Jacksonian and antebellum America represent the high-water mark of illiberal thought in the United States, a time in which intensive arguments in favor of social hierarchy, "natural" aristocracy, sexual paternalism, scientific racism, and economic caste gained enough believers to provoke a civil war that had the question of equality at its very center. In the constitution the Confederacy wrote in 1861, rather than simply ignoring equality, Confederate leaders defined inequality as the cornerstone of the slave-based caste society they intended to create. Preparing the ideological ground for this transformative event remains a breathtaking accomplishment; and it has had breathtaking consequences for those who stood behind it, and for the United States as a whole.

The antecedent changes in American values that made secession possible did not happen quickly. Defenses of slavery, and projects aiming to classify people by sex, race, ethnicity, and even economic standing, all participated in a decades-long campaign aimed at discrediting belief in human equality. Participants in the assault were an eclectic group, and they chipped away at Americans' faith in equality from a wide variety of angles. Among many others, participants included constitutional scholar Rufus Choate; the northern proslavery politician James Buchanan, who as president clearly signaled his willingness to accept the nationalization of slavery; and brigades of southern ideologues such as John C. Calhoun, Thomas Dew, and George Fitzhugh. Many participants simultaneously advocated equality in one area and inequality in another, such as labor organizer Ely Moore, who, as many populists have done, combined economic advocacy for workingmen with ethnocentric xenophobia; and Catharine Beecher, who defined a model of womanhood that sought equality of respect even as it maximized binary distinctions between men and women.

Yet all contributors to the assault on equality shared the conviction that the path to a more perfect American union was to clarify classification by identity and then to minimize social, economic, or conjugal fluidity among categories. As Steven Hahn describes the recurring rise and fall of this strain of "illiberal" thought in American culture, "Illiberalism develops and changes, transforms and reconstitutes itself, finds new bases of support while displacing others, and is rarely distant from the levers of power."[1] At the center of this rise in illiberal thought was an effort to discredit the antislavery movement, to define antislavery as the ringbolt that secured a broad range of egalitarian challenges to traditional prerogatives. Egalitarian movements of all kinds provoked accusations of radical leveling that would undermine a society ordered by natural hierarchy. To advocates of caste, connections between antislavery and other movements in favor of equality were easy to spot. Egalitarian thought was giving ideas to "boarding school misses and factory girls" who might turn their "sewing parties into abolition clubs."[2] Reform threatened the authority of husbands and fathers, business owners, political elites, and slave society as a whole. In its leveling, it would blur lines that allowed hierarchy to define people's boundaries and assign them to categories for regulation. Ultimately, many argued, antislavery would lead to miscegenation and the emergence of an ever-expanding conglomeration of people unclassifiable by race, the day's strongest metaphor for social chaos.[3] The assault on equality, at its most fundamental level, was about using modern forms of knowledge to strengthen justifications for old hierarchies. Rufus Choate appeals to exactly this anxiety when he tells the Whigs of Maine that unless the Republicans are defeated, the society will slip further into moral chaos. Victory for the Republicans would mean "the beginning of the end" of the country they knew: "flushed by triumph," the Republicans would "inaugurate freedom and put down the oligarchy; its constitution the glittering and sounding generalities of natural right which make up the Declaration of Independence."[4]

Emerson entered the debate over equality as a surprising convert. From the very early 1830s onward, he developed religious beliefs unconventional enough that shortly before his thirtieth birthday he chose to resign from an important and prestigious pastoral position in Boston. It was a brave and principled move. But few could fathom his reasons for walking away, especially given that he continued to preach for several more years. It was also surprising on a personal level. Throughout his education, he seemed content to live in a tradition of conservative liberalism that was suspicious of anything radical and that embraced many anti-egalitarian values. The republican spirit that Emerson absorbed from his social environment was steeped in the Federalists' belief that power rightly belonged in the hands of a "natural aristocracy."

The struggle between inclusive and exclusionary models of voting rights that peaked during Emerson's teens and twenties marked the first successful egalitarian reform movement in the young republic. Emerson's position in that debate should have been predictable. In 1821, when Massachusetts held a state constitutional convention to address property requirements for the franchise, Daniel Webster—the hero of Emerson's youth—voted to keep the franchise restricted to property owners. Ezra Ripley, Emerson's revered stepgrandfather, pastor in Concord for sixty years, supported the continuation of property restrictions too. If the conservatives had won, Massachusetts would have retained the exclusionary standard of the 1780 constitution written by John Adams. Yet Emerson warmed quickly to democratization and even wrote essays to explain how it could foster a society that was more individualistic.

Though he was always committed to a principle of spiritual equality, Emerson's allegiance to equality broadened and adapted to changing contexts. External obstacles to individuality and self-reliance forced him to rethink his early belief that liberating the internal faculties of the individual would be enough to allow one to become free and equal. But he concluded that you couldn't just plant yourself in the center, be true to your beliefs, and expect the world to emulate your independence of spirit. Thus, I think it is incorrect to say that Emerson's work evolved through a philosophical or spiritual logic. Rather, his positions on civil issues emerged from paying attention to and participating in the antebellum culture wars.[5] The evolution of Emerson's thought was political and civic rather than philosophical; his philosophy and spirituality never change in any major commitment. He never wavers from the core beliefs he articulates in the 1830s. Rather, as his thought develops, he recontextualizes these beliefs to suit a more cynical understanding of the society in which he lived.

In this book I have argued that Emerson held equality as a fundamental value and that his commitment to extending equality to more people is just as important in his thinking as is the idea that all people should be free. Less explicitly, I have tried to argue that these two beliefs intersect in the idea of individuality: every person should be free to achieve individuality and equally empowered from birth to pursue it.

Emerson's condemnation of Daniel Webster following the Massachusetts senator's choice to stand with slavery in the secession crisis of 1850 allows a vital insight into Emerson's understanding of how justice is linked both to egalitarian reform and to a grand struggle between forces of inequality and unfreedom on the one hand and forces of equality and liberty on the other: "Mr. Webster is a man who lives by his memory, a man of the past, not a man of faith or of hope. He obeys his powerful animal nature;—and his finely developed understanding only works truly and with all its force, when it stands for animal good; that is, for property. He believes, in so many words, that government exists for the protection of property" (*AW* 66). Though Emerson had revered Webster, had even been encouraged to emulate Webster's oratory by his aunt Mary Moody Emerson, Webster's political power had become symbolic of institutions intent on sustaining the norms of an oppressive past rather than idealistically leaning forward into a more just future. If nothing else, by the time of the Fugitive Slave Act controversy, Emerson had been immersed in antislavery long enough to know that plenty of people would have had Webster's back if he had made the right choice. Webster, a senator from Emerson's home state of Massachusetts, was going to stand for property, slavery, hierarchy, and the past.

As the assault on equality was racking up a series of wins that enabled Indian removals and expanded slavery, Emerson was articulating a stable, committed, and adaptable defense of equality. It was stable in the sense that it did not change much over time; committed in the sense that he tested his defense of equality against the claims of equality's antagonists and found equality to be true and inequality to be false; and adaptable in that it addresses social conditions relevant to everything from the value of international trade to the terms under which husbands and wives sit down to dinner. Seeing Emerson's career as a sustained defense of equality adds much to our understanding of the role that he played within the Transcendentalist movement and of the Transcendentalists' importance as advocates for the United States to become more and more a society of equals. His vision for equality begins and ends in the same place, with people giving one another the high respect of recognition as individuals. Most importantly, this meant speaking honestly, or at least striving to, the way one would in conversation with friends.

Among the many public questions that sustained his career was: What would it mean to live "a good and equal life" (*CW* 3:127). A crucial mode of addressing that question was to acknowledge that inequality was a problem in justice, to keep equality in the foreground as a personal value, and to aid its expansion through both personal transformation and support for egalitarian reform activism.

His interest in conversation is the bridge that links his focus on honesty in personal relationships and integrity in public discourse. His whole theory of politics, from the concept of the citizen to the role of public opinion, revolves around the issue of sincerity in public speech. In his thought about topics related to communication, which I have grouped under the aspirational goal of "the domestication of the idea of culture," honesty and sincerity serve Emerson as powerful standards for analysis (*CW* 1:65). At the center of the aspirational "air-pictures" of a society in which norms of private intimacy also characterize public debate, Emerson locates the task of making institutional borders porous so that people can communicate as equal *persons*. Fostering an ability to communicate across widely diverse institutional positions and individual experiences links his communication theory both to his praise of the way capitalism liberates creative energy and to his criticism of the way it distributes the benefits of innovation. It also directs his thought toward ideals of the universalization of human rights along a cosmopolitan model. Imagining equality in cosmopolitan terms is the necessary complement of Emerson's effort to imagine autonomy in individualistic terms.

Of all Emerson's books, *Representative Men*, his book on heroes, has the most yearning quality, even more than *The Conduct of Life*. He asks why certain individuals are able to become representative of a certain quality and cast shadows so dense that everyone else lives in their shadow. In *Representative Men*, Emerson is not advertising greatness. On the contrary, analyzing great men is more like opposition research, and it is part of his effort to envision a more aspirational equality than even greatness can offer. In the introductory essay, "The Uses of Great Men," Emerson asks: "But *great men*:—the word is injurious. Is there caste? Is there fate? What becomes of the promise to virtue?" (*CW* 4:17). The very idea threatens his own belief in universal equality.

The closest civil approximation Emerson ever witnessed to the egalitarian condition he imagines as an air-picture was at the Chardon Street Convention, a set of three conferences held in Boston between November 1840 and November 1841. The conference was called by the "Friends of Universal Reform," an ad hoc group that had convened in an empty meeting room right after a gathering of the Non-Resistance Society. Emerson had delivered his lecture "War" to the latter group three years earlier. Accompanied by Lidian, Emerson attended most of the first three-day convention. The only conference review that *The Dial* ever published was Emerson's short report.

The Universal Reform group, which included Bronson Alcott and William Lloyd Garrison, thought it timely to call a convention to discuss three basic questions in religion: (1) Is the Sabbath biblical? (2) What is the status of ministers as spiritual leaders? And (3) How should people think about churches as a setting for spiritual life? The agenda sounds obscure and technical—but everyone could see that it was a Trojan horse that the reformers would use to advance anti-institutional and radically individualist ideas against the interests of old-line Protestant churches like Presbyterianism and Congregationalism. These churches had recently been disestablished and thus no longer received direct subsidies from their states, but their ministers considered them to be the true foundation of order and justice in American society.

Even though New England was saturated with reform activity in 1840, this program was met with special anticipation. The call set the stage for a freewheeling discussion in which spiritual autonomy would stand toe to toe with orthodox Christian worship. Emerson did not speak at the convention, but he would attend all three meetings as an eager observer. What Emerson saw in the advertisement was very much in line with his interest in individual freedom, especially as it related to spirituality. He teased Lidian in a letter leading up to the conference, asking her: "A week from today will be the Convention of Universal Reform. Do you not wish to go there & speak for the old Sunday?" (*L* 2:360–61). Though they would sit side by side, she would ally with the orthodox and he would ally with the reformers.

But what he took away from the experience had nothing to do with theology. He focused on the diversity of people in the room and on how they conducted themselves as they argued from deepest conviction. The Chardon Street Convention struck him as a model of equality like none he had ever known before. We can't say how much of the event he actually attended, but he was definitely there at the beginning, and he was probably still there at the very end. Just before the final adjournment, having discussed the Sabbath, the ministry, and the church, Bronson Alcott moved that they hold another convention to discuss the authority of the Holy Bible. Emerson either accepted or was put on the organizing committee.[6]

Emerson's review of the Chardon Street Convention has become the standard account and the most widely read. But his semi-satirical essay describes the conference very differently than do other reports. Most records express shock at the diversity of the attendees. An observer from Hingham, on the shore just south of Boston, observes that "since the day of Pentecost, we don't believe such a conglomeration of strange tongues has even been known. . . . Clergymen were there as well as laymen . . . Atheists and Deists, Mormons and Socialists, white men and black men, men with beards and men without, No-money men and Anti-property men, and so on, including 'Women lecturers,' who too freely claimed the floor."[7]

At one point in the first session, Edward Taylor, the fierce Methodist pastor of the Seamen's Bethel in New Bedford, was confronted by Abby Kelley, a well-known advocate of civil equality for women and African Americans. As Taylor "commenced his remarks" in defense of the Sabbath, Kelley rose and interrupted.

"Brother Taylor! Brother Taylor!"

"Don't you brother me, madam. I am in no way related to you unless it is in Adam, and I am sorry for that."

"Brother Taylor! Brother Taylor! I will be a swift witness against you in the coming day."

"What have I done, madam?"

"I was a stranger and ye took me not in."

"Ah! Madam! There are a great many strange women in and about Boston. I hope I will not be severely dealt with, for not taking them all in."[8]

Another observer reads the diversity of the group as a subject for mockery: "Down in front of the pulpit, I could see quite a number of lovely looking creatures plying their pretty fingers with remarkable industry in knitting, who, if they had been in almost any other congregation and place, might have been deemed worthy the appellation of *ladies*; . . . I could see, perched upon the top of a seat, or something more elevated than others occupied, a *Jew*, venerable and imposing in his exterior as Abraham himself." During a speech on the economy, he comments on the speaker and the convention's response. The speaker "screeched out the malignity of his heart—for *soul* he has none, according to his atheism—at the top of his voice, that those who get their living without 'manual labor are *thieves!*' 'That's true,' said the old Jew, backed up by a squeaking response from some of the pretty 'knitters' down near the pulpit." Altogether, it was too much: "It was a compounded mass of factious religionists, and 'believers in all unbelief'; men, and women too, who are seeking to uproot all existing organizations, civil, social, and religious. The Convention in its elemental character was a rank, rabid democracy, let loose from all restraint,—baptizing with a raving, malignant, disorganizing spirit—the legitimate offspring of obtuseness, of intellectual perception, and of obliquity of heart."[9] The conference did attract an eclectic audience of participants and observers. The register of the convention includes the signatures of nineteen women. Two accounts of the conference remark on the attendance of African Americans.

In his essay on the convention, Emerson adds his own list of notable participants. The attendees included "men of every shade of opinion, from the straightest orthodoxy to the wildest heresy.... Madmen, madwomen, men with beards, Dunkers, Muggletonians, Come-outers, Groaners, Agrarians, Seventh-day-Baptists, Quakers, Abolitionists, Calvinists, Unitarians, and Philosophers." But he emphasizes the norms of dialogue the conference established for itself: "This Convention never printed any report of its deliberations, nor pretended to arrive at any result by the expression of its sense in formal resolutions,—the professed objects of those persons who felt the greatest interest in its meetings being simply the elucidation of truth through free discussion." With a bare minimum of rules, "the most daring innovators, and the champions-until-death of the old cause, sat side-by-side" (CW 10:179–80).

At the Transcendentalist end of the spectrum, Bronson Alcott attended all three sessions and argued against privileging either the church or the Bible in spiritual life. At the orthodox end was minister Amos Phelps, who gave a four-hour lecture defending the biblical origins of the Sabbath. Nathaniel Whiting, a shoemaker from Marshfield, on the coast south of Boston, gave the most provocative speech, charging that the clergy and the Sabbath, in league with the business community, were at the center of an exploitative economy that supported slavery and degraded workmen like himself. He accused businessmen of having the same values as slaveholders and argued that workers had the same status as slaves. His speech was inflammatory enough that some feared the small businessmen and workers attending the convention might riot. Whiting was persuaded to give a public apology the following evening, saying that his critique was aimed at "the false system of society which is the cause of all our evils."[10] Emerson's first biographer reports that Emerson regarded Whiting's speech as the finest at the convention and implies that Emerson is referring to Whiting when he observes that "the still-living merit of the oldest New England Families . . . encountered the founders of families, fresh merit, emerging, and expanding the brows to a new breadth, and lighting a clownish face with sacred fire."[11] While prominent people, both men and women, spoke at the convention, Emerson describes it as though the newcomers and amateurs spoke while the elites sat and listened: "The assembly was characterized by the predominance of a certain plain, sylvan strength and earnestness, whilst many of the most intellectual and cultivated persons attended its councils" (*CW* 10:180). He sums up his report by remarking that although the event was exhausting, he was energized by it. There were

> signal passages of pure eloquence, by much vigor of thought and especially by the exhibition of character and by the victories of character. These men and women were in search for something more satisfying than a vote or a definition, and they found what they sought, or the pledge of it, . . . in the lofty reliance on principles, and the prophetic dignity and transfiguration which accompanies, even amidst opposition and ridicule, a man whose mind is made up to obey the great inward commander. (*CW* 10:180–81)

In "Self-Reliance" Emerson comments, "I like the silent church before the service begins" (*CW* 2:41). He appreciates the spiritual independence of a church full of souls all praying or preparing to pray in their own way. At the Chardon Street Convention, it was as though all the people were in church, speaking at once, and the result was something like the music of the spheres. People had gathered to voice "every shade of opinion from straitest orthodoxy to the wildest heresy, and many persons whose church was a church of one person only" (*CW* 10:179–80). Three years later he returns to his experience at Chardon Street and uses it as the central event in his essay "New England Reformers." Emerson emphasizes that convention as a gathering of the supreme individualists of his day. Those reformers and activists, battling for every cause, were also his admired colleagues in the antebellum culture wars. He remembers the participants criticizing everything, every institution, every practice—from "marriage as the fountain of social evils" to the founding of a society for "the protection of groundworms, slugs and mosquitos"—so that the convention seemed to him "like a congress of kings, each of whom had a realm to rule, and a way of his own that made concert unprofitable" (*CW*

3:150, 149). But they had come together, acting in concert to acknowledge one another's equality and to respect one another's dignity.

The Chardon Street Convention, and Emerson's effervescent response to it, is a metaphor for what he hoped to protect by defending equality. In his society in 1840 and 1841—before the Mexican War and the Fugitive Slave Act, before Webster's betrayal, but also before Seneca Falls, the Married Women's Property Act, the emergence of Frederick Douglass, the birth of the Republicans, and John Brown's raid—this gathering of individuals who asserted the high sovereignty to take the floor and represent how the world should be were also willing to gather as equal representatives in a congress; to speak and hear one another, claiming dignity for themselves and, by their tolerant attention, dignifying one another. For Emerson, it was a pledge of the possibility that little by little, the "domestication of the idea of culture," fostered by the vigorous defense of equality, would ultimately allow everyone to live in a fulfilling and creative society of equals.

Acknowledgments

Grants from the National Endowment for the Humanities and the American Philosophical Society were invaluable to me. They allowed me to reach materials not yet digitized at collections up and down the East Coast. Special collections librarians at Swarthmore and Bryn Mawr, and at the Concord Free Public Library, alerted me to collections of letters and pamphlets that added much to my understanding. I also owe a good deal to my college and university; both SUNY Brockport and SUNY-wide grant programs helped me obtain books, time, and graduate research assistance for this project. Amanda Heller's editing has added a valuable layer of clarity to the whole book. I also thank Kathleen McGarvey, Heather Dubnick, Aileen McGovern, Matthew Kilmer, Jose Maliekal, Ralph Black, Stefan Jurasinski, and Miriam Burstein.

Notes

PROLOGUE

1. Allan Nevins, *Ordeal of the Union*, 2 vols. (New York: Scribner, 1947), 2:156; Michael F. Holt, *Political Parties and American Political Development: From the Age of Jackson to the Age of Lincoln* (Baton Rouge: Louisiana State University Press, 1992), 820–24; Sean Wilentz, *The Rise of American Democracy: Jefferson to Lincoln* (New York: Norton, 2005), 675.
2. Lincoln and Stephens met in Congress during the late 1840s and occasionally corresponded throughout the rest of their lives. Stephens intended to patch up tensions between Stephen A. Douglas of Illinois and the sitting president, James Buchanan. Nonetheless, Lincoln's and Stephens's confidence was strong enough that their letters during the secession crisis are often cited to clarify the Republican and southern Democratic positions in the aftermath of Lincoln's election. For example, see Lincoln's letter of December 22, 1860, to Stephens in *The Portable Abraham Lincoln*, ed. Andrew Delbanco (New York: Penguin, 2009), 224; Nevins, *Ordeal of the Union*, 1:371–72; David Herbert Donald, *Lincoln* (New York: Simon and Schuster, 1995), 555–60; Holt, *Political Parties*, 467–70.
3. Henry Cleveland, *Alexander H. Stephens in Public and Private: With Letters and Speeches before, during, and since the War* (Philadelphia: National Publishing Company, 1866), 696–97, 713; Thomas Edwin Schott, *Alexander H. Stephens of Georgia: A Biography* (Baton Rouge: Louisiana State University Press, 1988), 306. James Read studies the personal correspondence Lincoln and Stephens maintained during the post-election secession crisis. What comes through is both the cordiality the two express and Stephens's feeling of humiliation by northern public opinion. James H. Read, "Hard Choices: Lincoln and 'the Public Estimate of the Negro': From Anti-amalgamation to Antislavery," in *The Political Thought of the Civil War*, ed. Alan Levine (Lawrence: University Press of Kansas, 2018), 133–34.
4. Cleveland, *Alexander H. Stephens*, 720.
5. Cleveland, *Alexander H. Stephens*, 721; Schott, *Alexander H. Stephens of Georgia*, 334–35.
6. Cleveland, *Alexander H. Stephens*, 721.
7. In regard to race, Jefferson is only slightly ambiguous regarding African Americans' inferiority to whites. Annette Gordon-Reed argues that he offered "as a suspicion only" that whites were superior, but "on one point he did not equivocate: the mixture with whites improved black people." Annette Gordon-Reed, *The Hemingses*

of Monticello (New York: W. W. Norton & Co., 2009), 141. Sean Wilentz studies the tone that civil rights leaders have taken in adopting Jefferson as an ally, noting that Martin Luther King Jr. maintained "a certain ironic detachment" that acknowledges Jefferson's contributions to egalitarian thought as well as his efforts against equality for free blacks in Virginia and his silence on race questions for much of his life. Wilentz concludes that "the greatest triumphs of the civil rights movement posed the greatest problems for Jefferson's reputation" (*Rise of American Democracy*, 86).

8. Thomas Jefferson, *Notes on the State of Virginia* (New York: Penguin Books, 1999), 163.
9. Gordon-Reed emphasizes Jefferson's patriarchalism over his racism and stresses that his posture changed over time: "The young man who had been very vocal, for one of his station and place, on the subject of emancipation, fell pretty much silent from middle age on.... Building the nation was Jefferson's true obsession, not the end of slavery and definitely not the racial question" (*The Hemingses of Monticello*, 566–67). Yet his white supremacist assumptions conditioned his behavior throughout his life. As Alan Taylor notes, into his seventies, Jefferson was writing in support of Indian removals and imagining ways to deport all black children from the South. Alan Taylor, *Thomas Jefferson's Education* (New York: W. W. Norton & Company, 2019), 141.
10. Cleveland, *Alexander H. Stephens*, 721–22.
11. Cleveland, *Alexander H. Stephens*, 722.

INTRODUCTION

1. Eugene D. and Elizabeth Fox-Genovese study the psychological justifications of slavery within the "mind of the master," as they phrase it. Eugene D. Genovese and Elizabeth Fox-Genovese, *Fatal Self-Deception: Slaveholding Paternalism in the Old South* (New York: Cambridge University Press, 2011), esp. chap. 4, "Loyal and Loving Slaves," and chap. 6, "Guardians of a Helpless Race."
2. Stanley Cavell develops this posture as a model of "aversive thinking" that links individuality to equality. In practice, this posture requires "a constitution of the public and at the same time, an institution of the private, a new obligation to think for ourselves to make ourselves intelligible in every word." Stanley Cavell, *Conditions Handsome and Unhandsome: The Constitution of Emersonian Perfectionism* (La Salle, IL: Open Court, 1990), 45, 33–51 passim.
3. Ralph Waldo Emerson, *Natural History of Intellect and Other Papers*, ed. Edward W. Emerson (Boston: Houghton Mifflin, 1893), 46.
4. Edward J. Larson, *The Creation-Evolution Debate: Historical Perspectives* (Athens: University of Georgia Press, 2010), 315.
5. Ralph Waldo Emerson, *Natural History of Intellect and Other Papers*, ed. Edward W. Emerson (Boston: Houghton, Mifflin, 1893), 66.
6. J. R. Pole, *The Pursuit of Equality in American History* (Berkeley: University of California Press, 1978), 13.
7. John Rawls's reading of Hobbes inverts the typical framework of the social contract. The "state of nature" is not a distant memory of universal war; rather, for Hobbes,

"the state of nature is not some *past* state of affairs, or indeed any actual condition, but an *ever present possibility to be avoided*." John Rawls, *Lectures on the History of Political Philosophy*, ed. Samuel Freeman (Cambridge, MA: Belknap Press of Harvard University Press, 2007), 32.
8. John Locke, *Two Treatises of Government and a Letter Concerning Toleration*, ed. Ian Shapiro (New Haven, CT: Yale University Press, 2003), 2.4.116.
9. Pole, *Pursuit of Equality*, 13–14.
10. Alexander Keyssar, *The Right to Vote: The Contested History of Democracy in the United States*, rev. ed. (New York: Basic Books, 2009), 10.
11. Pole, *Pursuit of Equality*, 6.
12. Ulrike Davy and Antje Flüchter, introduction to *Imagining Unequals, Imagining Equals: Concepts of Equality in History and Law*, ed. Ulrike Davy and Antje Flüchter (Bielefeld: transcript Verlag, 2022), 15.
13. Benjamin Rush, *Observations Upon the Present Government of Pennsylvania: In Four Letters to the People of Pennsylvania* (Philadelphia: Styner and Cist, 1777), 147.
14. Noah Webster, *Effects of Slavery* (Hartford, 1793), 32.
15. Whereas Sean Wilentz focuses his analysis of Jacksonian democracy on the Bank War, Daniel Walker Howe emphasizes the Indian removals crisis. Wilentz sees the period primarily in terms of a structural realignment of economic class in which people with few economic assets claimed political enfranchisement and tried to reorganize economic institutions to their advantage. Howe, by contrast, emphasizes culture over class and sees the Indian removals as representative of a broader pattern of determining the rights of different people within the republic. For Wilentz, the end of the Bank of the United States was a great victory for equality. For Howe, the removals were a great rejection of equality. See Sean Wilentz, *The Rise of American Democracy: Jefferson to Lincoln* (New York: Norton, 2005), 392–403; Daniel Walker Howe, *What Hath God Wrought: The Transformation of America, 1815–1848* (New York: Oxford University Press, 2007), 339–57.
16. Pole, *Pursuit of Equality*, 154–61; Charles Sellers, *The Market Revolution: Jacksonian America, 1815–1846* (New York: Oxford University Press, 1991), 23–27, 282–90. This issue is central to the motivation of early labor unions. See Eric Foner, *Free Soil, Free Labor, Free Men* (New York: Oxford University Press, 1995), 48–90. Mark Lause connects the issue of respect especially to the emergence of the Free Soil movement. Mark A. Lause, *Long Road to Harpers Ferry: The Rise of the First American Left* (London: Pluto Press, 2018), 102–14.
17. *New-York Gazette and General Advertiser*, November, 24, 1801; Howard B. Rock, *Artisans of the New Republic* (New York: NYU Press, 1979), 188–95; Sellers, *Market Revolution*, 26.
18. Pole, *Pursuit of Equality*, 157.
19. The boldest of these schemes was articulated in Thomas Skidmore's treatise *The Rights of Man to Property!* But this means of redefining equality through radical changes in property rights was important in the platform of the General Trades Union, headed by Ely Moore, and to the National Reform Association, led by George Evans. The latter organization, known as the NRA, sought to suppress land speculation by eastern bankers by funneling recent immigrants through coastal cities to western agricultural districts. This would, the NRA held, bring arable

western land into use, reduce competition for labor in coastal cities, and drive up wages through both the inflow of western produce and the tighter labor market. See Lause, *Long Road to Harpers Ferry*, 1–34; Foner, *Free Soil*, 112–14; Alexander Saxton, *The Rise and Fall of the White Republic* (London: Verso, 1990), 96–103.

20. Bruce Laurie, *Beyond Garrison: Antislavery and Social Reform* (Cambridge, UK: Cambridge University Press, 2005), 201–2, 213–25.
21. From the first Lincoln–Douglas debate, quoted in *The Portable Abraham Lincoln*, ed. Andrew Delbanco (New York: Penguin, 2009), 147–48.
22. As David Herbert Donald and Henry Louis Gates Jr. have detailed, Lincoln and Douglas were almost in competition to offer the sharpest vision of white supremacy in both the 1858 and 1860 campaigns. Despite Lincoln's commitment to preventing the spread of slavery, his speeches are replete with explicit claims of white supremacy. Donald concludes that throughout this period, "rather vaguely, he continued to think of colonization as the best solution to the American race problem." David Herbert Donald, *Lincoln* (New York: Simon and Schuster, 1995), 221. Gates emphasizes the complexity of Lincoln's views on race, how fully he separated race and slavery, but how difficult he found it to imagine blacks and whites sharing civil society as equals. Lincoln's attraction to the colonization movement, which Gates tracks, extended even past the Emancipation Proclamation. Henry Louis Gates Jr., *Lincoln on Race and Slavery* (Princeton: Princeton University Press, 2009), xx–lxiv.
23. Samuel Gilman Brown, *Life of Rufus Choate* (Cambridge: Legare Street Press, 2023), 322.
24. Brown, *Life of Rufus Choate*, 325, 324.
25. Brown, *Life of Rufus Choate*, 326.
26. Henry James Hammond, "Mudsill" speech or "Cotton is King" speech, March 4, 1858, https://www.americanantiquarian.org/Manuscripts/cottonisking.html.
27. An important strain of Emerson criticism tracks his movement from Transcendentalist idealism to some form of skepticism or pragmatism. Stephen Whicher's *Freedom and Fate: An Inner Life of Ralph Waldo Emerson* set the terms by defining the drama of Emerson's career as a struggle between human spiritual power and the irreducible facts of the world. John Michael did much to develop the debate between these impulses in his study of Emerson and Montaigne. This issue, as it has been expressed in a host of books and articles, is important to interpreting Emerson's sense of the practical power, or lack of it, that people can bring to bear on the world. The most basic understanding of it is that Emerson began his career as an idealist then shifted his perspective on human power toward an anti-foundationalist pragmatism, or even toward a form of stoic skepticism. This line of criticism is very important to my understanding of the debate over equality because it says much about ideas regarding the power of human beings over nature and even over themselves that underpinned arguments for the possibility of reform in relation to restrictions attributed to God and nature. See John Michael, *Emerson and Skepticism* (Baltimore: Johns Hopkins University Press, 1988); Barbara L. Packer, *Emerson's Fall: A New Interpretation of the Major Essays* (New York: Continuum, 1982); Stephen E. Whicher, *Freedom and Fate: An Inner Life of Ralph Waldo Emerson* (Philadelphia: University of Pennsylvania Press, 1953), esp. chap. 6, "Skepticism," 109–23, for foundational arguments on Emerson's skepticism. This theme is central, though

usually unstated in Michael Lopez, *Emerson and Power: Creative Antagonism in the Nineteenth Century* (Carbondale: Northern Illinois University Press, 1996), 165–90; and in Branka Arsić, *On Leaving: A Reading in Emerson* (Cambridge, MA: Harvard University Press, 2010). Arsić treats skepticism as a starting point for her analysis. See part 1, "Leave-Takings," 19–90, esp. 61–71; and Stanley Cavell, *In Quest of the Ordinary: Lines of Skepticism and Romanticism* (Chicago: University of Chicago Press, 1988). The Pragmatist strain has been drawn out by Jonathan Levin, *The Poetics of Transition: Emerson, Pragmatism, and American Literary Modernism* (Durham, NC: Duke University Press, 1999); Richard Poirier, *Poetry and Pragmatism* (Cambridge, MA: Harvard University Press, 1992); Michael Magee, *Emancipating Pragmatism: Emerson, Jazz, and Experimental Writing* (Tuscaloosa: University of Alabama Press, 2004); and Cornell West, *The American Evasion of Philosophy: A Genealogy of Pragmatism* (Madison: University of Wisconsin Press, 1989).

28. Bruce Baum explicitly connects Johann Gottlieb Fichte's and especially Friedrich Schlegel's nationalist thought with the emergence of proto-master race theories in the 1820s. Theories of linguistic anthropology that rooted Aryan master race thought in ancient India dovetailed with "scientific" studies of skeletal remains by natural historians in France, Germany, and the United States. This integration shifted assumptions about inherent biological differences. As Baum puts it, by the 1830s, "racialism—the conviction that [there] were physiologically distinct human 'races'—had become the prevailing view among European and North American scientists and, more and more, non-scientists." Bruce Baum, *The Rise and Fall of the Caucasian Race: A Political History of Racial Identity* (New York: NYU Press, 2008), 96–99; see also chap. 4 on "racialized nationalism"; and Micheline Ishay, *The History of Human Rights: From Ancient Times to the Globalization Era* (Berkeley: University of California Press, 2004), 175–90.

Links connecting the American school of anthropology to master race theories of the mid-twentieth century involve both direct influence and the rise of eugenic theories. John Humphrey Noyes and Victoria Woodhull both advocated scientific breeding of human beings as early as the 1860s. Also see Stefan Kuhl, *Nazi Connection: Eugenics, American Racism, and German National Socialism* (New York: Oxford University Press, 2002), 3–26. The eugenics movement was influential enough that many American states practiced forced sterilization from the beginning of the twentieth century through the 1970s. In crafting the Nuremberg Laws, German Nazi legal scholars combed the history of American racial legislation. In *Hitler's American Model*, James Whitman writes that "it is with the Blood Law that we discover the most provocative evidence of direct Nazi engagement with American legal models, and the most unsettling signs of direct influence. American law was expressly invoked in the key radical Nazi document establishing the initial framework for the Blood Law." James Q. Whitman, *Hitler's American Model: The United States and the Making of Nazi Race Law* (Princeton, NJ: Princeton University Press, 2017), 76.

29. Judith N. Shklar, *Redeeming American Political Thought* (Chicago: University of Chicago Press, 1998), 103.

30. F. O. Matthiessen, *Art and Expression in the Age of Emerson and Whitman* (New York: Oxford University Press, 1968), xi.

31. Carl Lotus Becker, *The Declaration of Independence: A Study in the History of Political Ideas* (New York: Harcourt, Brace, 1922), 279.

CHAPTER 1

1. *Richmond Whig*, quoted in *Globe* [Washington, DC], August 22, 1834. See also Alexander Keyssar, *The Right to Vote: The Contested History of Democracy in the United States*, rev. ed. (New York: Basic Books, 2009), 28–35; and Ronald P. Formisano, *The Transformation of Political Culture: Massachusetts Parties, 1790s–1840s* (New York: Oxford University Press, 1983), 128–35.
2. *American Review* 1 (January 1845): 3–4.
3. As political organizations, both the Whig and Democratic Parties trace their roots to Jeffersonian republicanism, as Michael Holt puts it in his history of the Whigs: "Massive research in the past forty years has shown that the Whig Party evolved not from the Federalists, but from divisions within the Jeffersonian Republican Party." Michael F. Holt, *The Rise and Fall of the American Whig Party* (New York: Oxford University Press, 1999), 2. For my purpose, the slipperiness of the Democracy is especially important. Sean Wilentz concludes that most historical accounts fail to recognize the "dynamic and unstable character of the Democracy's rise and development." Sean Wilentz, *The Rise of American Democracy: Jefferson to Lincoln* (New York: Norton, 2005), 509. To Emerson and those who leaned toward a Whig perspective, the Democracy embodied mass psychology, complete with violent and brutal pathologies. Historians such as Daniel Walker Howe, Alexander Saxton, and Michael Holt often echo this view of the Democracy. Howe, especially, aligns the Democracy with the assault on equality: "The Jacksonian movement in politics, although it took the name of the Democratic Party, fought so hard in favor of slavery and white supremacy, and opposed the inclusion of non-whites and women within the American civil polity so resolutely, that it makes the term 'Jacksonian Democracy' all the more inappropriate as a characterization of the years between 1815 and 1848." Daniel Walker Howe, *What Hath God Wrought: The Transformation of America, 1815–1848* (New York: Oxford University Press, 2007), 4.
4. Carl F. Strauch, "Emerson's Phi Beta Kappa Poem," *New England Quarterly* 23, no. 1 (1950): 90, https://doi-org.brockport.idm.oclc.org/10.2307/361592.
5. Rogers Smith and Daniel Walker Howe especially emphasize the sexism and racism of Jacksonian revisions of citizenship. Alex Keyssar interprets this period of reconstructing citizenship in terms that imply slightly less diabolical intentions. Sean Wilentz offers an analysis that defends the Jacksonians' efforts to expand democratic political rights even as it recognizes the exclusionary legacies they left in political equality. See Rogers M. Smith, *Civic Ideals: Conflicting Visions of Citizenship in U.S. History* (New Haven: Yale University Press, 1997), esp. chap. 8, "High Noon of the White Republic," 197–242; Howe, *What Hath God Wrought*, esp. chap. 11, "Jacksonian Democracy and the Rule of Law," 411–45; Keyssar, *The Right to Vote*, 22–43; and Wilentz, *Rise of American Democracy*, 23–24.
6. I put "universal" in quotations marks here to denote the idiomatic term with which contemporaries defined the expanded suffrage of the 1820s and 1830s, despite the

fact that it was profoundly exclusionary. In fact, a more universal suffrage was discussed frequently in constitutional conventions and franchise debates generally. The first important movement in the emergence of an antebellum culture of reform was the expansion of the franchise to men with little or no real property. See T. Gregory Garvey, *Creating the Culture of Reform in Antebellum America* (Athens: University Press of Georgia, 2006), 28–29; and Nancy Isenberg, *Sex and Citizenship in Antebellum America* (Chapel Hill: University of North Carolina Press, 1998), 25–31; Smith, *Civic Ideals*, 311–17.

7. Robert Richardson characterizes the period between Emerson's authorship of *Nature* and delivery of "The American Scholar," roughly from early 1836 through winter 1837, as the point at which his thinking coalesced. As Richardson puts it in reference to the "Philosophy of History" lecture series: "What often appear as scattered insights in . . . better-known essays appear here in this set of lectures as part of a major and coherent phase in Emerson's development. The moment when his thought reached its most systematic." Robert D. Richardson Jr., *Emerson: The Mind on Fire; A Biography* (Berkeley: University of California Press, 1995), 257. Neal Dolan makes a similar observation but expands the time frame to reach from the "Philosophy of History" lectures to the "Present Age" lectures (1839–40). Dolan writes: "This large group of lectures as a whole delivered over a four-year period, has a striking coherence and completeness." Neal Dolan, *Emerson's Liberalism* (Madison: University of Wisconsin Press, 2009), 111.

8. Peter Zogas reads this process in terms of a kind of Romantic dialectic in which "progress records forms of limitation that in turn energize the moral force of the individual." Peter Zogas, "Emerson and the Dissatisfactions of Progress," *ESQ* 60, no. 2 (2014): 209–49.

9. This tension between liberal and republican models reflects Michael Sandel's 1984 analysis of tension between an "unencumbered self" that is always free to make choices and a model of selfhood in which *following* certain values and life plans is essential. His model, and its predicament, I think, illustrate well the contradictions of Emerson's political ideals. On the one hand, for "a subject capable of an autonomous will," the moral law "is a law we give *ourselves*; we don't *find* it, we *will* it." This power brings Sandel to replicate Emerson's ideal of selfhood as a form of existential sovereignty: "The unencumbered self, and the ethic it inspires, taken together, hold out a liberating vision. Freed from the dictates of nature and the sanction of social roles, the human subject is installed as sovereign, cast as author of the only moral meanings there are." This position of extreme liberty might define a site from which the subject may genuinely claim to establish their own moral values, but it represents a deracinated pure Platonism that, when clothed in flesh, would mark a person "wholly without character, without moral depth." The problem that the republican side of the issue (in Sandel's frame it is associated with Utilitarianism) poses for Emerson is that certain allegiances "are more than values I happen to have, and to hold, at a certain distance. They go beyond the obligations I voluntarily incur and the 'natural duties' I owe to human beings as such. They allow that to some [people] I owe more than justice requires or even permits, not by reason of agreements I have made but instead on virtue of those more or less enduring attachments and commitments that, taken together, partly define the person I am."

Michael Sandel, "The Procedural Republic and the Unencumbered Self," *Political Theory* 12, no. 1 (1984): 81–96, esp. 85, 87, 91.

10. John Adams, *Correspondence between the Hon. John Adams, Late President of the United States, and the late William Cunningham, esq., Beginning in 1802 and ending in 1812* (Boston: True and Greene, 1823), 19. Stanley Elkins and Eric McKitrick write that "Adams had always believed that man was a creature of intractable passions, and that the central drama both of man within himself and of man in society was the ceaseless contest between his reason and his passions, paralleling that in the realm of government between liberty and power." Stanley M. Elkins and Eric McKitrick, *The Age of Federalism* (New York: Oxford University Press, 1993), 535.

11. Gordon Wood, *The Creation of the American Republic, 1776–1787* (Chapel Hill: University of North Carolina Press, 1998). Following John Adams's logic, Brian Balogh argues that Adams believed "getting governance right was a high-stakes venture. Properly ordered government *produced* virtue: this essential resource was political, not social in its origins.... Corruption, declining virtue, and social strife were symptoms, not causes of the poorly ordered republic." See, especially, Balogh's chapter "How Americans Lost Sight of the State: Adapting Republican Virtue to Liberal Self-Interest," in Brian Balogh, *A Government Out of Sight: The Mystery of National Authority in Nineteenth-Century America* (Cambridge, UK: Cambridge University Press, 2009), 18–53, quotation 27.

12. Mary Kupiec Cayton, *Emerson's Emergence: Self and Society in the Transformation of New England, 1800–1845* (Chapel Hill: University of North Carolina Press, 1989), 34.

13. Many legislative bodies still retain a trace of this model of representation through "at-large" representatives who give an overweight to something analogous to the Rousseauian "general will."

14. Cayton, *Emerson's Emergence*, 35; Wilentz, *Rise of American Democracy*, 182–96. Formisano emphasizes revivals, the rise of factory labor, and the emergence of mass politics (*Transformation of Political Culture*, 217–50).

15. See Elkins and McKitrick, *Age of Federalism*, for the long evolution of this change, beginning with the Democratic Societies of the 1790s, which emphasized the importance of reflecting a plurality of interests in the formal representations of a legitimate republican government (451–61).

16. *Memoirs of John Quincy Adams, Comprising Portions of His Diary from 1795–1848*, ed. Charles Francis Adams, vol. 1 (1874; Freeport, NY: Books for Libraries Press, 1969), 249.

17. James Traub, *John Quincy Adams: Militant Spirit* (New York: Basic Books, 2016), 109–20, 363–79; Robert V. Remini, *John Quincy Adams* (New York: Times Books, 2002), 33–40, 130–46. Michael Zuckert also addresses John Quincy Adams and the relationship between equality and aristocracy. See Michael Zuckert, *The Natural Rights Republic* (Notre Dame, IN: University of Notre Dame Press, 1997), 19–26.

18. See Douglass L. Wilson's chapter on Lincoln, "Breaking into Politics," in *Honor's Voice: The Transformation of Abraham Lincoln* (New York: Knopf, 1999), 142–70; and David Herbert Donald, *Lincoln* (New York: Simon and Schuster, 1995), 94–101. Robert Scholnick places the Whigs and Democrats as parties looking to the past in order to offer "competing concepts of past and future," especially as it related to

the responsibility of Jacksonians to regulate the "scope and responsibility of the national government." Robert J. Scholnick, "Whigs and Democrats, the Past and the Future: The Political Emerson and Whitman's 1855 Preface," *American Periodicals* 26, no. 1 (2016): 70–91.

19. On Ely Moore, see Walter Hugins, *Jacksonian Democracy and the Working Class* (Redwood City, CA: Stanford University Press, 1960), 63–73; Edward L. Widmer, *Young America: The Flowering of Democracy in New York City* (New York: Oxford University Press, 1998), 74; Sean Wilentz, *The Politicians and the Egalitarians: The Hidden History of American Politics* (New York: W. W. Norton, 2016), 413–18; John Ashworth, *"Agrarians" and "Aristocrats": Party Political Ideology in the United States, 1837–1846* (Cambridge, UK: Cambridge University Press, 1987), 40–41; Stephen P. Rice, "The Mechanics' Institute of the City of New-York and the Conception of Class Authority in Early Industrial America, 1830–1860," *New York History* 81, no. 3 (2000): 269–99; Jeffrey L. Pasley, "Minnows, Spies, and Aristocrats: The Social Crisis of Congress in the Age of Martin Van Buren," *Journal of the Early Republic* 27, no. 4 (2007): 600–610.
20. *Niles' Weekly Register*, November 1, 1834.
21. Emerson identifies his source as "Mr. H.," but he is surely referring to Philip Hone, former mayor and Whig organizer in New York. Later that year Hone traveled to Concord for its bicentennial celebration and was on hand when Emerson delivered his "Discourse on the History of Concord" (*L* 1:453).
22. Zakaras uses this condition to revise Stanley Cavell's more broad-based idea of "aversive thinking" as the starting point for individual consciousness. Talking of J. S. Mill and Emerson, Zakaras claims, "Both argued, in fact, that modern societies have made mass conformity everyone's point of existential departure." Individuals must "unsettle themselves" in relation to social forces so that they can define an individuality. Zakaras, *Individualism and Mass Democracy*, 27.
23. "Electoral College," *National Intelligencer*, June 13, 1835; Thomas Coens, "The Early Jackson Party: A Force for Democratization?," in *A Companion to the Era of Andrew Jackson*, ed. Sean Patrick Adams (Malden, MA: Wiley-Blackwell, 2013), 231–59.
24. Thomas Carlyle, "Characteristics," *Edinburgh Review*, December 1831, 359.
25. Henry David Thoreau, *Walden and Other Writings*, ed. Brooks Atkinson (New York: Modern Library, 1992), 85.
26. For the relationship of the demagogue to the genius, see Judith N. Shklar, *Redeeming American Political Thought* (Chicago: University of Chicago Press, 1998), 52–58; T. Gregory Garvey, "Emerson's Political Spirit and the Problem of Language," in *The Emerson Dilemma: Essays on Emerson and Social Reform*, ed. T. Gregory Garvey (Athens: University Press of Georgia, 2001), 14–19.
27. Charles Stewart Daveis was a lawyer, diplomat, and politician who grew up in Maine. He was a friend and frequent correspondent of both George Ticknor and Charles Sumner. From "An Address Delivered on the Commemoration of Fryeburg, May 19, 1825" (Portland, ME, 1825), 34–64.
28. Bancroft was deeply involved in the literary nationalism of the era. His politics combined populist democratic egalitarianism with expansionist nationalism. As an official in the Van Buren administration, he appointed both Orestes Brownson and Nathaniel Hawthorne to positions in the Customs Service. Serving in Polk's cabinet

in 1846, he was important in justifying and even provoking the Mexican War. John C. Pinheiro, *Manifest Ambition: James K. Polk and Civil-Military Relations during the Mexican War* (Westport, CT: Praeger Security International, 2007), 46–51; Jean H. Baker, *Affairs of Party: The Political Culture of Northern Democrats in the Mid-Nineteenth Century* (New York: Fordham University Press, 1998), 121–30.

29. George Bancroft, "The Office of the People in Art, Government, and Religion," in *Literary and Historical Miscellanies* (New York: Harper & Brothers, 1855), 409.
30. Bancroft, "Office of the People," 415, 422–23.
31. Bancroft, "Office of the People," 424–25.
32. Bancroft, "Office of the People," 427.
33. Wilentz, *Rise of American Democracy*, 294–303; Widmer, *Young America*, 27–64. Duff Green supported John C. Calhoun, then Jackson, then Calhoun again after 1830. Between 1829 and 1833 Green both edited the *United States Telegraph* and, through Jackson's patronage, held lucrative government printing contracts. Throughout his career he was a strident opponent of abolition. His journalism was an influential voice in antebellum white supremacism.
34. *United States Magazine and Democratic Review*, no. 1 (October 1837): 1.
35. *United States Magazine and Democratic Review*, no. 1 (October 1837): 14–15.
36. *United States Magazine and Democratic Review*, no. 1 (October 1837): 2.
37. The second party system emerged as the Democrats organized in the late 1820s and the Whigs organized as an opposition in the early 1830s. This system differed in nature from the parties of the early federal period. For my purposes, it is especially important to recognize that this emergence responded to the expanded franchise as a means of corralling voters and stamping them with party identities. See Holt, *Rise and Fall of the American Whig Party*, 60–88; Larry J. Reynolds, *Righteous Violence: Revolution, Slavery, and the American Renaissance* (Athens: University of Georgia Press, 2011), 111–14; Wilentz, *Rise of American Democracy*, 448–52, 484.
38. This district included Concord. It had been represented in Congress by Edward Everett and Samuel Hoar, both in opposition to Jackson. John Gorham Palfrey, a minister and historian, was elected in 1846 as a Whig and ran for reelection with the Free Soil Party. He lost the election, but the seat he occupied was not filled until another Whig was elected in 1851.
39. Lovejoy's killing became a cause célèbre, especially in Lovejoy's native Massachusetts. Emerson participated in a public meeting organized by William Ellery Channing to defend the right to free speech and denounce the rioting that killed Lovejoy. In a memorial biography published in 1838, John Quincy Adams contributed an introductory essay. In it he writes: "The incidents which preceded and accompanied, and followed the catastrophe of Mr. Lovejoy's death, point it out as an epocha in the annals of human liberty. They have given a shock as of an earthquake throughout this continent." Joseph C. Lovejoy and Owen Lovejoy, *Memoir of the Rev. Elijah P. Lovejoy; who was murdered in defence of the liberty of the press, at Alton, Illinois, Nov. 7, 1837* (New York: John S. Taylor, 1838), 12.

The most widely read account in the East was eyewitness Edward Beecher's *Narrative of the Riots at Alton, In Connection with the Death of Rev. Elijah P. Lovejoy* (Alton, IL: G. Holton, 1838). Lovejoy is also treated extensively in David Grimsted, *American Mobbing, 1828–1861: Toward Civil War* (New York: Oxford University

Press, 1998), 35–37, 72, 76; See also Len Gougeon, "Abolition, the Emersons, and 1837," *New England Quarterly* 54, no. 3 (1981): 347–50.

40. Jason Frank, "Standing for Others: Reform and Representation in Emerson's Political Thought," in *The Political Companion to Ralph Waldo Emerson*, ed. Alan Levine and Daniel Malachuk (Lexington: University Press of Kentucky, 2011), 399–400. Also see Gustaaf Van Cromphout on Emerson's theory of political representation in *Emerson's Ethics* (Columbia: University of Missouri Press, 1999), 54–59.

41. Joseph Story, "Statesmen: Their Rareness and Importance," *New England Magazine* 7 (August 1834): 93; Thomas Brown, *Politics and Statesmanship: Essays on the American Whig Party* (New York: Columbia University Press, 1985), 9.

42. Jacob E. Cooke, ed., *The Federalist* (Middletown, CT: Wesleyan University Press, 1961), 62.

43. Robert McKinley Ormsby, *A History of the Whig Party: Or Some of Its Main Features, with a Hurried Glance at the Formation of Parties in the United States, and the Outlines of the History of the Principal Parties of the Country to the Present Time* (Boston: Crosby, Nichols, 1859), 176.

44. In Daniel Walker Howe's synthesis of these positions, the "political culture" of the Whigs sought to bind the nation together through economic development and to advance liberal individualism by emphasizing self-control and individual responsibility. As he puts it: "While the Democrats favored economic uniformity and cultural diversity, Whigs favored economic diversity and cultural uniformity.... [M]uch more than Democrats, Whigs worried about lawlessness, violence, and demagogy" (*What Hath God Wrought*, 570–85, quotation 583). Also see Brown, *Politics and Statesmanship*, esp. chaps. 1 and 2 on the formation of the Whig Party; and Holt, *Rise and Fall of the American Whig Party*, 259–71.

45. Judith Shklar especially emphasizes Emerson's ambivalence about the status of talent and excellence in democracy. She characterizes his concern as an "inhibition" of democracy, that is, not so much a fear of the masses, but a recognition that an emphasis on mass opinion can inhibit both the achievement of genius and a general aspiration toward excellence (*Redeeming American Political Thought*, 52–58).

46. Alexis de Tocqueville, *Democracy in America*, ed. J. P. Mayer, trans. George Lawrence (New York: Harper & Row, 1966), 436.

47. Kenneth S. Sacks, *Understanding Emerson: "The American Scholar" and His Struggle for Self-Reliance* (Princeton, NJ: Princeton University Press, 2003), 32.

48. Sacks, *Understanding Emerson*, 31.

49. Michael Sandel distinguishes between "procedural" and "perfectionist" forms of liberalism. Advocates of the procedural model insist that "government should be neutral toward competing conceptions of the good life." Against this model of liberal government, Sandel defines what he calls "perfectionist liberalism," which is a hybrid of liberal and republican characteristics. In this model, government "gives up the aspiration to neutrality and promotes liberal virtues like autonomy and individuality as comprehensive moral ideals, qualities of character that figure prominently in the good life." Michael J. Sandel, *Liberalism and the Limits of Justice* (Cambridge, UK: Cambridge University Press, 1982), 210–11. Emerson is an advocate of perfectionist liberalism. His early thought, especially, is motivated by an impulse to influence democratic citizenship in that it privileges the qualities of character Sandel identifies.

CHAPTER 2

1. Ronald A. Bosco and Joel Myerson, *The Emerson Brothers: A Fraternal Biography in Letters* (New York: Oxford University Press, 2005), 266.
2. Robert D. Richardson, *Emerson: The Mind on Fire; A Biography* (Berkeley: University of California Press, 1995), 224.
3. Kenneth S. Lynn, *The Air-Line to Seattle: Studies in Literary and Historical Writing about America* (Chicago: University of Chicago Press, 1984), 27–32; Richard A. Grusin, "'Put God in Your Debt': Emerson's Economy of Expenditure," *PMLA* 103, no. 1 (1988): 35–44; Linda K. Kerber, *Toward an Intellectual History of Women: Essays* (Chapel Hill: University of North Carolina Press, 1997), 214.
4. Efforts to improve or undermine Emerson's value to the emergent women's rights movement tend to focus on his explicit organizational participation and thus miss his more important contribution to sexual equality. Emerson's value for women's rights lies only minimally in open and self-conscious advocacy. It lies more importantly in his effort to redefine the idea of privacy and in his lifelong effort to present deeply private forms of self-expression as sources of public authority. Joelle Million, *Woman's Voice, Woman's Place: Lucy Stone and the Birth of the Woman's Rights Movement* (Westport, CT: Praeger, 2003), 71. Stone met Emerson in 1850 and solicited his participation in a women's rights convention in 1851. Million, *Woman's Voice*, 116; *JMN* 11:443–44.
5. Norma Basch, *In the Eyes of the Law: Women, Marriage, and Property in Nineteenth-Century New York* (Ithaca, NY: Cornell University Press, 1982), 42.
6. Jean Bethke Elshtain, *Public Man, Private Woman: Women in Social and Political Thought* (Princeton, NJ: Princeton University Press, 1981), 127. Also Caroline Healy Dall provides a comprehensive review of changes that occurred between the 1820s and the 1860s in *Woman's Rights Under the Law: In Three Lectures, Delivered in Boston, January, 1861* (Boston: Walker, Wise, 1861).
7. The foundational legal text in America at this time was James Kent's *Commentaries on American Law*, ed. George Camstock, 4 vols. (Boston: Little, Brown & Co., 1867), 2:134. Kent merges Blackstone's legal focus with religious and cultural concerns, especially linking marriage to morality and child rearing. *Liberator*, January 5–February 16, 1838. Elizabeth Wilson's "Scriptural View of Marriage" (1849) follows Grimké's lead. Mary Gove and Henry C. Wright also made important statements for women's control over the sexual lives of married couples on the grounds of women's health. See Henry C. Wright, *Sex, Marriage, and Society* (1855; repr., New York: Arno, 1974). Throughout the effort to reform marriage and intimate relationships, reformers faced charges that they were advocates of free love, the unsexing of bodies, and atheism. This critique of marriage reform made public discussion of topics such as egalitarianism within marriage, women's health, and divorce even more transgressive. See Jean L. Silver-Isenstadt, *Shameless: The Visionary Life of Mary Gove Nichols* (Baltimore: Johns Hopkins University Press, 2002), esp. chap. 5, "Seminal Influence," 129–56.
8. Catharine Esther Beecher, *The American Woman's Home* (Hartford, CT: Harriet Beecher Stowe Center, 2002), 5. Alexis de Tocqueville, whom Beecher draws on

heavily in her *Treatise*, also emphasizes a kind of republicanization of the family in Jacksonian America. Fathers and sons are equal from the outset, and women have a higher sense of autonomy and responsibility through a kind of hybrid domestic citizenship. Beecher sought to amplify these qualities. In introducing a comprehensive analysis of the emergence of family law in the United States over the course of the nineteenth century, Michael Grossberg links these two features of family life. First, he argues, "jurists, legislators, and commentators" defined a "republican approach to domestic relations" which adapted the coverture tradition but retained unique distinctions between the head of household and dependents. "Second[,] . . . during the [nineteenth] century, legal change diminished paternal authority, enlarged maternal and filial prerogatives, and fixed more clearly the state's responsibilities in domestic affairs." Michael Grossberg, *Governing the Hearth Law and the Family in Nineteenth-Century America* (Chapel Hill: University of North Carolina Press, 1988), xi–xii.

9. Beecher, *The American Woman's Home*, 4.
10. Late in her career, Beecher compresses her overall vision into a single article titled "How to Redeem Woman's Profession from Dishonor." *Harper's*, November 1865, 710–716.
11. Beecher, *The American Woman's Home*, 3.
12. Mary Ryan amplifies this professionalization, listing professions that supported and stabilized gender spheres: "As Americans settled into industrial society in the 1850s, the family's specialized functions were supervised by scientists, professionals, proliferating institutions of social service: architectural firms, medical offices, and public schools." Mary P. Ryan, *The Empire of the Mother: American Writing about Domesticity, 1830 to 1860* (New York: Haworth Press, 1982), 99.
13. Beecher, *The American Woman's Home*, 42.
14. Beecher, *The American Woman's Home*, 19, 21.
15. Ellen Tucker Emerson, *Life of Lidian Jackson Emerson*, ed. Delores Bird Carpenter (East Lansing: Michigan State University Press, 1991), 126.
16. Beecher, *The American Woman's Home*, 263–64.
17. Beecher, *The American Woman's Home*, 144. In her study of women's petitions to Congress, Allise Portnoy extends this responsibility toward explicit political action by linking "the application of private standards of morality to conflicts in the public sphere," even connecting women's participation in the Indian removals debate to the definition of "home" for all Americans. Alisse Portnoy, *Their Right to Speak: Women's Activism in the Indian and Slave Debates* (Cambridge, MA: Harvard University Press, 2005), 70–71.
18. Quoted in Carol Faulkner, *Lucretia Mott's Heresy: Abolition and Women's Rights in Nineteenth-Century America* (Philadelphia: University of Pennsylvania Press, 2013), 159. Lori Ginsberg comments on the 1860 convention, noting that "even to discuss the topic" of divorce "whether with hope or trepidation, was to ensure that marriage would never be the same." Lori D. Ginsberg, *Untidy Origins: A Story of Woman's Rights in Antebellum New York* (Chapel Hill: University of North Carolina Press, 2005), 99. Joelle Million offers a detailed account of how the "marriage question," especially rhetorical tactics for discussing divorce, divided activists. See Million, *Woman's Voice*, 125–37, 140–48.

19. See Nancy F. Cott, *Public Vows: A History of Marriage and the Nation* (Cambridge, MA: Harvard University Press, 2002), 28–30, 47–53. Divorce is a major issue, especially in chapter 3, in Hendrik Hartog, *Man and Wife in America: A History* (Cambridge, MA: Harvard University Press, 2002), 62–92. Adam Tuchinsky's essay on Elizabeth Oakes Smith's opposition to divorce offers a good summary of the politics of divorce in the antebellum period. See Adam Tuchinsky, "'Woman and Her Needs': Elizabeth Oakes Smith and the Divorce Question," *Journal of Women's History* 28, no. 1 (2016): 38–59, 183.
20. William Blackstone, *Commentaries on the Laws of England*, ed. Thomas Cooley, 4th ed., 2 vols. (Chicago: Callaghan, 1899), 1:387, 430.
21. "Facetiousness of the Law: Husband and Wife," *New York Legal Observer* 3 (March 1845): 156.
22. John Stuart Mill, *On Liberty; and, The Subjection of Women*, ed. Alan Ryan (New York: Penguin, 2006), 177. For the legal restrictions of coverture, see Basch, *In the Eyes of the Law*, 42–54.
23. Margaret Fuller, *Woman in the Nineteenth Century*, in *The Essential Margaret Fuller*, ed. Jeffrey A. Steele. (New Brunswick, NJ: Rutgers University Press, 1992), 331, 282.
24. Stanton first published this argument as "Divorce" in Amelia Bloomer's journal *The Lily* 2, no. 4 (1850): 6.
25. Elizabeth Cady Stanton to Susan B. Anthony, March 1, 1853, in *Elizabeth Cady Stanton, Susan B. Anthony: Correspondence, Writings, Speeches*, ed. Ellen Carol DuBois (New York: Schocken Books, 1981), 55. In *Eighty Years and More*, Stanton records that she had torn pages on the discriminatory statutes from her father's lawbooks. Elizabeth Cady Stanton, *Eighty Years and More: Reminiscences, 1815–1897* (New York: Schocken Books, 1971), 31–33.
26. Elizabeth Cady Stanton to Susan B. Anthony, August 7, 1857, in *The Selected Papers of Elizabeth Cady Stanton and Susan B. Anthony*, ed. Ann D. Gordon (New Brunswick, NJ: Rutgers University Press, 1997–2013), 2:82.
27. Lucy Stone to Antoinette Brown, July 11, 1855, in *Friends and Sisters: Letters between Lucy Stone and Antoinette Brown Blackwell, 1846–93*, ed. Carol Lasser and Marlene Deahl Merrill (Champaign: University of Illinois Press, 1987), 144.
28. Antoinette L. Brown, "Lucy Stone at Oberlin College," *Woman's Journal*, February 10, 1894.
29. Stone's friendship with Brown became even more relevant to their lives as the two married brothers. They were thus both sisters-in-law and friends. Million, *Woman's Voice*, 194–98.
30. Lucy Stone to Francis Stone, May 12, 1845, Blackwell Family Papers, Library of Congress.
31. These letters are in the Blackwell Family Papers in the Library of Congress, but many are quoted in *Loving Warriors: Selected Letters of Lucy Stone and Henry B. Blackwell, 1853–1893*, ed. Leslie Wheeler (New York: Doubleday, 1981). With regard to anxiety about Blackwell's sexual expectations, Stone sent Blackwell a copy of Henry C. Wright's *Marriage and Parentage* (1855), in which Wright advocates for women's control of sexual activity in marriage. Blackwell's response is lost, but the issue abated and the courtship proceeded. Andrea Moore Kerr and Joelle Million offer significantly different readings of the Stone–Blackwell correspondence. See

Million, *Woman's Voice*, 153–57; and Andrea Moore Kerr, *Lucy Stone: Speaking Out for Equality* (Toledo, OH: Great Neck Publishing, 2005), 33–34.
32. Moira Gatens, *Feminism and Philosophy: Perspectives on Difference and Equality* (Cambridge: Polity, 1991), 113.
33. Jeffrey Steele, "The Limits of Political Sympathy," in *The Emerson Dilemma: Essays on Emerson and Social Reform*, ed. T. Gregory Garvey (Athens: University of Georgia Press, 2001), 115–38.
34. Significantly, Emerson seems to have persuaded Lydia Jackson to change her first name to Lidian. Most efforts to read this change conclude it probably had to do with the vowel glide from "Lydia" to "Emerson," which would have sounded something like "Lydier Emerson." Richardson, *Emerson*, 611; Ellen Tucker Emerson, *Life of Lidian Jackson Emerson*, xiii; *The Selected Letters of Lidian Jackson Emerson*, ed. Delores Bird Carpenter (Columbia: University of Missouri Press), 28–29.
35. Phyllis Cole, "Pain and Protest in the Emerson Family," in *The Emerson Dilemma: Essays on Emerson and Social Reform*, ed. T. Gregory Garvey (Athens: University Press of Georgia, 2001), 67–93, quotation 68.
36. Richardson, *Emerson*, 270; Len Gougeon. "Abolition, the Emersons, and 1837," *New England Quarterly* 54, no. 3 (1981): 345–64, 353–56; Cole, "Pain and Protest," 70–77.
37. Quoted in Ellen Tucker Emerson, *Life of Lidian Jackson Emerson*, 60–61.
38. Sandra Herbert Petrulionis, *To Set This World Right: The Antislavery Movement in Thoreau's Concord* (Ithaca, NY: Cornell University Press, 2006), 16.
39. Petrulionis, *To Set This World Right*, 24–25.
40. Gary L. Collison, "Shadrach in Concord," *The Concord Saunterer* 19, no. 2 (1987): 8.
41. Richardson sees the Emerson marriage as highly repressive, more so than Cole does, implying that Lidian "blossomed" late in life as her husband retired and daughter Ellen took over the housekeeper's role. Richardson, *Emerson*, 557–58.
42. Ellen Tucker Emerson, *Life of Lidian Jackson Emerson*, 47, 48.
43. Ellen Tucker Emerson, *Life of Lidian Jackson Emerson*, 145.
44. Joel Myerson, ed., "Margaret Fuller's 1842 Journal: At Concord with the Emersons," *Harvard Library Bulletin* 21 (1973): 328.
45. Megan Marshall includes a detailed analysis of this incident. She focuses on how it reinforced Fuller's sense of solitude as a single woman, even when she was among her most admiring friends. Megan Marshall, *Margaret Fuller: A New American Life* (Boston: Houghton Mifflin Harcourt, 2013), 190–97. Also see Bell Gale Chevigny, ed., *The Woman and the Myth: Margaret Fuller's Life and Writings* (Old Westbury, NY: Feminist Press, 1976), 127–32.
46. Myerson, "Margaret Fuller's 1842 Journal," 328–30.
47. Myerson, "Margaret Fuller's 1842 Journal," 330. Fuller is referring to Elizabeth Hoar, fiancée of Waldo's younger brother Charles, who died in 1836.
48. Ellen Tucker Emerson, *Life of Lidian Jackson Emerson*, 32, 73, 140.
49. Ellen Tucker Emerson, *Life of Lidian Jackson Emerson*, 80.
50. Ellen Tucker Emerson, *Life of Lidian Jackson Emerson*, 95.
51. Sacvan Bercovitch reads this paradox as one of Emerson's most characteristic tropes. In thinking about Emerson and politics, he singles out a journal entry from 1842 in which Emerson presents the political paradox of unity in isolation

as a mode of harmonizing equality and individuality. Recalling Emerson's sense of marriage as a process of increasing intimacy leading to an impersonal connection, Bercovitch finds Emerson's definition of the "good society in a similar paradox." In arguing about national unity, the political partisans get it all wrong, Emerson fumes: "This union is to be reached by a reverse of the methods they use. It is spiritual and must not be actualized. Union is only perfect when all the Uniters are absolutely isolated" (*JMN* 8:251). Sacvan Bercovitch, *The Rites of Assent: Transformations in the Symbolic Construction of America* (New York: Routledge, 1993), 312.

52. Emerson's attitude toward chastity most likely had a wide variety of influences, but in its connection to sexuality, it was probably most influenced by Margaret Fuller, through conversation and through her essays "The Magnolia of Lake Pontchartrain" and "The Great Lawsuit," both published in *The Dial*. See Marshall, *Margaret Fuller*, 160–61.

53. George Kateb, *Emerson and Self-Reliance* (Thousand Oaks, CA: Sage, 1995), 105.

54. Branka Arsić, *On Leaving: A Reading in Emerson* (Cambridge, MA: Harvard University Press, 2010), 2, 194–97.

CHAPTER 3

1. Louis Agassiz, "Evolution and Permanence of Type," *Atlantic Monthly* 33 (January 1874): 92–101, esp. 94.
2. Adrian J. Desmond, *Darwin's Sacred Cause: How a Hatred of Slavery Shaped Darwin's Views on Human Evolution* (Boston: Houghton Mifflin Harcourt, 2009), 18–21.
3. Theda Purdue and Michael D. Green initiated a broadening of the study of removals with *The Cherokee Nation and the Trail of Tears* (New York: Penguin, 2007). Their pioneering work has been developed in terms of antecedent removals, especially in New England, and in the connection between Indian removals and African colonization in the 1820s. See also Christina Snyder, "Many Removals: Re-evaluating the Arc of Indigenous Dispossession," *Journal of the Early Republic* 41, no. 4 (Winter 2021): 1–29; Jeffrey Ostler, *Surviving Genocide: Native Nations and the United States from the American Revolution to Bleeding Kansas* (New Haven, CT: Yale University Press, 2019); and Nicholas Guyatt, *Bind Us Apart: How Enlightened Americans Invented Racial Segregation* (New York: Basic Books, 2016).
4. Ned Blackhawk, *The Rediscovery of America: Native Peoples and the Unmaking of U.S. History* (New Haven: Yale University Press, 2023), 211–16, 239–40.
5. Jill Norgren, *The Cherokee Cases: Two Landmark Federal Decisions in the Fight for Sovereignty* (Norman: University of Oklahoma Press, 2004), 112–42.
6. Kenneth S. Sacks, *Understanding Emerson: "The American Scholar" and His Struggle for Self-Reliance* (Princeton: Princeton University Press, 2003), 5–21.
7. Thomas R. Hietala, *Manifest Design: Anxious Aggrandizement in Late Jacksonian America* (Ithaca, NY: Cornell University Press, 1985); Reginald Horsman, *Race and Manifest Destiny: The Origins of American Racial Anglo-Saxonism* (Cambridge, MA: Harvard University Press, 1981).

8. Priscilla Wald, "Terms of Assimilation: Legislating Subjectivity in the Emerging Nation," in *Cultures of United States Imperialism*, ed. Amy Kaplan and Donald E. Pease (Durham, NC: Duke University Press, 1993), 59–84.
9. Usually referred to as "cultural genocide," this priority in itself now meets the United Nations' definition of genocide, which contains both a "mental element" as well as a "physical element." https://www.un.org/en/genocide-prevention/definition.
10. Henry Mayer, *All on Fire: William Lloyd Garrison and the Abolition of Slavery* (New York: W. W. Norton, 2008), 244–49.
11. Norgren, *The Cherokee Cases*, 141.
12. John A. Andrews III, *From Revivals to Removals: Jeremiah Evarts, the Cherokee Nation, and the Search for the Soul of America* (Athens: University of Georgia Press, 1992), 133–36.
13. Alexis de Tocqueville, *Democracy in America*, ed. Jacob Peter Mayer, trans. George Lawrence (New York: Harper & Row, 1966), 339.
14. Francis Paul Prucha, *American Indian Policy* (Bloomington: Indiana Historical Society, 1971), 20–36.
15. In *The Enlightenment: And Why It Still Matters* (New York: Random House, 2013), Anthony Pagden places the push and pull between egalitarian and racist theories as central legacies of the Enlightenment. He especially details how both Kant and Rousseau moved from intense racism toward egalitarianism later in life. Kant did so in his thought about geopolitics and slavery, while Rousseau came to the conclusion that "if . . . there are slaves by nature it is because they have once been slaves contrary to nature." From *The Social Contract*, quoted in Pagden, *The Enlightenment*, 169. See also Micheline Ishay, *The History of Human Rights: From Ancient Times to the Globalization Era* (Berkeley: University of California Press, 2004), 75–107.
16. Adam Dewbury, "The American School and Scientific Racism in Early American Anthropology," *Histories of Anthropology Annual* 3, no. 1 (2007): 121–47, esp. 133.
17. This precedent eventually became part of the Nazi Nuremberg Laws. On "blood law," see James Q. Whitman, *Hitler's American Model: The United States and the Making of Nazi Race Law* (Princeton, NJ: Princeton University Press, 2017), 73–131.
18. Louis Agassiz, "The Diversity of Origin of the Human Races," *Christian Examiner*, July 1850, 144.
19. Lewis Henry Morgan, *Ancient Society; or, Researches in the Lines of Human Progress from Savagery through Barbarism to Civilization* (Chicago: Charles H. Kerr & Company, 1909), 27.
20. Adam Dewbury, "The American School and Scientific Racism in Early American Anthropology," *Histories of Anthropology Annual* 3, no. 1 (2007): 135.
21. Louis Agassiz, "Sketch of Natural Provinces of the Animal World and Their Relation to the Different Types of Man," in Samuel George Morton, J. C. Nott, and George R. Gliddon, *Types of Mankind: or, Ethnological researches based upon the ancient monuments, paintings, sculptures, and crania of races, and upon their natural, geographical, philological and Biblical History* (Philadelphia: Lippincott, Grambo & Co.,1854), lviii, lxi.
22. Agassiz, "Sketch," lxvii.

23. Agassiz, "Sketch," lxxv.
24. Christopher Irmscher, *Louis Agassiz: Creator of American Science* (New York: Houghton Mifflin Harcourt, 2013), 247–51.
25. Agassiz, "Sketch," lxxvi.
26. Irmscher, *Louis Agassiz*, 150–53; John G. T. Anderson, *Deep Things Out of Darkness: A History of Natural History* (Berkeley: University of California Press, 2012), 221.
27. Agassiz, "Sketch," lxxvi. See also Anderson, *Deep Things*, 208–25.
28. This is part of Agassiz's argument for the "permanence" of type. Irmscher, *Louis Agassiz*, 23–25; Laura Dassow Walls, *Emerson's Life in Science: The Culture of Truth* (Ithaca, NY: Cornell University Press, 2003), 172–75.
29. Anderson, *Deep Things*, 94–98.
30. Walls, *Emerson's Life in Science*, 167; Adrian Desmond and James Moore, *Darwin's Sacred Cause: Race, Slavery, and the Quest for Human Origins* (Chicago: University of Chicago Press, 2011), 109.
31. This debate persists into the present. It spiked especially in the early twenty-first century with advocacy of teaching "intelligent design" in schools as an equal and alternative theory to evolution. See Michael Shermer, *Why Darwin Matters: The Case against Intelligent Design* (New York: Holt, 2007); and John Brockman, *Intelligent Thought: Science versus the Intelligent Design Movement* (New York: Vintage Books, 2006).
32. See Walls, *Emerson's Life in Science*, 176–86; and Bruce Baum, *The Rise and Fall of the Caucasian Race: A Political History of Racial Identity* (New York: NYU Press, 2008), chap. 3, "Passage into 'Our Ordinary Forms of Expression': The Caucasian Race, ca. 1795–1850."
33. Whitman, *Hitler's American Model*, 1–17.
34. Walls, *Emerson's Life in Science*, 186.
35. Lawrence Buell, *Emerson* (Cambridge, MA: Belknap Press of Harvard University Press, 2003), 142–57, 261–77.
36. Branka Arsić, *On Leaving: A Reading in Emerson* (Cambridge, MA: Harvard University Press, 2010), 250.
37. Gregg D. Crane, *Race, Citizenship, and Law in American Literature* (New York: Cambridge University Press, 2002), 98.
38. John Rawls, *Lectures on the History of Political Philosophy*, ed. Samuel Freeman (Cambridge, MA: Belknap Press of Harvard University Press, 2007), 144–54.
39. Ian Finseth, "Evolution, Cosmopolitanism, and Emerson's Antislavery Politics," *American Literature* 77, no. 4 (2005): 729–60, quotation 730.
40. In very literal terms, consistent with Finseth's argument, this bias means the connection of blood in the sense of a fluid that carries genetic traits trackable from generation to generation. But in the more philosophical terms of Stanley Cavell, it represents an "aversion" to fixity, racial or social. Shortly after quoting Tocqueville's assessment that Americans "have all a lively faith in the perfectibility of man, . . . they all consider society as a body in a state of improvement, humanity as a changing scene, in which nothing is, or ought to be, permanent; and they admit that what appears to them today to be good, may be superseded by something better tomorrow," Cavell talks about "transformative nextness" as a possibility that pervades Emersonian thought and is essential to Emerson's perfectionist bias. Stanley

Cavell, *Conditions Handsome and Unhandsome: The Constitution of Emersonian Perfectionism* (La Salle, IL: Open Court, 1990), 15–16.
41. Finseth, "Evolution, Cosmopolitanism," 745.
42. Finseth, "Evolution, Cosmopolitanism," 731.
43. Kwame Anthony Appiah, *Cosmopolitanism: Ethics in a World of Strangers* (New York: W. W. Norton, 2006), 99–105; Ishay, *History of Human Rights* 69–78, 87–91; Pagden, *The Enlightenment*, xvi–xvii.
44. Stanley Cavell also emphasizes the connection between "Fate" and antislavery. He discusses this passage in "Emerson's Constitutional Amending," which is republished in *Emerson's Transcendental Etudes* (Stanford, CA: Stanford University Press, 2003), 196.
45. My reading of "Fate" is closer to Cavell's in its emphasis on freedom than it is to Barbara Packer's, which underscores the way "Fate" rolls back Emerson's optimism. See Barbara Packer, "Historical Introduction" to vol. 6 of *The Collected Works of Ralph Waldo Emerson* (Cambridge, MA: Belknap Press of Harvard University Press, 2003), xv–lxvii, or her essay "History and Form in Emerson's 'Fate,'" in *Emerson Bicentennial Essays*, ed. Ronald A. Bosco and Joel Myerson (Boston: Massachusetts Historical Society, 2006), 432–52.
46. Theodore Parker, *The Collected Works of Theodore Parker*, ed. Francis Power Cobbe, 14 vols. (London: Trübner, 1863–1871), 2:57. This line is adapted from a sermon that Parker delivered in 1853 titled "Of Justice and the Conscience." The full and accurate quotation is: "Look at the facts of the world. You see a continual and progressive triumph of the right. I do not pretend to understand the moral universe; the arc is a long one, my eye reaches but little ways; I cannot calculate the curve and complete the figure by the experience of sight; I can divine it by conscience. And from what I see I am sure it bends towards justice. Things refuse to be mis-managed long. Jefferson trembled when he thought of slavery and remembered that God is just. Ere long all America will tremble."
47. Whitman, *Hitler's American Model*, 51–52.
48. Len Gougeon, "Emerson's Abolition Conversion," in *The Emerson Dilemma: Essays on Emerson and Social Reform*, ed. T. Gregory Garvey (Athens: University Press of Georgia, 2001), 170–96.
49. In his study of New World slavery, *American Crucible*, Robin Blackburn divides the history of slavery in the Americas into four periods: critique, abolitionism, emancipation, and "slavery resurgent." He accurately situates Emerson among a set of "liberal" abolitionists who "attacked slavery, but sometimes in terms that seemed to give ground to racial 'Darwinism.'" Robin Blackburn, *The American Crucible: Slavery, Emancipation and Human Rights* (London: Verso, 2011), 387.
50. Michael Ignatieff, *Human Rights as Politics and Idolatry* (Princeton: Princeton University Press, 2011), 12.
51. Blackburn, *American Crucible*, 234–42.
52. Blackburn, *American Crucible*, 221–29, 281–82.
53. Len Gougeon, "Abolition, the Emersons, and 1837," *New England Quarterly* 54, no. 3 (1981): 345–64, quotation 360–61.
54. Thomas R. Dew, *Review of the Debate in the Virginia Legislature of 1831 and 1832* (Richmond, VA: T. White, 1832), 109.

55. Dew, *Review*, 111–12.
56. *United States Telegraph*, June 18, 1833; Sean Wilentz, *The Rise of American Democracy: Jefferson to Lincoln* (New York: Norton, 2005), 430.
57. John C. Calhoun, "Remarks of Mr. Calhoun, of South Carolina, On the Reception of Abolition Petitions, Delivered In the Senate of the United States, February [6,] 1837" (Washington, DC: W. W. Moore, 1837), 1–16, Library of Congress locator: https://www.loc.gov/item/11016620/.
58. Emerson's closest recorded relationship with an African American was with John Garrison, a longtime resident of Concord who did carpentry and woodchopping for the Emerson family. Robert A. Gross, *The Transcendentalists and Their World* (New York: Farrar, Straus and Giroux, 2021), 103–6.
59. Nell Irvin Painter, *The History of White People* (New York: W. W. Norton, 2010), 184–90.
60. See Frederick Douglass's explanation of his return from England in 1847 and negotiations with Garrison and his other Boston colleagues in *My Bondage and My Freedom* (1855; New Haven, CT: Yale University Press, 2014), 314–18; and Mayer, *All on Fire*, 371–74, 429–33.
61. Henry Louis Gates Jr., *Lincoln on Race and Slavery* (Princeton: Princeton University Press, 2009), xviii–xxix.
62. Parker, *Collected Works*, 2:90.
63. Theodore Parker, "Thoughts on Labor," *The Dial*, April 1841, in *Critical and Miscellaneous Writings of Theodore Parker* (New York: D. Appleton, 1864), 122–51.
64. Reginald Horsman, *Race and Manifest Destiny: The Origins of American Racial Anglo-Saxonism* (Cambridge, MA: Harvard University Press, 1981), 178.
65. Habermas argues that an "ideal speech situation" is characterized by an effort to achieve "undistorted communication free from domination." Strategically distorted communication, by contrast, relies on an auditor's trust that a speaker is sincere when they are cynically aiming to advance a hidden agenda. He calls this "intentional distorted communication." See Jürgen Habermas, *Justification and Application: Remarks on Discourse Ethics* (Cambridge: MIT Press, 2013), 41–49, 71.
66. For example, in *Loving v. Virginia* (1967).

CHAPTER 4

1. *New-York Evening Post*, November 2, 1836; Sean Wilentz, *The Rise of American Democracy: Jefferson to Lincoln* (New York: Norton, 2005), 449.
2. The campaign of 1836 marked a high point for the Democrats and an organizational turning point for the Whigs. See Wilentz, *Rise of American Democracy*, 446–55; David Reynolds, *Waking Giant: America in the Age of Jackson* (New York: Harper, 2008), 308–15; Daniel Walker Howe, *What Hath God Wrought: The Transformation of America, 1815–1848* (New York: Oxford University Press, 2007), 485–91.
3. Elected in 1836 to succeed Jackson, Van Buren was hobbled by the financial panic and depression that began with the collapse of commodity prices a few months after his inauguration. In combination, a Democratic Party weakened by financial panic and an opposition empowered by successful adaptation to mass partisan

politics made the Democrats and Whigs relative equals in political power until the Whigs collapsed in 1856. See Michael F. Holt, *The Rise and Fall of the American Whig Party* (New York: Oxford University Press, 1999), ix–xiv; Howe, *What Hath God Wrought*, 18–20; Wilentz, *Rise of American Democracy*, 411–12.

4. On Emerson and the Panic of 1837, see Joseph Fichtelberg, *Critical Fictions: Sentiment and the American Market, 1780–1870* (Athens: University Press of Georgia, 2003), 125–33; and Philip F. Gura, *American Transcendentalism: A History* (New York: Hill and Wang, 2007), 120–28. For a counterargument on "Emerson's journey from social revolutionary (after his fashion) to liberal accommodationist (also after his fashion)," see Robert Milder, "The Radical Emerson?," in *Cambridge Companion to Emerson*, ed. Joel Porte and Sandra Morris (New York: Cambridge University Press, 1999), 49–75. Neal Dolan's thoughts on this topic are concentrated in chapter 2, "Property, Culture," in *Emerson's Liberalism* (Madison: University of Wisconsin Press, 2009), 108–38.

5. A textile mill was built on the outskirts of Concord in 1808, and "by 1820 one man was engaged in manufacturing for every two in agriculture." When Emerson settled in Concord in 1835, rivalry between the older village and the upstart mill towns was already a staple of local politics. Robert A. Gross, *The Transcendentalists and Their World* (New York: Farrar, Strauss and Giroux, 2021), 94–98, quotation 94.

6. This transition in Emerson's thought has many versions going back at least to the distinction Stephen Whicher makes, in *Freedom and Fate: An Inner Life of Ralph Waldo Emerson* (Philadelphia: University of Pennsylvania Press, 1971), between spiritual "freedom" and contextual "fate." It has also been defined in terms of movement from idealism to pragmatism by David Van Leer in *Emerson's Epistemology: The Argument of the Essays* (New York: Cambridge University Press, 1986); by David Jacobson in *Emerson's Pragmatic Vision: The Dance of the Eye* (University Park: Pennsylvania State University Press, 1993); and by David Robinson in *Emerson and the Conduct of Life: Pragmatism and Ethical Purpose in the Later Work* (Cambridge, UK: Cambridge University Press, 1993). More recently, it has taken the form of a growing awareness of historical constraints that led to a more active involvement in the culture of reform from the mid-1840s onward. Len Gougeon, *Virtue's Hero: Emerson, Antislavery, and Reform* (Athens: University of Georgia Press, 1990); and Alfred J. Von Frank, *The Trials of Anthony Burns: Freedom and Slavery in Emerson's Boston* (Cambridge, MA: Harvard University Press, 1998), are the most thorough texts for this line of analysis. Also see T. Gregory Garvey, ed., *The Emerson Dilemma: Essays on Emerson and Social Reform* (Athens: University Press of Georgia, 2001). In Robert Gross's study *The Transcendentalists and Their World*, this turn in Emerson's thought structures Gross's treatment of Emerson's career from the 1840s onward.

7. Orestes A. Brownson, "The Laboring Classes: An Article from the Boston Quarterly Review" (Boston: Benjamin H. Greene, 1840); Theodore Parker, "Thoughts on Labor," in *Critical and Miscellaneous Writings of Theodore Parker* (New York: D. Appleton, 1864), 109; Seth Luther, *An Address to the Working Men of New England, on the State of Education, and on the Condition of the Producing Classes in Europe and America* (George H. Evans, 1833). Mark A. Lause, in *Long Road to Harpers Ferry: The Rise of the First American Left* (London: Pluto Press, 2018), 44–75, offers a thorough analysis of this aspect of the debate over property rights, especially as

it pertains to inherited wealth and the ability of workingmen to buy land. Thomas Skidmore broached the topic the earliest, publishing his analysis of the right to property in 1829 in *The Rights of Man to Property! Being a Proposition to Make It Equal among the Adults of the Present Generation, and to Provide for Its Equal Transmission to Every Individual of Each Succeeding Generation* (New York: A. Ming Jr., 1829). Brownson, whose long intellectual and spiritual journey led him to become the most influential advocate of Catholicism in antebellum America, advocates the abolition of inheritance, somewhat defensively, at the end of his influential 1840 essay "The Laboring Classes."

8. Neal Dolan, in *Emerson's Liberalism*, offers a deep and subtle analysis of Emerson's understanding and use of the idea of property. As Dolan puts it, "In the context of an economy characterized by an ever more finely differentiated division of labor and a seemingly limitless proliferation of commodities, the activities of culture all serve to restore their participants, however, briefly, to a holistic consciousness of nature and of other human beings as radiant ends in themselves rather than as means to any particular practical end" (*Emerson's Liberalism*, 296).

9. In *Emerson and Self-Reliance* (Thousand Oaks, CA: Sage Publications, 1995), George Kateb's reading of *Nature* as a foundation for the perspective that makes self-reliance possible is a useful parallel reading: "It is one thing for Emerson to find all vocations and activities and worldly experiences unequal to his expectations. It is quite another thing for Emerson to find the very stuff of the world unsatisfying and hence in need of metaphysical enlargement." For Kateb, *Nature* prepares the way for individuals to reinvent the "matter" of their lives in order to practice a fuller, more "ravenously religious," and more self-reliant life. This "enlargement" is also pointed toward the culture as a whole. "Vocations, activities, and worldly experiences" may be unsatisfactory, but they needn't be. By thinking of them in terms more connected to the improved welfare of all, they also achieve "metaphysical enlargement" (70).

10. This idea of progress as "reflection" of an ideal is at the center of Daniel Malachuk's reading of the Transcendentalists' political thought, especially in its contrast between an Augustinian City of God and an experienced "city of man." Daniel S. Malachuk, *Two Cities: The Political Thought of American Transcendentalism* (Lawrence: University Press of Kansas, 2016), 137–51.

11. See Dolan, *Emerson's Liberalism*, 118–24.

12. Kris Fresonke, *West of Emerson: The Design of Manifest Destiny* (Berkeley: University of California Press, 2003), 89–90.

13. Emerson is fully aware of the oppression that Columbus brought with him. In 1849 he remarks that "the Indians were a sort of money, it seems in Spanish Colonies.... Columbus seems to have been the principal introducer of American slavery" (*JMN* 11:77).

14. Dolan also analyzes this set of figures in the "Discipline" chapter of *Nature*; see Dolan, *Emerson's Liberalism*, 93–96.

15. Henry Vane and Lord Russell were both important figures in the Reformation in England. Vane, who was governor of Massachusetts Bay Colony at the time of the antinomian crisis, was executed in 1662, largely for his liberal stand on religious tolerance. Lord Russell, an early Whig, was executed in 1683 for his effort to resist royal authority during the reign of Charles II.

16. Margaret Fuller, *Woman in the Nineteenth Century*, in *The Essential Margaret Fuller*, ed. Jeffrey A. Steele (New Brunswick: Rutgers University Press, 1992), 265.
17. The tension it mediates between inner will and outer form embodies what Michael Lopez terms the "creative antagonism" or "reverential hostility" in the relation between an imagined world of unfettered power and an experienced world of immutable laws. Michael Lopez, *Emerson and Power: Creative Antagonism in the Nineteenth Century* (DeKalb: Northern Illinois University Press, 1996), 18–22.
18. Lopez, *Emerson and Power*, 53–106.
19. Lopez, *Emerson and Power*, 84.
20. Alan Hodder's *Emerson's Rhetoric of Revelation* is especially useful in interpreting Emerson's effort to collapse external nature and human "nature" into a paradoxical "apocalypse of the mind." Alan D. Hodder, *Emerson's Rhetoric of Revelation: Nature, the Reader, and the Apocalypse Within* (College Park: Pennsylvania State University Press, 1996), 9–11. Also see David Robinson, *Apostle of Culture: Emerson as Preacher and Lecturer* (Philadelphia: University of Pennsylvania Press, 1982), 166–67.
21. Malachuk, *Two Cities*, 12–17.
22. Daniel Howe characterizes this perspective as a form of "democratic mysticism" rooted in "Neoplatonic categories . . . which give it its particular intensity and spiritual quality." Daniel Walker Howe, *Making the American Self: Jonathan Edwards to Abraham Lincoln* (Cambridge, MA: Harvard University Press, 1997), 190–91.
23. Douglas A. Irwin, *Against the Tide: An Intellectual History of Free Trade* (Princeton: Princeton University Press, 1996), esp. chap. 6, "Free Trade in Classical Economics," 87–100. Micheline Ishay, in *The History of Human Rights: From Ancient Times to the Globalization Era* (Berkeley: University of California Press, 2004), situates the emerging belief that capitalism is inherently degrading and thus makes a transition to socialism inevitable in the period between 1840 and 1900. Not only Proudhon and American socialists, and later Marx, but also the English Fabians concluded, as Sidney Webb wrote, that industrial production and the centralization of capital set the stage for "the inevitable convergence of all the economic tendencies toward socialism." Sidney Webb, *Socialism in England* (London: S. Sonnenschein, 1890), 3. It is worth emphasizing, though, that a counter-tradition that criticizes private property but remains committed to it runs through Mill to John Rawls. Whereas "welfare state capitalism permits a small class to have a near monopoly of the means of production," Rawls writes, "the background institutions of property-owning democracy work to disperse the ownership of wealth and capital" as long as they can resist monopolies. John Rawls, *Justice as Fairness: A Restatement* (Cambridge, MA: Harvard University Press, 2001), 139.
24. Richard Cobden to Henry Ashworth, April 12, 1842, quoted in John Morley, *The Life of Richard Cobden*, 2 vols. (London: Macmillan and Co., 1908), 1:155.
25. Adam Smith devotes book 4 of *Wealth of Nations* to a critique of the mercantile system built around protective tariffs. He notes sarcastically that "it is unnecessary, I imagine, to observe, how contrary such regulations are to the boasted liberty of the subject, of which we affect to be so very jealous; but which, in this case, are so plainly sacrificed to the futile interests of our merchants and manufacturers." Adam Smith, *An Inquiry into the Nature and Causes of the Wealth of Nations* (1776), ed. Kathryn Sutherland (New York: Oxford University Press, 2008), 377–78, 376;

Smith's free trade bias is echoed in Immanuel Kant, "Idea for a Universal History with Cosmopolitan Intent" and "To Eternal Peace," in *Basic Writings of Kant*, ed. Allen W. Wood (New York: Modern Library, 2001), 117–32, 433–41. This critique has more recently been reproduced in analysis of the social cost of globalization. Pheng Cheah links Kant's standard of "cosmopolitan right" to Habermas's post-discourse ethics turn toward cosmopolitanism. Pheng Cheah, *Inhuman Conditions: On Cosmopolitanism and Human Rights* (Cambridge: Harvard University Press, 2006), 45–52.

26. Charles Davenant, *An Essay on the East-India-Trade* (1696), 25–28, https://quod.lib.umich.edu/cgi/t/text/text-idx?c=eebo;idno=A37163.0001.001. J. G. A. Pocock reads Davenant's free trade advocacy as a foundation for both the work ethic and civic republicanism. Pocock speculates that "frugality could appear the civic virtue of the trader; assuming the circulation of goods to be a public benefit, he displayed in frugality and reinvestment his willingness to subordinate private satisfaction to the public good." J. G. A. Pocock, *The Machiavellian Moment: Florentine Political Thought and the Atlantic Republican Tradition* (Princeton: Princeton University Press, 1975), 446. Henry Martyn (attributed), *Considerations Upon the East-India Trade* (1701), 58–59, https://archive.org/details/ConsiderationsUponTheEASTINDIATRADE 58–59; Jacob Vanderlint, *Money Answers All Things, or, An Essay to Make Money Sufficiently Plentiful amongst All Ranks of People, and Increase Our Foreign and Domestick Trade* (London: T. Cox, 1734); Frances Hutcheson, *System of Moral Philosophy*, 3 vols. (Glasgow: A. Millar, 1755), 1:293–94.

27. Kathryn Sutherland, introduction to Smith, *Wealth of Nations*, xi.

28. J. S. Mill, *Principles of Political Economy, with Some of Their Applications to Social Philosophy*, 4 vols., ed. W. J. Ashley, vol. 4 (London: A. M. Kelley, 1965), 17.14.

29. Richard Cobden, *Speeches on Questions of Public Policy* (Manchester: Macmillan, 1870), 363.

30. John Locke, *Two Treatises of Government: And a Letter Concerning Toleration*, ed. Ian Shapiro (New Haven: Yale University Press, 2003), 2.26 and 27. Waldron contrasts the Lockean connection of property to transformative labor against a later, Hegelian model that treats the right to property as a universal human claim based on the fact that subsistence requires material resources. The Hegelian argument for the universal right to property runs parallel to the anti-mercantilist argument for the right to free trade. Both ground rights in "natural" impulses, such as the desire to clothe oneself and to build a habitation, and, in the case of free trade, the impulse to travel and socialize with other persons. See Jeremy Waldron, *The Right to Private Property* (New York: Oxford University Press, 1989), 31.

31. Dolan, *Emerson's Liberalism*, 116.

32. See especially Stanley Cavell, "Emerson's Constitutional Amending: Reading 'Fate,'" in *Emerson's Transcendental Etudes*, ed. Stanley Cavell and David Justin Hodge (Stanford, CA: Stanford University Press, 2003), 192–216. Emerson's development of the word "constitution" as a complex metaphor is also notable in the essay on Rawls in Cheah, *Inhuman Conditions*, and in "Appendix A: Hope against Hope," 101–27, 129–39, of the same text.

33. Kateb, In *Emerson and Self-Reliance*, 171.

34. Some of the meanness comes out of this comment when one reads it as biography. Emerson's mother, Ruth Haskins Emerson, was widowed at forty-three, when Waldo was eight years old. She raised her four sons in straitened circumstances.
35. See the note earlier in this chapter on Skidmore and Brownson and the attack on property.
36. George Fitzhugh, *Cannibals All! Or, Slaves without Masters* (Cambridge, MA: Belknap Press of Harvard University Press, 1960), 47.
37. Fitzhugh, *Cannibals All!*, 51, 62, 61, 67, 70, 82–83.
38. Stephen Simpson, *The Working Man's Manual: A New Theory of Political Economy, on the Principle of Production the Source of Wealth* (Philadelphia: Thomas L. Bonsal, 1831), 17–18, 14.
39. Simpson, *Working Man's Manual*, 19.
40. Simpson, *Working Man's Manual*, 27.
41. In Philip Foner's reading, antebellum workers' efforts at organization were divided between attempts to form political parties and compete for legislative power and attempts to form unions and negotiate with capital. Philip S. Foner, *History of the Labor Movement in the United States*, vol. 1, *From Colonial Times to the Founding of the American Federation of Labor* (New York: International Publishers, 1947), 101–41, 167–70. Charles Sellers emphasizes the role of Christianity in moderating political responses to the economic vulnerability of people with little or no property. As he puts it, "Under peaking market pressures in the 1820s and 1830s, Americans found religious salvation more compelling than political salvation." Charles Sellers, *The Market Revolution: Jacksonian America, 1815–1846* (New York: Oxford University Press, 1994), 202. J. R. Pole underscores the underlying liberalism of Americans who were being precipitated into the working class. Resistant to a communitarian perspective, workers were unable to form and sustain either parties or unions, and this motivated an emphasis on equality of opportunity over the redistribution of wealth or strong government control of prices, wages, and working conditions. J. R. Pole, *The Pursuit of Equality in American History* (Berkeley: University of California Press, 1978), 132–50.
42. At the end of the report, published by the Manayunk Working People's Committee, the workers add: "We should like to hear from the different Trades Unions throughout the U. States, concerning their regulations, & etc." See *The Pennsylvanian*, August 28, 1837, in *A Documentary History of American Industrial Society*, 10 vols., ed. John Roger Commons et al. (Cleveland, OH: Arthur H. Clark, 1910), 5:330–34.
43. In chapter 2 of *Uncle Tom's Cabin*, George Harris, a mixed-race slave, is introduced as the inventor of "a machine for the cleaning up of hemp, which, considering the education and circumstances of the inventor, displayed quite as much genius as Whitney's cotton-gin." In the next chapter, Stowe makes it clear that this accomplishment serves as a significant source of pride for George and adds to the degradation of his enslavement. Harriet Beecher Stowe, *Uncle Tom's Cabin, or, Life among the Lowly* (1852; New York: Oxford University Press, 2016), 18.
44. When George Ripley and his wife, Sophia, were organizing Brook Farm just outside Boston, they met with Bronson Alcott and Margaret Fuller at Emerson's house. Despite George Ripley's high hopes, Emerson was never strongly attracted

to utopian communities as a vehicle for changing property relations or for the opportunities they represented. In his study of Brook Farm, Sterling Delano inserts Emerson's note that "Lidian gives the true doctrine of property when she says 'No one should take more than his own share, Let him be ever so rich'" into the middle of his discussion of Ripley's plan (*JMN* 7:404). Sterling Delano, *Brook Farm: The Dark Side of Utopia* (Cambridge, MA: Belknap Press of Harvard University Press, 2004), 28. See also Carl J. Guarneri, *The Utopian Alternative: Fourierism in Nineteenth-Century America* (Ithaca, NY: Cornell University Press, 1991), 47–49.
45. *Jean Jacques Rousseau: Political Writings*, ed. Fredrick Watkins (Madison: University of Wisconsin Press, 1986), 40–42.
46. Len Gougeon, "The Anti-Slavery Background of Emerson's 'Ode Inscribed to W. H. Channing,'" *Studies in the American Renaissance* (1985): 63–77, esp. 68.

CONCLUSION

1. Steven Hahn, *Illiberal America: A History* (New York: W. W. Norton & Co., 2024), 351.
2. Leonard Richards, *"Gentlemen of Property and Standing": Anti-Abolition Mobs in Jacksonian America* (New York: Oxford University Press), 69, 70.
3. Hahn, *Illiberal America*, 112.
4. Samuel Gilman Brown, *Life of Rufus Choate* (Cambridge: Legare Street Press, 2023), 326.
5. John C. Calhoun, "Speech on Slavery," US Senate, 24th sess., *Congressional Globe*, February 6, 1837, 157–59.
6. Chard Powers Smith, "The Chardon Street Convention" (MA thesis, Columbia University Faculty of Political Science, 1949), 110.
7. "Church, Ministry, and Sabbath Convention," *Hingham Patriot*, November 5, 1841.
8. Wesley T. Mott, "'All Kinds of Extravagant Isms': An Orthodox View of the Chardon Street Convention," *The Concord Saunterer* 19, no. 2 (1987): 17–25.
9. "Chardon Street Convention," *New Hampshire Observer*, December 5, 1840.
10. Transcribed in A. A. Phelps, *A Sketch of the Proceedings of the Convention for the Discussion of the Sabbath* (Boston, 1841), 26.
11. George Willis Cooke, *Ralph Waldo Emerson: His Life, Writings, and Philosophy* (1881; Honolulu, HI: University Press of the Pacific, 2003), 93.

Index

abolitionism. *See* antislavery movement
Adams, Abigail, 2
Adams, John, 29–30, 31, 32, 43, 47, 158, 206, 224n10, 224n11
Adams, John Quincy, 31–32, 43, 224n17, 226–27n39
African Americans, 16, 146, 210–11, 217–18n7, 236n58
Africans, 136–37
Agassiz, Louis, 4, 21, 104–5, 108, 113, 115–19, 132, 147
Alcott, Bronson, 209–10, 211, 241–42n44
American Party, 18, 158
American Peace Society, 175
American race, 124, 128, 132–34
American Renaissance, 19
American Revolution, 28, 155
anaconda, metaphor of, 130–31
Anthony, Susan B., 65, 80–81
anthropology, 113; cosmopolitan, 104, 125; racist, 142–56, 221n28
Anti-Corn Law League, 172, 191, 192
anti-egalitarianism, 5, 6–7, 17–18, 19, 20, 149, 206
anti-miscegenation laws, 155
antislavery movement, 2, 4, 64, 134–42, 144–45, 150, 205, 226n33, 235n44, 235n49; antislavery press, 2, 45; antislavery societies, 4; effort to discredit, 205; the Emersons and, 84–91; free speech and, 31, 144, 146; gag rule on antislavery speech, 31, 144; global, 139–42; organized, 45; as transformative, 106; white, 147; women and, 84–85
aristocracy, "natural," 204, 206

"arrested undertype," 132–42
Arsić, Branka, 100–101, 126
assimilation, 107, 108–12
Association movement, 192–93
Augustine, 170
authenticity, 21, 73. *See also* sincerity
autonomy, 169, 172, 174, 176, 178–79, 188, 195; individualism and, 208; liberal, 179, 182, 184–85; private property and, 185; spiritual, 209

Balogh, Brian, 224n11
Bancroft, George, 39–41, 42, 43, 123, 225–26n28
Bank of the United States, 14–15, 36, 157
Bank War, 14–15, 219n15
banking system, 185–86
banknotes, 157–58
barbarism, 177
Baum, Bruce, 221n28
beauty, 164–65, 166, 189
Becker, Carl, 19–20
Beecher, Catharine, 1, 21, 64, 66, 83, 205, 228–29n8, 229n10; definition of housekeeper, 90–91; Emerson and, 72–77; *Treatise on Domestic Economy*, 67–72, 76, 77
Beecher, Edward, 226–27n39
Beecher Stowe, Harriet, 191, 241n43
Bercovitch, Sacvan, 231–32n51
Bigelow, Ann, 85
Blackburn, Robin, 235n49
blacks, 140–41, 155–56. *See also* African Americans
Blackstone, William, 78–79, 82–83, 228n7

Blackwell, Antoinette B., 78
Blackwell, Henry Browne, 81–82, 230–31n31
blood: "blood cosmopolitanism," 128, 129; as metaphor, 122–23, 127, 128–29; multiple meanings of, 127
Boudinot, Elias, 111
Britain, 42; abolition of slavery in, 4; aristocratic legacy of, 38; British pre-eminence, 120–23, 134; Emancipation Act (UK) in, 140; House of Commons in, 46. *See also* British West Indies, emancipation in
British West Indies, emancipation in, 85, 135, 137–41
Brooks, Mary, 85
Brooks, Nathan, 85
Brown, Antoinette, 81
Brown, John, xii, 213
Brownson, Orestes, 160, 182, 225–26n28, 237–38n7
Bryant, William Cullen, 110, 123
Buchanan, James, 204, 217n2
Buell, Lawrence, 126
Burke, Edmund, 46
Burns, Anthony, 85, 109–10, 149
Byron, George Gordon, 176

Calhoun, John C., 144, 149, 204, 226n33
capital: access to, 15; vs. labor, 185–86, 188, 197
capitalism, 158–59, 160, 172, 174, 177–78, 180, 185–86, 188, 190; character and, 178; creativity and, 208; critique of, 191–203, 208; degradation and, 239n23; Emerson's move away from, 190–95; selfhood and, 197; suspicion of, 178; as transitional, 191–95
Carlyle, Thomas, 37, 132, 133
caste, 204–5
Cavell, Stanley, 179, 218n2, 225n22, 234–35n40, 235n44, 235n45
Cayton, Mary Kupiec, 30
Central America, 112; independence movements in, 176
Channing, W. H., 199, 226–27n39

character, 83; capitalism and, 178; citizenship and, 49–50; home life and, 72; models of, 195; politics and, 57; representative, 54–55
Chardon Street Convention, 23, 208–13
Charles II, 164–65, 238n15
Chartists, 183
chastity, 96, 232n52
chauvinism, Emerson's resistance to, 125
Cheah, Pheng, 239–40n25
Cherokee Indians, 107–12. *See also* Cherokee removals debate
Cherokee removals, 84, 107–12, 123, 138, 156, 207. *See also* Indian Removal Act
Child, Lydia Maria, 91
child labor, 160
child rearing, 77
Choate, Rufus, 17–18, 150, 155, 204, 205
citizens: as idealized embodiment of individual character, 49–50; independence to speak in public, 46–47; self-government of, 39
citizenship, 25–60, 200; affiliative model of, 111; alienation from, 112, 156; aspirational ideal of egalitarian, 53; definitions of, 20–21, 29–30; Emersonian model of, 29, 44, 52–53, 57–60, 108, 110, 208; grounded in aspirational ideal, 108; grounded in liberal political assumptions, 59–60; grounded in sincere communication, 65; heritage and, 133; individuality and, 55, 60; Jacksonian revisions of, 222n5; liberal vs. classical republican model of, 29; race and, 107–12; republican model of, 157, 171; "self-reliance" model of, 29; virtuous, 157; Whig model of, 31
civic republicanism, 31, 46–47, 50, 60, 193, 203
civil society, 112, 170
Civil War, xiii, 19, 20, 127
civility, 139, 170
class, 2, 48, 74, 157, 179, 219n15. *See also* caste; *specific classes*
Cobden, Richard, 172, 174–75, 176, 185, 192

Cole, Phyllis, 84, 231n41
College of William & Mary, 143
Columbus, Christopher, 164, 165, 238n13
commerce, 3, 23, 158–61, 189; critique of, 189; danger posed by, 189, 195; Emerson's ambivalence about, 200; human rights and, 195; as intercultural dialogue, 185; for the public good, 161–69; socialism and, 193–94; as transitional social form, 191, 203
commodification, 190, 195, 196, 197
commodities, 197, 198, 203. *See also* private property
common good, 60, 157, 160–69
Common Sense philosophy, 22
communication, 190, 193; egalitarian, 10–11; friendship and, 67; globalization of, 126; sincerity in, 9, 10–11, 23, 63–64, 65, 73, 77, 101–2, 207, 208; strategic, 198; "strategically distorted," 149–51
communism, 191, 193. *See also* socialism
communitarianism, 169, 188, 193
community, 29, 161–62, 169, 200
Concord, Massachusetts, 10, 48, 84, 124, 146, 152–53, 187, 206, 225n21, 226n38, 237n5
Concord Female Anti-Slavery Society, 85
Confederate States of America, xi, xii, xiii, xvi; constitution of, 204; establishment of, 19; repudiation of equality in, xiii, xv–xvi, 1
conformity, domesticity and, 73–75, 76, 83, 102
Congregationalism, 130, 209
Congress of Nations, 2, 173, 176, 177
consensus, 127–28
"constitution," 179, 240n32
constitution making, political process of, 127
"constitutional cosmopolitanism," 129
conversation, 44, 100–101, 201–2, 208
conversion, 44
Copernican revolution, 27, 28, 48, 105, 188
cosmopolitan anthropology, 104, 125

cosmopolitan democracy, 131–32
cosmopolitan egalitarianism, 126–32, 136–37, 142, 147, 172, 178, 185, 188
cosmopolitan universalism, 108, 130, 132
cosmopolitanism, 126, 175, 208, 239–40n25; "blood cosmopolitanism," 128, 129; constitutional, 127–28, 129; Enlightenment, 113; equality and, 146; erosion of, 112–13; human rights and, 146; Kant and, 173; universalizing, 170; validation of, 139
cotton boom, 1
coverture marriage, 21, 77, 78–79
Crane, Gregg, 127–28, 129
creativity, 178, 188, 189, 190, 203, 208
Creek Indians, 111–12
crisis of 1850, 10
cultural leadership, Emerson's critique of, 52–54
cultural nationalism, 107
culture, "domestication" of idea of, 52, 56–57, 65, 91–93, 100, 110–11, 127, 141, 208, 213
culture wars, 18–19, 204–13
Cunningham, William, 29–30
currency, 157–58

dana, Richard Henry, 123
Darwin, Charles, 104–5, 108, 113, 114, 119–20, 125, 128
Darwinism: proto-social Darwinist ideas, 1–2; "racial," 235n49
Daveis, Charles Stewart, 38–39, 40, 42, 43, 225n27
Davenant, Charles, 173, 240n26
Davis, Pauline, 81
Davy, Ulrike, 13
Declaration of Independence, xiii, 14, 17–18, 20, 150, 155
Declaration of Seneca Falls Convention, 77–78
degradation, 190, 199
Delano, Sterling, 241–42n44
demagoguery, 20, 26, 36, 37, 158, 161
the Democracy, 25–27, 29, 44–49, 158, 171, 222n3

democracy, 29, 65, 161, 177, 180, 219n15, 227n45; cosmopolitan, 131–32; democratic discourse, 44; direct, 46, 203; Emersonian citizenship in, 57–60; Emersonian citizenship in mass, 57–60; Emerson's ambivalence about, 189; expansion of, 56, 178; factionalism of, 39; individuality and, 49–57; Jacksonian, 29, 36–38, 47, 65, 161, 219n15; Jeffersonian, 47; as majoritarian form of government, 159; meaning of, 154–55; vs. meritocracy, 36–37; public opinion and, 36–38, 47; representative, 46, 50, 202–3; slavery and, 154–55. *See also* mass democracy

Democratic Party, 16, 18, 25, 32–33, 36, 45–46, 60, 157, 217n2, 224–25n18; of Boston, 39; as demotic force, 48; election of 1836 and, 158; John Quincy Adams's opposition to, 32; model of citizenship and, 26; Panic of 1837 and, 236–37n3; political equality and, 27; proslavery, xii; public opinion and, 41, 43, 44, 46, 47; rival factions of, xi–xii; roots in Jeffersonian republicanism, 222n3; second party system and, 226n34

Democratic Societies, 224n15
democratization, 3, 46–47, 56–57, 59–60, 206
despotism, 158
Dew, Thomas R., 143–44, 149, 204
Dewey, Orville, 110
Dickens, Charles, 137
dignity, 119, 190, 195, 196, 203
discipline, 166, 175, 180, 184–85
disunionism, 199
divorce, 77, 78, 80
Dolan, Neal, 179, 238n8
domesticity, 21, 65–66, 67; conformity and, 73–75, 76, 83, 102; conservative views of, 67–72, 83; critique of, 102; cult of, 90, 102; debates over, 65; Emerson's critique of, 64, 72–77; individuality and, 72–75, 83; metaphors of, 23, 60, 201–2
dominion, 198

Donald, David Herbert, 220n22
Douglas, Stephen, 16, 220n22
Douglass, Frederick, 132, 146, 147, 150, 213
Dred Scott decision, 149

economic issues, 157–69; economic independence, 30, 203; economic inequality, 15–16, 185–86; economic opportunity, 66, 185–87
economic theorists, 173
egalitarianism, 12, 23, 25–26, 56, 59, 74, 132, 139, 194, 202–3, 206, 208; conflicted, 135–37; cosmopolitan, 136–37, 142, 147, 172; democratic, 56, 59, 225–26n28; dialogue and, 201–2; egalitarian movements, 205; egalitarian pluralism, 128, 129; egalitarian racial recognition, 127; egalitarian reform, 207; egalitarian universalism, 91; Emerson as surprising convert to, 205–6; Enlightenment and, 20; "European" mode of, 67–68; free trade and, 172; friendship and, 100; liberalism and, 65–67, 76, 83; Lincoln and, 16–17; marriage and, 91–92, 98, 228n7; progress and, 21; racial, 112–13, 156; vs. racist impulses, 147–48, 155–56; radical, 200–201; sexual, 77; socialist, 160–61; tension in aspiration of, 168–69; universalized, 102
egotism, 160, 169
election of 1834, 32–35, 47–48
election of 1836, 157–58, 236n2
election of 1858, 16
election of 1860, xi–xii, 16–17
election of 1864, 158
Electoral College, Jackson's effort to eliminate, 36
elites, 36, 53
elitism, 30, 36, 53, 125, 132
Elkins, Stanley, 224n10, 224n15
Elshtain, Jean Bethke, 65–66
emancipation, xv, 4; in British West Indies, 85, 135, 137–41; compensated, 152
Emancipation Act (UK), terms of, 140

Emancipation Proclamation, xiii, 220n22
Emerson, Charles, 61, 62
Emerson, Edith, 87
Emerson, Edward, 61, 87, 155
Emerson, Ellen (daughter), 70, 87, 89, 90
Emerson, Lidian, 84–91, 149, 209, 231n34, 231n41, 241–42n44
Emerson, Mary Moody, 61, 89, 207
Emerson, Ralph Waldo, 2, 4, 55, 62, 83, 241n34; abolitionism and, 84, 134, 135–37, 144–45, 149–53, 235n49; accepts position at Second Unitarian Church, 62; ambivalence about talent and excellence, 227n45; as antinationalist, 126; attends Whig rally, 33–34, 48; Beecher and, 72–77; chauvinist comments by, 148–49; completion of divinity school, 61; conservatism and, 32; cosmopolitanism and, 126; defense of equality and, xvi, 1–23; in the Democracy, 32–36; election of 1834 and, 33–35, 47–48; eulogy for Lincoln, 124–25; evolution of his thought, 206; evolutionary theories and, 22, 104–6, 126; expansion of franchise and, 20–21; household of, 83; importance in history of equality, 5; inheritance from Tucker, 62–63; liberalism and, 29–30, 32; libertarian impulses of, 4; as literary nationalist, 41, 126; marriage to Ellen Louisa Tucker, 62; marriage to Lydia Jackson, 83, 84–91, 231n34, 231n41; masculinist bias of, 21; model of citizenship and, 29; move away from capitalism toward socialist egalitarianism, 160–61, 190–95, 239n23; movement from Transcendentalist idealism to skepticism/pragmaticism, 220–21n27, 237n6; perfectionist bias of, 234–35n40; prejudices of, 4; proposal to Lidian, 85–86; reaction to Kansas-Nebraska Act, 12; rejection of partisan organizations, 26, 33–35, 41; as religious rebel, 4; republicanism and, 32; resigns as pastor to become social reformer, 2, 63, 205–6; resolution on equality, 4; response to Stephens's "Cornerstone Speech," xiii; roots of his politics, 29–32; seeks alternative to political parties, 27; sharp move to ideological left, 178; skepticism of, 220–21n27; on spiritual equality, 4; as surprising convert to egalitarianism, 205–6; theory of self-reliance, 3; time warp and, 185; Transcendentalism and, 18–19, 47, 63, 66, 85, 220–21n27; women's rights movement and, 228n4. *See also* Emerson, Ralph Waldo, works of

Emerson, Ralph Waldo, works of: "Address on Emancipation in the British West Indies," 137–38, 147; address on fourth anniversary of Webster's speech, 149–52; "Address to the Citizens of Concord on the Fugitive Slave Law," 10, 130, 149, 151–53; "American Civilization," 167; "The American Scholar," 21–22, 36, 50–54, 55, 56, 58–59, 76, 85, 107–8, 112, 180, 195, 202, 223n7; antislavery speech at Second Church, 84; *The Conduct of Life*, 11, 130, 178, 208; "Culture," 178; "Discourse on the History of Concord," 225n21; "The Divinity School Address," 6–7, 85, 140, 180, 201; "Domestic Life," 11, 72–77, 82, 90; *English Traits*, 120–22; *Essays* (first series), 91, 98; *Essays* (second series), 180, 188; "Experience," 130, 188, 201; "Fate," 106, 118, 130–31, 134, 235n44, 235n45; "The Fortune of the Republic," xiii; "Friendship," 63, 91, 98–99; "Heroism," 45, 63; "History," 28, 147; "Human Culture" lecture, 28; "Human Culture" series, 45; "The Individual," 56; lecture at women's rights convention, 1855, 63–64; "Love," 82, 91–98, 189; "Natural History of Intellect," 6, 11; *Nature*, 7–8, 28, 39, 55, 63, 85, 130, 154, 157–59, 161–69, 180, 186, 189, 203, 223n7, 238n9; "New England Reformers," 7–8, 212–13; "Ode, Inscribed to

Emerson, Ralph Waldo, works of: (*continued*)
W. H. Channing," 199–200; "The Over-Soul," 9; Peace Society address, 176–77; Phi Beta Kappa poem, 26; "Philosophy of History" series, 55–56, 162, 171, 223n7; "The Poet," 3–4, 5, 6, 8, 188; "Politics" (1837), 22, 51–52, 56–58, 126, 169–78, 179, 180–81, 182, 185, 188, 195; "Politics" (1844), 8, 10–11, 22, 41, 134, 178, 180, 185, 188–89, 190–91, 195–203; "Present Age" series, 189, 190; public letter to Van Buren, 108–9, 111, 112, 138; *Representative Men*, 82, 208; second essay on Fugitive Slave Law (1954), 149–50, 153–54; "Self-Reliance," 5, 9, 42–43, 63, 118, 137, 194, 212; "Society," 44; statement at 1856 Kansas relief meeting, 154, 155; "Swedenborg," 82, 95–98; "War," 175, 209; "Wealth," 178; "Worship," 11; "The Young American," 43, 124, 134, 167, 175, 188–95

Emerson, Ruth Haskins, 86–87, 89, 241n34

Emerson, Waldo (son), 87

Emerson, William, 61

Emerson family, 61, 75, 84

enfranchisement. *See* voting rights

Enlightenment, xii, xvi, 20, 125, 172, 233n15

enslaved persons: advocacy for, 2; equality of, 146; escaped, 85, 109–10, 146, 149, 199; freed, 140–41; manumission of, 143

equality, 42, 60, 156, 159, 170, 200, 208; of access to resources, 166, 179; for African Americans, 16; as aspirational, 10–11, 47; belief in, xii–xiii; chaos of, 183–84; in conversation, 100–101; cosmopolitan, 126–32, 146, 185; debate over, 22; Emersonian, 5–11; of esteem, 11; expansion of, 178; four kinds of, 11–12; freedom and, 3, 23, 81, 179, 182–84; as fundamental value, 206–7; history as voyage through, 203; as immanently social, 9; individuality and, 77, 206–7, 218n2; intimacy and, 102–3; Jefferson on, xiv–xv, 1; before the law, 11–12, 13; liberal ideas of, 81, 82–83; Lincoln's defense of, 16–17; marriage and, 76–77, 91–92, 95, 98–99; meanings of, 1–23; as normative value, 4; of opportunity, 14–16, 196; political discourse and, 59; prioritization of, 200–201; progress and, 27–29; property and, 11, 15, 16, 180, 219–20n19; racial, 134–35, 144; of respect, 11; self-respect and, 3–4; sexual equality, 228n4; sincerity and, 102; Spirit and, 126; spirituality and, 4–5, 8, 18–19, 206; struggle for, 60; theory of, 5; universal, xii–xiii, xvi, 3, 13, 18–20, 63–64, 77, 83, 106, 127, 132, 156, 177, 200, 208; universalization of, 66; universalizing model of, 7–8, 156; women and, 63–64, 66, 77. *See also* economic equality; political equality; sexual equality; spiritual equality; women's rights movement

ethnic cleansing, 107, 108, 110, 111–12

ethnic hybridization, 120, 122

ethnicity, race and, 125

ethnocentricity, progress and, 111

ethnographic mapping, polygenetic theory and, 146

ethnography, 142, 146, 147

ethnology, 106, 113, 155

Europe, independence movements in, 175–76

Evans, George, 182, 219–20n19

Everett, Edward, 65, 226n38

evolutionary theories, 22, 104–6, 108, 112–20, 122, 125, 128, 130, 134, 171, 234n31, 235n49

exceptionalism, 19, 41

exploitation, 182–84, 194, 196–98

expulsion, vs. assimilation, 107–12

Fabians, 239n23

factory towns, 4, 15

the Fall, 50–51

family life, 21, 66, 72, 228–29n8. *See also* marriage

fatalism, 62–63, 130

fate, 131–32
Federalism, 29, 30, 31, 206
Federalist Papers, 46
femininity, 66, 83, 97, 102
feudalism, 175, 177, 180, 191
Fichte, Johann Gottlieb, 221n28
Finseth, Ian, 128, 129, 234–35n40
Fitzhugh, George, 182–84, 204
Flint, Almira, 90
Flüchter, Antje, 13
Foner, Philip, 241n41
Founders, xii, xiii, xiv–xv
France, 191
Frank, Jason, 46
free land policies, 182
free market, 159–60
Free Soil Party, 45, 158, 226n38
free speech, 31, 144, 146
free states, living standards for laborers in, 15
free trade, 169–78, 182–84, 188, 195
freedmen, restraint of, 140–41
freedom. *See* liberty
Fresonke, Kris, 164
"Friends of Universal Reform," 209
friendship, 9, 21, 156; aspirational nature of, 103; communication and, 67; egalitarian universalism and, 91; Emersonian, 98–100; hero worship of, 101; as highest possible relationship attainable, 101; individuality and, 101; intimacy and, 102–3; as perfect egalitarianism, 100; self-expression and, 100; sincerity and, 65, 101
Fugitive Slave Law, 9, 10, 130, 135–37, 149–53, 207, 213
Fuller, Margaret, 21, 63, 64, 80, 82, 96, 106, 231n45, 232n52, 241–42n44; Lidian and, 87–89; *Woman in the Nineteenth Century*, 80, 165

Garrison, Ellen, 85
Garrison, John, 236n58
Garrison, Susan, 85
Garrison, William Lloyd, 2, 53, 106, 132, 142, 145, 199, 209
Garrisonians, 147

Gatens, Moira, 82
Gates, Henry Louis, Jr., 220n22
gender, 97; fluidity of, 95–96, 97, 102; gender equality, 77, 166; gender spheres, 65–66, 67–72, 76–77, 205, 228–29n8, 229n12; liberalism and, 65; models of, 64, 65. *See also* gender spheres
General Trades Union, 219–20n19
Genesis, 50–51
genius, 132; achievements of, 163–67, 227n45; communal value produced through labor of, 163–69; republican ideal of, 37; transformative power of, 155, 189
Georgia, xi, xii, xiii, 107–12
Germany, 191
Gettysburg, battle of, xiii
Gettysburg, Pennsylvania, Everett's oration at, 65
Gettysburg Address, 65
Ginsberg, Lori, 229n18
Gliddon, George R., 114, 115
global diplomacy, 2
global disarmament movement, 2
globalization, 239–40n25
Gordon-Reed, Annette, 217–18n7, 218n9
Gove, Mary, 228n7
government: critique of, 192–93; defense of human rights over property rights, 198–99; as "evil," 41; of force vs. grounded in egalitarian dialogue, 201–2; provisional nature of, 195–96
Greek Revolution, 176
Greeley, Horace, 33
Green, Duff, 41, 226n33
Grimké, Angelina, 67, 84–85
Grimké, Sarah, 65, 66, 67, 84–85, 228n7
Grimsted, David, 226–27n39
Grossberg, Michael, 228–29n8

Habermas, Jürgen, 149, 236n65, 239–40n25
Hahn, Steven, 205
Haiti, 142
Hale, Sarah Josepha, 21, 66
Harrington, James, 169–70

Harvard Divinity School, 6–7
Haudenosaunee People (Iroquois Federation"), 114
Hawthorne, Nathaniel, 225–26n28
hereditary power, discrediting of, 177
heroic individuality, 45
heroism, 45–46
hierarchy, 155, 204–5
"higher" law, statute law and, 152
history, 27, 137, 155; Emerson's conception of, 126, 134; end state of, 202; as evolutionary process, 147; as voyage through equality, 203
Hoar, Elizabeth, 61, 89
Hoar, Samuel, 226n38
Hobbes, Thomas, 12, 169–70, 183, 201, 218–19n7
Holt, Michael, 222n3
Hone, Philip, 35, 225n21
Horsman, Reginald, 148
Howe, Daniel Walker, 219n15, 222n3, 222n5, 227n44
human rights, 20–21, 23; boundaries of, 138; commerce and, 195; cosmopolitan language of, 146; cosmopolitanism and, 146; free trade and, 195; mocking of, 155; vs. property rights, 1, 5, 22, 180, 184, 188, 196–97, 198–99, 200–201; trade and, 172–75; universalization of, 208
human rights law, 184
human similarity, 129
Humboldt, Alexander von, 117
Hungarian Revolution, 176
Hutcheson, Francis, 173–74
hybridization, 120, 123–24, 127. See also racial combination
hypocrisy, 149

the ideal, reasoning from, 170–71
idealism: aspirational, 196; progressive idealism, 203; public benefits of, 163–67
identity politics, 130–32
illiberalism, 204–5
Illinois, xi, 16
independence, 26, 47, 184, 203
independence movements, 175–76
Indian Removal Act, 107, 219n15
Indian territories, conquest of, 41
"Indian Territory," in Oklahoma, 107, 153
Indigenous people, 107–12. See also Cherokee removals debate
Indigenous sovereignty, 107
the individual: alienation of, 43; emergence of, 55; Emerson's libertarian emphasis on, 40; empowerment of, 171–72, 180; liberation from arbitrary institutions of power, 27; mass politics and, 60; rights of, 159; as sovereign state, 26, 34, 40, 52, 55, 59, 170, 171, 177–78; sovereignty of, 28, 32, 43–46, 51–52, 100, 132, 161, 182, 184, 194–95, 200
individual character, public stage and, 45
individualism, 32, 55, 142, 200–201, 206; autonomy and, 208; liberal, 227n44; possessive, 184, 185–86, 188, 189; Romantic, 55
individuality, 26, 40, 47, 49, 52, 156, 159; as alternative to partisan identity, 29; citizenship and, 55; the democracy and, 44–49; democratic representation and, 49–57; domesticity and, 72–75, 83; equality and, 206–7, 218n2; friendship and, 101; masculine, 72–75; nonconformist, 20; obstacles to, 206; partisan politics and, 35–36, 60; public debate/dialogue and, 55; right to, 63, 64; right to achieve, 78; Transcendentalism and, 71; as universal human right, 23, 76–77; of the "wise man," 202
industrial production, 15, 184–85, 187, 239n23
inequality, 11–23, 207, 208; amplification and institutionalization of, 2; antebellum inequalities, 11–23; as cornerstone of Confederate society, 204; defense of, xiii–xv, 13, 154; economic, 185–86; freedom and, 13; marriage and, 22; "natural" vs. "contrived," 198; private property and,

22; property rights and, 180–81; racial, 148–49; in wealth, 15–16
insincerity, 152, 154–55
institutions: evolution of, 126; internalization of functions of, 52; as prosthesis only necessary in immature society, 54–57; repressive force of, 63
intellectual property, as contradiction in terms, 166
intelligent design, tradition of, 119, 234n31
interest-group liberalism, 30–31, 39
intermarriage, 111
international courts, 2
intimacy, 21, 208; equality and, 102–3; friendship and, 102–3; growth of, 93–94; language of sexual, 100; marriage and, 93, 96, 98; metaphors of, 23; spiritual growth and, 96
invention, 163–67, 189. *See also* creativity
the Irish, 155–56
Irving, Washington, 123

Jackson, Andrew, 25, 31, 36, 53, 157, 158, 226n33, 226n38; election of, 59–60; first message to Congress, 36
Jackson, Lydia, 84–91, 231n34, 231n41
Jacksonian movement, 14–15, 32–33, 179, 186–87, 222n3; anti-bank stand of, 14–15; emphasis on majoritarian public opinion, 46; Jacksonian liberalism, 32; Jacksonian materialism, 162
Jacksonian press, 38–39
Jamaica, 140
Jefferson, Thomas, 29, 143; on equality, xiv–xv, 1; legacy of, xiii–xvi; *Notes on the State of Virginia*, xiv–xv; race and, 217–18n7, 218n9; on slavery, xiv–xvi
Jeffersonians, 31, 47
jurisprudence, racist, 107
justice, 2, 22, 127, 207, 208

Kansas Relief Meeting, 154, 155
Kansas-Nebraska Act, xi, 10, 12, 149, 155
Kansas-Nebraska Debate, 149
Kant, Immanuel, 172–73, 184, 233n15

Kateb, George, 100, 180, 238n9
Kelley, Abby, 67, 210
Kent, James, 228n7
Kerr, Andrea Moore, 230–31n31
Keyssar, Alexander, 13, 222n5
King, Martin Luther, Jr., 217–18n7
Knox, Robert, 121
Kossuth, Lajos, 176

labor: vs. capital, 185–86, 188, 197; as civic contribution, 180; commodification of, 190, 195; commodification of, 196; forced, 175; "free" labor market, 185; labor market, 186; property as product of, 180; property rights and, 240n30; self-ownership and, 159, 176; as standard for ownership, 180; unalienated, 203. *See also* labor movement; laborers
labor movement, 2, 15, 187, 191–92, 241n41, 241n42. *See also* unions
laborers: advocacy for, 2; compensation of, 186; deteriorating power of, 187; dignity of, 186; vs. elites, 36; public nature of, 161; respect for, 15, 16; rights of, 4
Lamarck, Jean-Baptiste, 118–19, 122
language, distortion of, 149–52
Lawrence, Massachusetts, 15
legislators, responsibility of, 46
Leonidas, 164, 165
liberalism, 32, 126, 171–74, 178, 190, 192, 200, 241n41; vs. classically republican politics, 29; conservative, 206; cosmopolitan, 176, 188; egalitarianism and, 65–67, 76, 83; gender and, 65; interest-group, 30–31, 39; Jacksonian, 32; laissez-faire, 193; liberal identity, 184–85, 188; liberal individualism, 227n44; liberal selfhood, 194; liberal utopia, 55–56; philosophical, 170; pluralist, 50; "procedural" vs. "perfectionist" forms of, 227n49; redemption of, 200; rise of, 60; self-ownership and, 188; universalization of, 65–66
liberals, 29–32
The Liberator, 2, 66, 142

Liberia, 152, 176
libertarianism, 40, 188. *See also* free trade
liberty, 23, 157–203, 207; creativity and, 188; economic, 14–15; equality and, 3, 23, 81, 179, 182–84; individual, 209; inequality and, 13; liberalism and, 188; property and, 22, 23; radical, 202. *See also specific freedoms*
Liberty Party, 158
Lincoln, Abraham, xi, 142, 157, 217n2, 217n3; campaign of 1860 and, xi–xii; defense of equality and, 16–17; egalitarianism and, 16–17; election of, xii, xiii, 16–17, 158; election of 1860 and, 16–17; Emerson's eulogy for, 124–25; Gettysburg Address, 65; inauguration of, xii; Lincoln-Douglas debates and, 16; race and, 147, 220n22; sincerity of, 65; in Whig Party until formation of Republican Party, 31–32; white supremacy and, 220n22
Lincoln-Douglas debates, 16
Linnaean tradition, 21
literary nationalism, 41–42, 107, 126, 225–26n28
Locke, John, 12–13, 169–70, 178–79, 180, 240n30
Lopez, Michael, 167, 239n17
Louverture, Toussaint, 142
love, 3, 21, 91–98; as beginning of "domestication of the idea of culture," 92–93; marriage and, 92–103; power of as basis of a state, 201–2
Lovejoy, Elijah, 45–46, 226–27n39
Lowell, Massachusetts, 15, 187
Luther, Martin, 27, 28
Luther, Seth, 160

Macpherson, C. B., 184
Madison, James, 46
Maine, 17, 18, 155, 205
majoritarianism, 45, 47, 48, 159
Malachuk, Daniel, 238n10
Manayunk Working People's Committee, 241n42
Manchester, England, 172

mandate model of representation, 47
"mandate-independence" debate, 46, 47
manifest destiny, 41, 134
manumission, 143
Mark, Gospel of, 78
marriage, 3, 9, 61–67, 91–103, 156; 1860 convention and, 229n18; as act of unification, 95; chivalrous monogamous, 91; class identities and, 74; conservative views of, 83; "conversation" and, 98; coverture marriage, 77, 78–79; critiques of, 66; difficulty of discussing publicly, 65, 77; doctrine of marital unity, 78–79; egalitarianism and, 11, 91–92, 98, 228n7; Emerson's theory of history and, 91; equality and, 76–77, 79, 91–92, 95, 98–99; as gendered process of leading and following, 98; idea of unification and, 78; individual growth within, 95; inequality and, 22; intimacy and, 93, 96, 98; marriage reform, 21, 65–66, 73, 77–83, 80–81, 228n7; as metaphor for society of equals, 103, 231–32n51; as Platonic ideal, 96; Plato's allegory of the cave and, 93–94; problem of, 77–84; property rights and, 78–79; salvation and, 97; sexual duty imposed on women in, 79–80; as sharing of single thought, 98; sincerity and, 65; social contract philosophers and, 82–83; subordination of women and, 79; Swedenborg's theory of, 95–98. *See also* marriage reform
Married Women's Property Act, 213
Marshall, Megan, 231n45
Martyn, Henry, 173
Marx, Karl, 190, 191–92, 239n23
masculinity, 73, 83, 97, 102
Massachusetts, 150, 152–53, 199, 226–27n39; 1780 constitution of, 206; emergence of interest-group liberalism in, 30–31; factory towns in, 4, 15; Fourth Congressional District, 45; Fugitive Slave Law and, 10; state constitutional convention of 1821, 206

master race theories, anthropology and, 221n28
master-slave relationship, compared to familial affection, 143
materialism, 160, 162, 189, 190, 195, 200
Matthew, Gospel of, 78
Matthiessen, F. O., 19
Maxwell, Mr., 34
McKitrick, Eric, 224n10, 224n15
mercantilism, 171, 172, 239–40n25
meritocracy, 36–37, 159–60, 227n45
Mexican-American War, 147–48, 213
Mexicans, 148
Mexico, 157
Michael, John, 220–21n27
Michigan, 108
Mill, John Stuart, 79, 174, 175, 185, 239n23
Million, Joelle, 230–31n31
minority rights, 44
miscegenation, 111, 112, 128, 155, 205
mob rule, fear of, 47–48
monarchy, 175
money, corrupting influence of, 195
monogenesists, 113–14, 116–17
Montaigne, Michel de, 220–21n27
Montesquieu, 174
Moore, Ely, 31, 33, 205, 219–20n19
morality, xvi, 44, 152
Morgan, Lewis Henry, 114
Morton, Samuel George, 21, 113, 114
multiculturalism, egalitarian, 128. *See also* pluralism
mutability, 22, 118–19, 135, 156
mysticism, 8, 102

nakedness, 100
Napoleon Bonaparte, 37
Napoleonic Wars, 173
Nat Turner rebellion, 142–43, 149
National Reform Association, 182, 219–20n19
nationalism, 19, 221n28; cultural, 107; Emerson's resistance to, 126; expansionist, 225–26n28; literary, 40, 42, 107; literary nationalism, 225–26n28; melting pot, 134
nationality, 121, 127, 132–34

nativism, 132–34
natural history, 104–6, 113–14, 136, 137, 147, 155–56
natural law, 12, 14–15, 152, 188, 198–99
natural rights, 172–75
nature: fecundity and diversity of, 117; mastery over, 107–8; private vs. public values of, 166; society and, 8; state of, 182, 183, 218–19n7
Nazism, 19, 221n28
Nebraska, xi
New England intellectuals, diminishing authority of, 52–53
New Testament, 78
New York, 110
Non-Resistance Societies, 2, 209
the North, 154; expansion of factory production in, 1; political discourse in, 17. *See also* free states; *specific states*
Nott, Josiah, 114, 115
Noyes, John Humphrey, 221n28
Nullification Crisis, 123
Nuremberg Laws, 221n28

Odd-Fellows, 183
Oklahoma, "Indian Territory" in, 107, 153
"one man" metaphor, 51–52, 195–96, 202
opportunity, equality of, 14–16, 144, 190, 196
organicism, 50, 51, 52
Ormsby, Robert McKinley, 46
O'Sullivan, John L., 40, 42, 43, 47, 123

pacificism, 2, 172–73, 175
Pagden, Anthony, 233n15
Palfrey, John Gorham, 45, 226n38
Panic of 1837, 90, 158, 236–37n3
Parker, Theodore, 4, 132, 147–48, 160
partisanship, 20, 39, 40, 45, 58, 157–58; alternatives to, 27; emergence of, 29; Emerson's ambivalence about, 26, 27, 33–35, 41, 45, 48, 60, 189; vs. individuality, 29, 60; public rhetoric of, 26; second party system and, 226n34. *See also specific organizations*
paternalism, 204

patriarchy, 1
patriotism, meaning of, 150–51
peace, trade and, 172–75
peace movement, 172–73, 176–77
Peace Societies, 176–77
personal identity, property and, 200
personhood, idea of unification and, 200
Petrulionis, Sandra Herbert, 85
Phelps, Amos, 211
Phi Beta Kappa Society, 52–54, 107
Phillips, Wendell, 78
physical bodies, defined in term of inherent hierarchy, 155
plantations, 182–84
Plato: allegory of the cave, 93–94; *The Republic*, 170
Platonism, 223–24n9
pluralism, 127, 129
Pocock, J. G. A., 240n26
Pole, J. R., 11–12, 13, 15–16, 241n41
political equality, 13–14, 26–27, 44, 47, 144, 171; economic equality and, 15–16; economic opportunity and, 186–87; expansion of, 25–27, 29; free trade and, 172; "furious democracy" and, 25–60; possibilities of, 45; validation of, 27; wealth equality and, 15–16; women's rights movement and, 65–66. *See also* political equality; political representation; voting rights
political identity, metaphor for, 26
political representation, models of, 30–31, 46, 47, 50
Polk, James, 225–26n28
polygenetic theory, 21–22, 104, 112–20, 125, 133, 136, 146, 148, 155, 171
Portnoy, Allise, 229n17
Portuguese Empire, 176
Presbyterianism, 130, 209
Prescott, William Hickling, 123
the press, 46, 107
private discourse, vs. public discourse, 65–67, 73
private property, 159, 160, 172, 174, 176; accumulation of, 189; coercive power of, 185; critique of, 195–203; defended by natural law, 198–99; elimination of legal protection under statute law, 198–99; Emerson's critique of, 178, 188; inequality and, 22; as legitimate institution, 180; as obstacle to equality and progress, 180; as obstacle to liberal autonomy, 185; public value and, 203; right to, 180; unalienated labor and, 203. *See also* property rights
private relationships, 21. *See also* family life; marriage
private sphere: priority of, 66; vs. public sphere, 72–77, 91–92
professionalization, 229n12
progress, 21, 54–57, 127, 130, 137, 139, 147, 160, 223n8, 238n10; cosmopolitan, 177; egalitarianism and, 21; Emerson's standard of, 190–91; equality and, 27–29; ethnocentricity and, 111; evolutionary theories and, 104–6, 105; measures of, 65; private property as obstacle to, 180; race and, 111
progressive idealism, 161–62, 203
"progressive" theory, 161–62
property, 23, 157–203; Emerson's understanding of idea of, 238n8; equality of, 11, 15, 16; integration of, 200; liberty and, 22, 23; philosophy of, 180; political defense of, 197–98; power of, 13–14; as pun linking will and matter, 179; rethinking role of in politics, 196–97; role in society, 158; selfhood and, 22. *See also* private property; property rights
property crimes, 180–81
property law, 159, 188
property rights, 3, 22, 77, 178–87; equality and, 219–20n19; exploitation and, 196; vs. human rights, 1, 5, 22, 180, 184, 188, 196–201; inequality and, 180–81; labor and, 240n30; marriage and, 78–79; reinvention of, 23; as weapon, 200; Whigs and, 45
proslavery politics/rhetoric, 17–18, 135–37, 142–44, 204; biblical criticism and, 18; change in aspect of, 149–52; Emerson's critique of, 9; hypocritical

cynicism of, 149–51; post–Nat Turner, 149. *See also specific politicians*
prosperity, 23
Protestant Reformation, 27, 48
Protestantism, 66, 71, 130, 209
public discourse and debate, 40, 44, 48–49, 65; "domestication" of, 65; egalitarian, 84; individuality and, 55; integrity in, 208; model of, 45, 46–47; vs. private discourse, 65–67, 73; sincerity in, 50, 150–52. *See also* conversation; public opinion
public good: commerce for, 161–69; creative science in service to, 188
public opinion, 13, 32, 44, 47, 50, 208, 227n45; authority of, 39–43, 45, 46; Jacksonian democracy and, 36–38, 46, 47; lowest common denominator and, 46; as political legitimacy, 40; sovereignty of, 38–40, 42–43; spirit and, 36–43
public power, democratization and, 59–60
public selfhood, 50
public service, 30, 32
public sincerity, 142–56
public speech, equality of access to, 144
public sphere: vs. private sphere, 72–77, 91–92; reimagining of, 44; subsumed into private realm, 64–65
public stage, individual character and, 45

Quincy, Edward, 2
Quincy, Josiah III, 2

race, 77, 127, 217–18n7, 218n9, 220n22; citizenship and, 107–12; civil society and, 112; definition of racial identity, 113; Enlightenment and, 233n15; ethnicity and, 125; evolution of Emerson's ideas on, 142–56; "formidable doctrine of," 120–25; integration and, 128; mutability of, 123–24, 132–34, 137; nation and, 121; progress and, 111; racial combination, 127–28, 132–34; racial difference, 113–14; slavery and, 144–45

race theories, 19, 21–22, 120–25, 155–56
racial combination, 129, 132–34, 137
racial equality, 108, 112–13, 123–24, 134–35, 144, 156, 177
racial inequality, xii, 4, 110–11, 130–31, 132, 146, 147–49, 155–56, 170
racial pluralism, 111
racial progress, 136–37
racial purity, 112–20, 122, 124–25, 127, 128, 132, 134, 142, 155
racial succession, 147
racialism, 221n28
racism, 1–2, 111, 120–25, 137, 139, 147–48, 221n28, 222n5; vs. egalitarian principles, 147–48, 155–56; Emerson's resistance to, 125; Lincoln, Abraham and, 147; racist anthropology, 3, 4, 142–56; racist jurisprudence, 107; scientific, 18, 19, 83, 85, 127, 129, 132, 142, 148–49, 155, 204. *See also* white supremacism
Rawls, John, 218–19n7, 239n23
Read, James, 217n3
reform: culture of, 2; possibility of, 6–7; science and, 106
reform movements, 2, 19, 205, 209, 212–13; egalitarian, 206, 208; in New England, 209; Transcendentalism and, 82; women's rights movement and, 65, 106
religion, 152, 155, 209. *See also* theology; *specific religions*
representation, theories of, 46–47
representatives, authority of, 46
Republican Party, xi, 17, 18, 29–32, 205, 213, 217n2
republicanism, 32; civic, 203; Federalist, 29, 30–31, 32, 157, 206; Jeffersonian, 222n3
respect: equality of, 11, 144, 166; for laborers, 15, 16
Richardson, Robert, 223n7, 231n41
Richardson, Samuel, 29–30
Ridge, John, 111
Ripley, Ezra, 206
Ripley, George, 31, 241–42n44
Ripley, Sophia, 241–42n44

Romanticism, 55, 169
Rousseau, Jean-Jacques, 197–98, 233n15
Rush, Benjamin, 14
Russell, Lord William, 165, 238n15
Russia, 176
Ryan, Mary, 229n12

Sacks, Kenneth, 52–53
Sandel, Michael, 223–24n9, 227n49
Saxton, Alexander, 222n3
Schiller, Friedrich, 55
Schlegel, Friedrich, 221n28
Scholnick, Robert, 224–25n18
science, 106, 107–8
scientific racism, 83, 85, 127, 132, 142, 148–49, 155, 204
scientific revolution, 188
scientific sexism, 83
Scott, Winfield, 110
secession crisis, xii, xvi, 204, 207, 217n2
secessionism, resistance to, xi
Second Unitarian Church, Boston, 62, 63, 84, 205–6
self-expression, 50, 77, 100, 102
self-government, 50, 200–201, 202
selfhood: authenticity and, 73; capitalism and, 197; conservative, 223–24n9; liberal, 29, 194, 223–24n9; property and, 22; public, 50; theory of, 55
self-interest, 29, 60
self-liberation, 179
self-ownership, 159, 176, 178–87, 188, 196
self-reflection, 42, 43, 73
self-reliance, 26, 37, 43, 45–46, 156, 169, 186, 206, 238n9; Columbus and, 164, 165; egalitarian, 28; Emerson's theory of, 3; ethic of, 23; "mental," 180
self-representation, 46, 47
self-respect, 3–4
Sellers, Charles, 241n41
Seneca Falls Convention, 77–78, 213
sensualism, 189
"sentiment," rhetoric of, 65, 66
Seward, William Henry, 18, 157
sexism, 83, 222n5
sexual equality, 64, 65, 69, 77, 228n4

sexual submissiveness, expectation of, 79–80
sexuality, 92–93, 102–3, 232n52
Shakespeare, William, 6
Shklar, Judith, 19, 227n45
Simpson, Stephen, 185–86
"simular man," 132–42
sincerity, 21; in communication, 9, 10–11, 23, 77, 101–2, 207, 208; equality and, 102; loss of, 149–54; in personal relationships, 101, 208; in public dialogue, 142–56; self-expression and, 102
skepticism, 220–21n27
Skidmore, Thomas, 182, 219–20n19
skill, power of, 13–14
slave society, 183–84
slave states, xi, 17, 146. *See also specific states*
slave trade, 4, 138, 173, 184
slaveholders, 140, 143–44
slavery, 4, 22, 129–31, 150, 182, 197; abolition of, xvi, 4; chattel, 182, 185, 200; debate over, 4; defense of, 17–18, 170, 204; democracy and, 154–55; expansion of, xi, xiii, xv, 17, 207; Founders' view of, xiv–xv; history of, 135–37, 138, 145–46, 235n49; ideology underpinning, 129; illegalization of, xv; as institution rather than fact of nature, 130–31; legitimization of, 144, 149–51, 183–84; obsolescence of, 152; opposition to, 2; post–Nat Turner defense of, 149; presidential campaign of 1836 and, 157–58; race and, 144–45; wage, 182
Smith, Adam, 172–73, 174, 193, 239–40n25
Smith, Rogers, 222n5
social contract philosophers, 12–13, 82–83, 169–70, 218–19n7
socialism, 22, 157–203, 239n23; "beneficent," 192–93; commerce and, 193–94; Emerson's move toward, 160–61, 190–95; experimental communities, 188; slave society argued to be, 182–84; socialist egalitarianism, 160–61;

socialist movements, 22; utopian, 23, 31
the South: political discourse in, 17; slavery deeply rooted in, 1; war of ideas of, 19. *See also* slave states; *specific states*
South America, 112, 175–76
South Carolina, 144
southern plantations, 182–84
southern unionists, xi
Spanish conquest, 112
Spanish Empire, 112, 176
Spirit, 51, 132, 147, 189, 196; authority of, 203; communication and, 63–64; definition of, 36, 169; Emerson's effort to popularize idea of, 37–38; equality and, 37, 126; evolutionary progress of, 106; masculinity and femininity as expressions of, 83; as metaphor for shared interest, 60; mutability and, 125; public opinion and, 36–43; Romantic definition of, 169; Transcendentalist, 37–38, 47, 126; universal equality and, 106; universality of, 37, 168–69, 170
spiritual equality, universal, 18–19, 20, 206
spirituality, 3, 63, 102; Emerson's radical views on, 84; equality and, 5, 8; intimacy and, 96; spiritual autonomy, 209; spiritual movements, 13; spiritual obligations, 77; theory of, 55
Stanton, Elizabeth Cady, 64, 78, 80–81, 90, 230n25
stasis, 129, 135
statute law, 12, 188; Emerson proposes elimination of regarding private property, 198–99; natural law and, 152; property and, 200; provisional nature of, 195–96
Steele, Jeffrey, 83
Stephens, Alexander H., xi, xv, 17, 18, 217n2, 217n3; appointment as vice president of Confederacy, xii; "Cornerstone Speech" of, xii, xiii–xiv, xv, 19; defense of inequality by, xv–xvi; embrace of anti-egalitarian worldview, xii–xvi, 3; rejection of racial equality, 4
Stone, Lucy, 21, 64, 65–66, 67, 78, 81–82, 106, 230–31n31
Story, Joseph, 46–47
Stowe, Cyrus, 48, 133
submission, duty of, 143
suffrage. *See* voting rights
Sumner, Charles, 225n27
Sutherland, Kathryn, 174
Swedenborg, Emanuel, 95–98, 102
synthesis, 128

talent, 30, 227n45
tariffs, 173, 174–75, 239–40n25
Taylor, Alan, 218n9
Taylor, Edward, 210
technology, 107–8
temperance, divorce and, 80
temperance activists, tactics of, 44
Temperance societies, 183
Tennessee, Cherokee removals and, 107–12
Texas, xv, 157
textile industry, 159, 237n5
theocracy, 158
theology, 169–70
Thoreau, Cynthia, 85
Thoreau, Helen, 85
Thoreau, Henry David, 37, 82, 85, 109–10
Thoreau, Sophia, 85
Ticknor, George, 225n27
Tocqueville, Alexis de, 47, 48, 67, 111–12, 228–29n8, 234–35n40
Tories, 33, 35, 173
Torrey, Charles Turner, 199
trade, 158–60, 189, 190, 191; as communicative act, 177; human rights and, 172–75; in Jacksonian America, 189; natural rights and, 172–75; peace and, 172–75; utopia and, 175–76. *See also* commerce
trade unions. *See* unions
traditions: arbitrary power of, 159; as prosthesis only necessary in immature society, 54–57

Trail of Tears, 107. *See also* Cherokee removals debate; Indian Removal Act

Transcendentalism, 63, 207, 211, 220–21n27, 238n10; cosmopolitan equality and, 126–32; Emersonian, 18–19, 37–38, 43, 47, 50, 66, 85, 126–32, 220–21n27; individuality and, 71; reform movements and, 82

transparency, metaphor of, 154

tuberculosis, 61, 62

Tucker, Ellen Louisa, 61–63

Tucker family, wealth of, 61–62

Turner, Nat, 142–43, 149

union: meaning of, 150, 154; trope of, 231–32n51

unionists, in Maine, 18

unions, 15, 183, 187, 191, 219–20n19, 241n41, 241n42

Unitarian Church, 2, 5, 32, 52, 62, 63, 84, 113, 130, 205–6

United States: expansion of, 107–8; geography of, 192; national shame and, 138–39

universal possibility, egalitarian ideal of, 125

universal reason, 39

Universal Reform group, 209

universalism: cosmopolitan, 108, 132; egalitarian, 91

universality, 40, 42, 56

universalization, principle of, 21, 60, 150, 168–69

US Congress, xi, 1, 50; Cherokee removals debate and, 107; gag rule on antislavery speech in, 31, 144; Jackson's first message to, 36; lifting of gag rule on antislavery speech in, 31; US House of Representatives, 31; US Senate, 16, 17, 150; women's rights movement and, 229n17

US Constitution, xiii, 18

US Senate, 16, 17, 150

US Supreme Court, 149

utopia, 55–56, 167–78, 202

utopian associations, 183, 241–42n44

utopianism, aspirational, 135

Van Buren, Martin, 107–9, 111–12, 138, 157, 158, 225–26n28, 236–37n3

Van Leer, David, 237n6

Vanderlint, Jacob, 173

Vane, Henry, 164–65, 238n15

venture capital market, regulated by natural law, 14–15

Virginia, xii, 110, 143

voting rights, 2, 15–16, 20–21, 26, 171, 200; expansion of, 25, 26–27, 29, 30, 47, 48; inclusive vs. exclusive models of, 206; as natural right, 13; "universal" (white male) suffrage, 26–27, 59, 65–66, 171, 222–23n6

Wald, Priscilla, 108

Waldron, Jeremy, 179, 240n30

War of 1812, 31

Ware, Henry, Jr., 62

Washington, George, 31

wealth, 158, 188; accumulation of, 14; coercive power of, 196; distribution of, 180, 182, 186, 187, 188; hereditary, 158, 160; inequality and, 14, 15–16, 158, 160, 180, 182, 186, 196; political equality and, 15–16

Webb, Sidney, 239n23

Webster, Daniel, 17–18, 123–24, 133, 136–37, 149–52, 153–54, 206; chooses to stand with slavery in secession crisis, 1, 10, 38, 207, 213; at dedication of Bunker Hill monument, 153; Emerson's condemnation of, 207; Emerson's disappointment in, 38; Emerson's youthful idolization of, 4; Fugitive Slave Law speech and, 149–54; on government's role in protecting property rights, 1; talent as orator, 153–54, 207

Webster, Noah, 14

Weld, Theodore, 150

West Indies, British colonies in, 4, 85, 135, 137–41

Whicher, Stephen, 220–21n27, 237n6
Whig Party, xi, 16–18, 25, 31–33, 38, 40, 42, 157–58, 179; civic republicanism and, 50; disintegration of, 17; election of 1836 and, 236n2; Emerson attends rally of, 33–34, 48; Emerson's political bias toward, 60; emphasis on character over interest, 46; in Maine, 17, 155, 205; model of citizenship and, 26, 31; political culture of, 227n44; property rights and, 45; public works projects and, 32; roots in Jeffersonian republicanism, 222n3; second party system and, 226n34; theory of representation, 46–47
white supremacism, 77, 120, 125, 129, 132, 136–37, 144, 147–49, 155
Whiting, Nathaniel, 211–12
Whitman, James, 221n28
Wilentz, Sean, 217–18n7, 219n15, 222n3, 222n5
Winkelried, Arnold von, 164, 165
the wise man, 202–3
womanhood, 67, 73
women: advocacy for, 2; antislavery movement and, 84–91; conservative views of, 83; discourses of sentimental influence and, 65–66; Emerson's friendship with women reformers, 4; empowerment of, 1; equality and, 4, 21, 63–64, 66, 77 (*see also* women's rights movement); subordination of, 79
women's rights movement, 2, 21, 22, 63, 228n7, 229n17; antebellum conservative, 67–68; divisions within, 65, 78; economic opportunity and, 66; Emerson, Ralph Waldo and, 228n4; marriage reform and, 73, 77–83; political equality and, 65–66; reform movements and, 65, 106; US Congress and, 229n17
Wood, Gordon, 30
Woodhull, Victoria, 221n28
workingmen of Pennsylvania, 187
Wright, Henry C., 228n7

xenophobia, 129
Xerxes, 164

Zakaras, Alex, 225n22
Zogas, Peter, 223n8
Zuckert, Michael, 224n17

GREG GARVEY is professor of literature at SUNY-Brockport. He is author of *Creating the Culture of reform in Antebellum America* and editor of *The Emerson Dilemma: Essays on Emerson and Social Reform*. His other publications include scholarship on Frederick Douglass, William Lloyd Garrison, Margaret Fuller, and Abraham Lincoln, among others. As a Fulbright Senior Scholar, resident at Moscow State University, Garvey spent several years teaching courses in the history of American reform in Russia, Ukraine, Poland, Lithuania, Azerbaijan, and Kirgizstan. His research has also earned support from the National Endowment for the Humanities, The American Philosophical Society, and the New York Council for the Humanities. He lives in the Finger Lakes area of western New York.

www.ingramcontent.com/pod-product-compliance
Lightning Source LLC
Chambersburg PA
CBHW030531230426
43665CB00010B/848